ABOUT THE AUTHOR: John S. Dacey received his PhD from
Cornell University. He is Director of the Educational
Psychology Division at Boston College.

NEW WAYS TO LEARN:
The Psychology of Education

NEW WAYS TO LEARN:
The Psychology of Education

By John S. Dacey

GREYLOCK PUBLISHERS
Stamford, Conn.

Graphics by: Jody Taylor
   Chapter Nine sketches by Bob Harnden
   Chapter Nine photos by Ron Fortunato

To Linda Schulman-

the best teacher I know

CONTENTS

Preface

Teachers need more than ever to understand and apply the principles of psychology in their classrooms. Increased stresses of growing up are making it harder for their students to learn. To be effective, teachers must become more adept at helping children deal with these stresses. Fortunately, psychology can now provide much more assistance than it did even a decade ago.

The purpose of this book is to explain the current applications of psychology in the classroom. This is the goal of most books on educational psychology, but this one goes about it differently.

A number of traditional subjects in educational psychology have been replaced in this book by subjects of greater relevance to teachers. Among these are the development of moral judgement, creative problem solving, values clarification, non-classroom education, communications skills, and process-centered education.

The elaborate referencing and detailed description of research studies typical of the other books are excluded here. The investigations of important contributors to the field are explained, of course, and bibliographies of their works are provided.

Where possible, technical jargon has been eliminated. Educational psychology has been guilty of proliferating such terminology; it is hoped that its reduction here will aid understanding of the concepts.

Many psychologists, educational and otherwise, seem to find it beneath them to suggest specific uses of the theory and research. "My job is to describe these findings accurately," some say. "It's up to the practitioner to apply them." However, most of us seem to understand concepts better when we have a clear view of how they can be used in our day-to-day work. Consequently I have attempted to unite the skeletons of theory and research with the flesh and blood of actual classroom applications. I hope that this balance will bring to the reader a sense of the excitement I find to be so much a part of educational psychology today.

One final note: as most authors these days, I have struggled with the sex of pronouns. Should I use he/she, him/her, (s)he, hir, hersh? Every suggestion I considered sounded absurd, so I have decided to stick with the time-worn masculine case. I hope it doesn't offend.

J.S.D.
Boston, Ma.
September, 1976

Acknowledgements

To Agathon Press, for a passage from *Studies in Open Education*, 1975, by B. Spodek and H. Walberg.

To the American Management Association for a passage from: "Building a Democratic Work Group," by L.P. Bradford and R. Lippitt, in *Personnel*, vol. 22, 1954.

To the American Psychological Association, for a passage from "A Locus of Control Scale for Children," by S. Nowicki, Jr., and B.R. Strickland, in *Journal of Consulting and Clinical Psychology*, vol. 40, 1973.

To Grune and Stratton for a passage from *Phenomenological, Existential, and Humanistic Psychologies: A Historical Survey*, by H. Misiak and V.S. Sexton, 1973.

To Charles E. Merrill for passages from *Early Childhood Education Today*, by G.S. Morrison, 1976.

To M.I.T. Press for a passage from *The Full and Open Classroom*, by P. Morrison, 1971.

To Random House for a passage from *Future Shock*, by Alvin Toffler, 1970.

I suppose that most books are the result of the ideas and critical suggestions of many people; this book is no exception. I would especially like to thank the following:

To those who helped with the manuscript: Julie Dacey, Louise Demers, Karen Zikoras, Carol Silbert, Anna Kolodner, Rita Wright, Nancy Weisner, Ann Robinson, Ralph Titus, Mike Cauley, Judy Dumont and especially to my most helpful critics, Phil Churchill, Linda Schulman and Rick Williams.

To colleagues who encouraged me: John Jensen, John Travers, Kirk Kilpatrick, John Walsh, Les Przewlocki, Mary Griffin, Ray Martin, Bob Belenky, and the late John Schmitt.

To those who helped to make camp-school a reality: Sue DiBerto, Jim Earley, Len Myers, Mike Gardner, John Cullinane, Sally Atkins, Maggie Diamond, George and Rosemary Murphy, John Hennelly, John and Marcia Bergman, Matt Leona, Stephanie Biziewski, Emily Stein, Marlene Godfrey, Jean Keith, Sam Turner, Donald Cushing and Helen Thomas.

To my typists, who are so much more than that: Elena Vitug and Ann Sibley.

Finally and with much gratitude, to my mother, the late Margaret Dacey, and my father, Stewart Dacey.

Part I

Chapter 1

Why We Need New Ways To Learn

...if the last 50,000 years of man's existence were divided into lifetimes of approximately 62 years each, there have been about 800 such lifetimes. Of these 800, fully 650 were spent in caves.

Only during the last 70 lifetimes has it been possible to communicate effectively from one lifetime to another—as writing made it possible to do. Only during the last six lifetimes did masses of men ever see a printed word. Only during the last four has it been possible to measure time with any precision. Only in the last two has anyone anywhere used an electric motor. And the overwhelming majority of all the material goods we use in daily life today have been developed with the present, the 800th, lifetime (Toffler, *Future Shock*, 1970, p. 148).

We are beginning to get a radically new view of the nature of humanity. In this latter half of the Twentieth Century, the research of psychologists and futurists (a new breed of scientists who try to anticipate the future) has produced a number of innovative insights. Of most importance to educators are eight discoveries, which will be considered in detail in this book. They are:

1. The amount, types, and rate of change in our daily lives have increased drastically in this century. The bewildering swirl of change, involving all areas of our lives, may cause psychological and physical illness in many people.

2. Our personality develops throughout our lives in a series of eight specific crises. Failure to adequately resolve any of these crises results in inadequate resolution of all remaining crises.

3. The development of our intellect occurs in four distinct stages, the last beginning in adolescence. Inadequate development at any one stage adversely affects all later stages.

4. As a result of the electronic age, there has been a major change in the thinking patterns of today's youth. Rather than relying on the logical, sequential approach to problem-solving used by their parents, their thinking is "non-linear." They have rejected the rational approach in favor of a more spontaneous, intuitive one.

5. Many children have an "external locus of control," that is, they feel that life is just a matter of chance, over which they personally have no control. Since they take neither credit nor blame for their actions, reinforcements given them by teachers for learning tend to have little effect.

6. We have six inherent human needs, which are arranged hierarchically. Only when lower level needs have been fulfilled can we hope to meet those at higher levels.

7. Children develop distinctive learning styles; each child learns best when teaching is geared to his or her own style.

8. Imagination is becoming more important than knowledge.

Each of these insights has ramifications for educators, but the implications of the first one are probably the most sweeping and the most urgent. Sociologist Alvin Toffler, in his best-selling book, *Future Shock*, provides evidence that we are experiencing an explosive increase in the rate of change in our lives. Because the consequences of this are so crucial to all that follows in this book, I want to describe this phenomenon more fully here.

Future Shock

Future shock is the illness which results from having to deal with too much change in too short a period of time. Toffler compares it to culture shock, the feeling we get when arriving in a foreign country for the first time. Nothing seems the same. The language is different, the customs are different, the scenery is different. We become disoriented and anxious. But in the back of our minds we know that if this discomfort becomes too great, we have only to hop on a plane and go back to our own culture where we can feel safe again. Future shock is the same kind of feeling, except that there is no going home.

As Orson Welles put it in a television program on the subject, future shock is the "premature arrival of the future." We have only to look at our own grandparents to observe future shock. We see their irritation that "Everything is changing. No one cares about traditions, nothing is the same any more." We are harrassed by hordes of choices we must make. Commercials insist that we keep up with the latest. We live in a throw-away society.

We find ourselves constantly changing everything, not only our possessions but even our friends. We make many more friends than our grandparents did, and our friendships endure for shorter periods of time and are not as deep. Our mobility is wrecking not only our relationships with friends, but the basic solidarity of our families. This disruptive uprooting is creating a "new race of nomads." Instead of the familiar family stucture of one father, one mother, children and some relatives, we find a whole new set of alternatives. We see people living together, unmarried, in group marriages, in homosexual marriages.

Toffler's main point is that the *rate* of change in our daily lives has different implications, and is often a more crucial factor in our well being, than the *direction* of change. There are three major aspects of the rate of change, each of which is rapidly increasing:

Transience. This has to do with the lack of permanence of things and people in our lives. Toffler documents in great detail how much more transient our lives have become in this century.

Novelty. In addition to duration, changes differ as to how different they really are. The dissimilarity of new situations in our lives from old situations is greater than it used to be.

Diversity. Changes differ not only in how quickly they come and how different they are, but also in how many there are. People used to maintain stability in the great proportion of their lives, allowing only a few aspects to change at any one time. This stable proportion is much smaller for most of us now.

The implications of future shock for education are many and great. The main one is that today's schools were designed at the turn of the century to meet the needs of an increasingly industrialized society, and are now outdated. Toffler describes these schools:

> The whole idea of assembling masses of students (raw material) to be processed by teachers (workers) in a centrally located school (factory) was a stroke of industrial genius. The whole administrative hierarchy of education, as it grew up, followed the model of industrial bureaucracy. The very organization of knowledge into permanent disciplines was grounded on industrial assumptions. Children marched from place to place and sat in assigned stations. Bells rang to announce changes of time.

> The inner life of the school thus became an anticipatory mirror, a perfect introduction to industrial society. The most criticized features of education today—the regimentation, lack of individualization, the rigid systems of seating, grouping, grading, and marking, the authoritarian role of the teacher—are precisely those that made mass public education so effective an instrument of adaptation for its place and time. (Toffler, 1970, p. 400).

What must the schools of the future be like?

> It is no longer sufficient for Johnny to understand the past. It is not even enough for him to understand the present, for the here-and-now environment will soon vanish. Johnny must learn to anticipate the directions and rate of change. He must, to put it technically, learn to make repeated, probabilistic, increasingly long-range assumptions about the future. And so must Johnny's teachers. (Toffler, 1970, p. 403).

> Why, for example, must teaching be organized around such fixed disciplines as English, economics, mathematics, or biology? *Why not around stages of the human life cycle:* a course on birth, childhood, adolescence, marriage, career, retirement, death. Or around contemporary social problems? Or around significant technologies of the past and future? Or around countless other imaginable alternatives? (Italics mine). (Toffler, 1970, p. 410).

Toffler argues that people living in super-industrial societies will need skills in three crucial areas:

Learning: We must teach people how to classify information, evaluate it, reclassify it when necessary, open-mindedly look for new directions, and to do all this *by themselves*. Psychologist Herbert Gerjuoy predicts that the illiterate of tomorrow will not be the person who cannot read, but rather the person who has not learned how to learn.

Relating: There is a growing sense of loneliness and an inability to "open up" with others today. As the rate of change in the world increases, so will our need to learn how to be intimate with others.

Choosing: Adaptation involves making successive choices. As the number and variety of alternatives in our lives grow, the greater will be our need for a clear-cut sense of values. Yet there is considerable evidence that our values, and particularly those of our children, have never been *less* clear. Simply taking dogmatic stands on questions will not make the problem go away, either. At least to some extent, we are going to have to learn to tolerate the ambiguity which rapid change brings to our lives. Chapters Five, Six, and Seven deal with this problem further.

Toffler believes that we have gained an enormous increase in our ability to control our lives, and he documents the many techniques being offered by psychology, genetics, etc. Nevertheless, much current change is out of our control. We must learn to deal more effectively with the complicated consequences of our actions. Primarily, education must help us to deal with ambiguity.

In response to concerns such as future shock and the seven concepts mentioned above, a new force has sprung up in our schools. It started some fifteen years ago as a revolt among psychotherapists and is known as "humanistic" psychology. More recently its followers have urged that this approach be applied in the schools. Called "humanistic education," it has provoked a great deal of debate.

Humanistic Education

Are schools inhumane to students?

It seems fair to ask an obviously inflammatory question like this because so many critics these days are suggesting that it is so. On the average, one-third of the students entering the first grade will not finish high school. When asked how they feel about school, most students in a large survey indicated that at best, their attitude, is a passive acceptance of it. Even more disturbing is that one-sixth of those who are above average in intelligence do not finish school today. Only ten years ago, virtually all students above average in I.Q. completed high school. It appears, therefore, that at least as far as students are concerned, schools are frequently unpleasant places to have to spend a large part of one's day.

Making schools responsive to children's emotional as well as intellectual needs has long worried psychologists as well as educators. Representatives of the two main schools of psychology, psychoanalysis and behaviorism, have concerned themselves with this problem for decades. Both of these schools of thought have made considerable, though haphazard, contributions to American curriculum.

Psychoanalysis views human development as moving through a series of five stages, based largely on the growth of the nervous system.

According to this theory, people mature as the innate needs of their erogenous zones (oral, anal, and genital) are successfully met. If in the course of this development, the needs of the currently pre-eminent zone are not met, the individual becomes fixated at that stage, and maturation is halted. This process is regulated by forces not under the person's control (his parents, teachers, genes, etc.). Life is seen as a constant war between one's Id (basic drives) and Super-ego (socially induced conscience). The Ego (reason) has the responsibility of arbitrating this constant conflict. Psychoanalysis views the role of education as helping the person obtain the best balance he can between these warring factions.

The school of behaviorism also sees the person's actions as being caused by forces beyond his control. People learn to make responses, some of which then become habitual, because they are reinforced for making those responses. Hence, one's behavior, and ultimately his personality, are determined by the actions of others. The role of education is seen by behaviorists as the appropriate use of reinforcers in order to shape the child by controlling what and how he learns. Chapter Four describes this approach to learning in detail.

Both of these theories see man as passive, with his actions totally determined by two forces: his environment (past and present), and his genetic inheritance. Under these circumstances, the individual has no responsibility for the kind of person he becomes.

Humanistic psychology sees the human being as a basically active organism, who is responsible for a major part of his behavior. As the person develops, he has a natural drive toward self-fulfillment, through which he gains greater and greater influence over his actions. In Abraham Maslow's words, "Man is, or should be, an active, autonomous, self-governing mover, chooser, and center of his own life..." Humanistic education proposes that teachers start this process early by helping students be more and more responsible for the means and direction of their own learning. As historians Henryk Misiak and Virginia Sexton put it:

> Humanistic psychology rejects the blind authority and competitiveness of traditional education and substitutes internal development and self-reinforcement. It shifts the focus of education to the growth potential of the learner and his human need for self-actualization. Essentially, humanistic psychology's program has demanded reforms in the traditional thinking and training of teachers and school administrators as well as modifications in methods of instruction. Although much has been written about the humanistic perspective in education and its key role in shaping the future of American education, only meager beginnings have been made in instituting the humanistic orientation in American schools up to now (Misiak and Sexton, 1973, pp. 118-119).

Affective Education vs. the Three R's

Proponents of humanistic education view the affective development of the child as the most central concern. They charge that American schools have always devalued the child's emotional and interpersonal needs, and have emphasized cognitive goals instead. Cognitive goals are relatively less complicated and more easily measured than affective goals. Teachers, they say, have "copped out" on helping children learn to express their emotions and deal with personal difficulties in a healthy manner. They feel that most teachers are afraid to become personally involved with their students. School administrators have bowed to school committee demands for "accountability" and have thus emphasized growth in achievement scores rather than the child's overall growth, Such scores are used in evaluating teacher effectiveness. Teachers, fearing for their jobs in a restricted job market, have also acquiesced.

Other educators counter-charge that the humanistic approach, though in its infancy, is already too pervasive. They claim that schools have no place dealing with affective needs, which should be left to the church and the home. They point to erosion in our standards for cognitive learning and blame the problem on the "permissive " attitudes of the humanists.

Although the data showing serious drop in average achievement in schools is undeniable (see *Newsweek*, Dec. 8, 1975, for example), a considerable amount of this data has been misinterpreted. It is true, for instance, that average Scholastic Aptitude Test scores, used to evaluate ability to do college level learning, have been dropping. Much of the decrease may be due to three factors, however:

1. When college entrance requirements were more demanding, it was a common practice for high school students to take the S.A.T. in both junior and senior years. These students hope for, and usually received, a higher second score. Today, many of the brighter seniors are no longer retaking the test, which lowers the overall average.

2. Students in general know they don't need scores as high as previously needed. Hence, they don't bother to prepare as carefully as they might have.

3. A larger percentage of all students are now taking the S.A.T., than 10 years ago. This increased percentage includes many lower ability students.

Math scores have been dropping, and this has been blamed on the "new math" curricula introduced in the late 1950's. It is true that the new math emphasized comprehension at the expense of computation skills. However, this "negative" effect is greatly exaggerated by the strong emphasis placed by the S.A.T. on computation. Gains made by students in comprehension are thus undervalued.

No doubt the greatest cause for concern has been in the area of writing ability, with the most notable decline in spelling and grammar. The angry accusations of businessmen and college professors, as well as declining S.A.T. scores, document the severity of the problem. This problem has been blamed almost solely on humanistic English teachers who, it is alleged, have paid far too much attention to creative writing. It is argued that since high quality reading is the best spur to good writing, teachers should assign more reading, as well as drill in spelling and grammar. It is probable that today's student does not value reading as much as is desirable, though certainly English teachers are not solely responsible. Marshall McLuhan (cf. Chapter Three) has attempted to demonstrate that the days of avid readers and eloquent writers are nearing an end regardless of what schools do. According to his studies, the impact of television and the other electronic media is so great that there is no feasible way to return verbal skills to their once-high pinnacle. It is not even desirable to try, he says, because the world is gradually becoming a "global village," in which immediate, face-to-face communication through electronics will again be pre-eminent, as it was before the print era began in 1451. He urges that educators understand and help implement this trend away from writing skills and toward interpersonal skills.

Thus, the battle between humanistic education and the three R's, and between affective and cognitive objectives, is on. I predict it will be the major concern of teachers in the next five years. It is my fervent hope that this conflict will result in innovative solutions of benefit to all children. This book is a presentation and evaluation of some alternatives already central to the educational scene.

A note of warninig is necessary here, however. Although change has been slow to come, the critics of education have fostered powerful pressure, especially from newly involved parents, to adopt alternative approaches in the schools. There is real danger that changes will be made simply to give the appearance of being up-to-date. Educational philosopher Harry Broudy has suggested that there are four myths increasingly heard about "alternative education." Here is a list of these assumptions, and a summary of Dr. Broudy's evaluation of them:

1. Alternatives promote freedom.

Broudy: The advocates of freedom usually wish to help children be more natural. But education, by definition, tries to change the child from what he would be otherwise. It opposes the child's "nature," in its basic effort to make him or her occupationally, culturally, and personally capable in today's complex society. The reformer's goal of freedom too often means freedom from these necessary responsibilities.

2. Alternatives promote better choices.

Broudy: Children are far too short-sighted to know what they will need in the future. Parents know better than their children, and educators know better than parents. Most alternatives are alternatives to the appropriate, time-tested way, and should be avoided.

3. Alternatives provide for individual differences.

Broudy: Individuals are not really all that different, and what diffrences there are, traditional classrooms can handle. Besides, the school should not do all the adjusting to the needs of the individual; he will benefit from doing some adjusting, too.

4. Alternatives promote creativity.

Broudy: Creative diversity does not mean variety for its own sake, but rather imaginative variations on a theme. Some alternatives may promote creativity, but there is no evidence that change in and of itself increases creativity.

If I make Dr. Broudy sound as though he is opposed to all change, I do him an injustice. Although his position is a bit too conservative for me, I agree with him that making no change will usually be better than jumping on the bandwagon with an alternative that has not been well thought out. *The primary guideline by which any educational innovation must be judged is the developing needs of the child.* Fortunately, psychological research in the last three decades has made great progress in improving our understanding of these needs. Chapter Two details what I consider the most relevant of these findings as to the development of personality. Chapter Three attempts the same objective in terms of the intellect. I believe that a clear awareness of the ideas presented in these two chapters is critical to a teacher's ability to grasp and apply the ideas presented in the remaining chapters of this book, which take a more "how-to-do-it" approach.

In Part Two, the fourth chapter looks at the three major schools of learning theory and presents suggestions for implementing them. The next three chapters are concerned with aspects of human behavior which until recently have received much less attention in schools than has the subject of learning. Creativity, morality, and communication skills are increasingly the province of public education; partly because of society's increased need to foster these characteristics, and partly because we now know better how to foster them.

The four chapters in Part Three deal with ways of organizing learning. Chapter Eight compares three positions on the continuum of contol, from the direct control of the traditional classroom through indirect control in the open classroom to almost no control in a free school. Chapter Nine explores what I feel is one of the most exciting innovations in education, the "camp-school" idea. Chapter Ten combines concepts from these first two chapters into a model for process-centered education, as opposed to the traditional content-centered model. Chapter Eleven looks at the changing role of the teacher from the standpoint of psychology, and in view of the innovations evaluated in this book. It presents ideas that help teachers look at their own behavior as it affects the growth of the learners in their charge.

Although the eight insights into the developing needs of children which were listed at the beginning of this chapter may not yet be considered "proven facts," I believe they have been well enough established to serve as guidelines in evaluating the "new ways to learn" currently emerging in the schools. Professional educators in America are trying to become more humanistic; even in the face of angry demands that we go "back to basics," responsible teachers are striving more than ever to meet the needs of the whole child. This book represents an attempt to aid in this difficult process.

References

Brown, George I., ed. *The Live Classroom.* New York: Viking Press, 1975

Featherstone, Joseph. *Schools Where Children Learn.* New York: Avon, 1971.

Freud, Sigmund. *A General Introduction to Psychoanalysis.* New York: Washington Square Press, 1965.

National Media Specialist Institutes. *The Affective Domain.* Washington, D.C.: Gryphon House, 1972.

Rich, John M. *Innovations in Education: Reformers and their Critics.* Boston: Allyn and Bacon, 1975.

Ringness, Thomas A. *The Affective Domain in Education.* Boston: Little Brown, 1975.

Rubin, Louis J. *Facts and Feelings in the Classroom.* New York: Viking Press, 1973.

Schwartz, Barry N., ed. *Affirmative Education.* Englewood Cliffs, N.J.: Prentice-Hall, 1972.

Thatcher, David A. *Teaching, Loving, and Self-directed Learning.* Pacific Palisades, Calif: Goodyear, 1973.

Troost, C.E., ed. *Radical School Reform.* Boston: Little Brown, 1973.

Zahorik, John A., and Dale L. Brubaker. *Toward More Humanistic Instruction.* Dubuque, Iowa: Wan C. Brown, 1972.

Chapter 2

Understanding Personality Growth

The subject matter taught in each of our schools today is remarkably similar. It would be reasonable to assume that this is the result of the agreement among American educators on a common view of human needs. Nothing could be farther from the truth. It is the result, rather, of a series of bits and pieces tacked together over the course of our history. In the relatively stable world of the past, when it was possible to predict with some accuracy our children's future needs, this worked no serious hardship. In the fast-paced world of the present, it will not do.

This is not to say that educators have disregarded the insights of scientific study. The ideas of a number of psychologists have played a vital role in the formation of our national curricula. Most notable among these have been Sigmund Freud, Jean Piaget, John Dewey, and B.F. Skinner. But Freud's description of human development really only covers the first five years of life, Piaget's is entirely cognitive, and Dewey and Skinner do not have a developmental theory.

We need to take a fresh look at what we are teaching, and how we are going about it. We should start from the standpoint of a clearer, more unified view of the goals of life. Educational innovations, and there have been many of late, must be judged on the basis of how well they coincide with such a guiding developmental theory. I think we are extremely fortunate that at this crucial point in our history, this needed overview of human nature has come into existence.

In 1950 Erik Erikson first offered his theory of human development in his ground-breaking book, *Childhood and Society*. He has spent most of his time since then embellishing it. A major source of the humanistic movement, it is a lucid and at times poetically beautiful picture of the way humans should grow. In this section, I will describe Erikson's theory as concisely as possible. In later chapters, I will use it as a basis from which to analyze the proposed educational alternatives.

Erik Erikson's Stages of Development

Erikson views human development as a series of eight life crises (Table 2-1), which follow each other in a fixed sequence. The ages at which people go through the stages vary, but to successfully complete the fourth stage, for example, it is necessary to have successfully completed the first three stages. Inadequate resolution of a crisis at any stage will hinder development at all succeeding stages (unless special help is received). Of course, no one ever completes the stages perfectly; Erikson's theory is mainly a picture of ideal development toward which we should strive.

In each crisis, the individual's development lies between two alternatives which Erikson terms the "psychosocial crises." These alternatives are in opposition to each other, for example, trust vs. mistrust. How the person resolves a crisis, for example, whether he becomes basically trustful or mistrustful, is determined by his interactions with his environment.

During the course of each crisis, there are two external factors that influence these interactions. First is "the significant other"—the person or persons who are most important in the individual's life at the time of the crisis, such as one's mother. Second is the "related element of social order"—the aspect of the culture that the child should come to understand during each crisis, for example, ideological perspectives. In each crisis, these roles are played by different persons or groups, who are catalysts of development.

Basic Trust vs. Mistrust: 0-1 1/2

The first stage is the most important, in which a sense of basic trust should develop. Erikson gives the word "trust" an unusually broad meaning. In his sense of the word, trust comes about only to the extent that the infant learns that the world is an orderly, *predictable* place. It is not so much that the world is safe, but rather that there are causes and effects which one can learn to anticipate. We only trust that which we understand.

Therefore a great deal of regularity in the infant's environment is essential. This regularity must be of a certain sort, however. This child needs variation in his surroundings, variation that occurs in a reliable order and that is easily discerned. Thus, the soft music of an FM radio station provides changes in sound level which the child can learn to anticipate. So do the regular attentions of a mother who is not overtaxed by other responsibilities.

The child born in poverty typically begins life with irregular and inadequate care, with noise and drab colors, and surrounded by disruptions and ever-changing comings and goings. We would expect such a child to be less trusting, because such a world is so unreliable. To the extent that he is untrusting, we can expect him to be hostile, antisocial, and under certain circumstances, even criminal. This is the real cost of poverty, and it is not easily overcome.

It seems to me that our penal system is frequently an example of an institution specifically designed to destroy any trust left in the inmate, especially so in the juvenile part of the system. Consider this note written by a fourteen-year old girl:

"Locked up. Going on my third day. In a freezing cold room . You sleep in there. Look at four walls. They don't give you nothing but one blanket. The bed is just a rubber mattress and a wooden block for it to go on. A little window with chicken wire. And a pail. And a door and nothing else but four walls. They let you out three times a day for a few minutes and they don't let you speak to nobody. They got nothing in here. You're not even supposed to have a book to read. It's freezing. It's an icebox. One blanket. One.. You feel like you want to scream. You feel like you're in a mad house. There's no need of putting kids in solitary confinement. I see no need of it at all. I wouldn't put a dead dog in this room. I wouldn't...I don't know. You can't really describe this place unless you're here. You've got to live here before you can really tell. They should send a real good kid here, you know, one that people would believe and have her come to live here for about a week. Or two, three weeks, you know. Then let her report back everything! Tell the people. Just let that person describe this. I know the State Senate is investigating this place and I hope they tear it down because it needs to be torn down. But I don't think the Senate is really going to do anything because it's going to take a lot of people to close this place; to tear it down."

She is talking about solitary confinement in a girl's vocational training school in Massachusetts. She was sent there in 1970 after running away from home three times. Her alcoholic mother had signed a warrant for her arrest. I have visited that school, and the girl was not exaggerating. The school was closed in 1973, but it is far too typical of our societal reaction to even slight deviation on the part of children. The major difference between the girl whose pathetic note you just read and the "good" girl she refers to, is a difference in basic trust. She doesn't believe we will find her trustworthy, and by providing experiences such as this, society is ensuring that she will not be.

Basic trust is critical, not only for a person to be loving and lovable, but also as an aid to effective learning. Curiosity and risk-taking are not possible without a sense of trust. It is the absence of this basic trust which so distinguishes emotionally disturbed youngsters.

As mentioned before, each of the crises take the form of opposing characteristics (e.g., trust vs. mistrust). Successful resolution is in favor of the first of the two characteristics, but this resolution is a matter of balance; we need *some* of the second characteristic, too. It is good to be basically trusting, but the totally trusting person would be continuously in danger of being duped. Appropriate mistrust is healthy. Erikson believes that in most people, however, the main problem is having too little of the first characteristic.

The "significant other" (column C in Table 2-1) during this first stage is the "maternal person." This may or may not be the infant's mother. In one Polynesian tribe, the father is the full-time maternal person; the mother returns to her work in the fields immediately after the birth of the child. Recently in Western cultures, the father is coming more and more to share this maternal role. This change will make fathers less forbidding to their children, thereby increasing the likelihood of a spirit of basic trust.

"Related elements of the social order" (column D in Table 2-1) refers to the aspect of the culture which predominates during the crisis. "Cosmic order" seems a heavy burden to lay on an infant, but it is one of many insights Erikson has into the human condition. By "cosmic order" he means the child's world view; his underlying, pervasive assumption as to what the whole of life is all about. The infant begins either to come to see his world as a predictable and trustable place, or he sees it as chaotic and hostile.

This attitude will be resistant to change. Erikson believes that the infant's desires should be fulfilled whenever and as much as possible, because this leads to basic trust. Children at so young an age are not really "spoilable," and the world will teach them soon enough that not everyone can be trusted.

Autonomy vs. Shame and Doubt: 1½-3

At about one and one-half years, the child should move into the second stage, Autonomy vs. Shame and Doubt. At this stage the child begins to gain control over his body and its functions. If encouraged to explore his body and his surroundings, he begins to develop a sense of self-confidence. If, on the other hand, his decisions are regularly belittled and countermanded, he comes only to doubt himself; he becomes ashamed and afraid to try.

The danger of self-doubt at this stage seems largely the result, at least in the past, of the father's introduction as the "significant other" person in the child's environment. As fathers diminsh their role as the family disciplinarian and become more of an understanding helper, this danger will subside.

Erikson puts the term "Law and Order" (column D in Table 2-1) in quotes because he does not mean a slavish adherence to the law. Rather, he is referring to the child's growing comprehension of the rules of this society, and his growing appreciation of the value of living an orderly life in compliance with these rules.

Initiative vs. Guilt: 3-5

At about three years old, the second crisis leads into the third; Initiative vs. Guilt. Controlling himself and learning to have some influence over others in his family becomes essential to the child. This is the stage at which his creativity should bloom. But if his parents and others make him feel incompetent through frequent denial of his wishes, the child develops a generalized feeling of guilt. In the second stage, he can be made to feel ashamed by others, but in the third stage the child is able to make himself feel ashamed. This is necessary for his social development, but if guilt begins to pervade his sense of self, he will be incapable of dealing with the crises ahead.

Now the child's brothers and sisters and other close relatives begin to play an important role in his life. At this stage, as Freud suggests, his superego, or conscience, emerges and the child looks to his basic family for models of proper behavior. These "ideal prototypes" give him indications as to the appropriateness of his own behavior.

Industry vs. Inferiority: 5-12

For those interested in the classroom, the next two stages are of special interest. The fourth stage, Industry vs. Inferiority, corresponds closely to the child's elementary school years. At this stage, the task is to go beyond looking for models and "ideal prototypes" (as in the third stage). Now the child who has developed appropriately becomes fascinated with learning the skills and elementary technology of his culture. He expands his horizons beyond the family and begins exploring the neighborhood. He begins to understand the basic conflicts of life that will be with him throughout his adulthood, and his play becomes more purposefully oriented toward resolution of these conflicts. The child now seeks knowledge in order to *complete* the tasks he sets himself.

The danger at this stage is the development of a deep and lasting sense of inferiority. This could happen due to failures in making, building, and learning. It could also happen because he has not yet resolved earlier crises. As Erikson puts it, he may still want his mother more than he wants knowledge. Erikson suggests that the typical American elementary school, staffed almost exlusively by women, can make it difficult for children (especially boys) to make the break from home and mother. The concern is that the child will learn to view his productivity merely as a way to please his mother substitute (his female teacher) and not as something good for its own sake. In his efforts to be the "good little worker," and the "good little helper," he fails to realize the enjoyment of pleasing himself with his industry.

Identity and Repudiation vs. Identity Confusion: 12-18

In the fifth stage, Identity and Repudiation vs. Identity Confusion, the task of the child is to achieve a state of identity. Erikson, who invented the term "identity crisis," uses the word "identity" in a specialized way. Identity is not just the picture one has of himself or herself. Identity is a *state* in which the various aspects of one's self- images come to be in agreement with each other. Take, for example, the case in which a person decides he will quit smoking. At first, he feels self-congratulatory. However, as the time since the last cigarette increases, that part of him that does not agree that he should quit smoking comes into conflict with his moralistic side. A person in the ideal state of identity would not have had such a conflict. All of his aspects of self would have been in agreement with each other when the decision to quit smoking was made. Identity also requires a correspondence between the individual's sense of self and the views that other people have of him, so that his sense of inner sameness is confirmed by those about him.

Repudiation is an essential aspect of reaching personal identity. Each of us builds his own personality through the choices he makes. In any choice, the selection we make means that we have repudiated all the other possibilities, at least for the present.

Major choices that the adolescent makes involve which clique he shall try to join, and who shall lead it. Erikson believes that these choices, and the many changes of them, are the adolescent's way of experimenting with ideological perspectives. We allow him a moratorium on final life decisions so that he can try out several "ways-to-be." It is one of the luxuries that Western industrial society can afford (although some have questioned its benefits).

The primary danger in this fifth stage is identity confusion. Erikson suggests as an example this statement by Biff, in Arthur Miller's *Death of a Salesman:* "I just can't take hold, Mom, I can't take hold of some kind of life." Biff has come to see himself as many different people, a person who sometimes acts one way in one situation and the opposite way in another—a hypocrite. He refuses to make choices. He abstains from commitments. There is no cohesiveness in his personality.

Erikson says that identity confusion is much more likely in a democratic society, because there are so many choices as to what or whom one can be. The Hitler Youth of the 1930's were not troubled with identity confusion, because clever propaganda gave children in Nazi Germany a clear-cut identity. In democratic societies, however, a great deal of emphasis is placed on autonomy in decision-making, and choices abound. Children who feel threatened by the overabundance of choices tend to over-identify with their parents or other adults they admire. This may be temporarily necessary, but it is essential that children be assisted to a unified personality of their own.

The typical elementary school meets the needs described in Erikson's fourth stage, Industry vs. Inferiority, rather well. Kids and teachers seem relatively happy there. But this is not the case with the junior high school. The students, who frequently hate the place, are labelled "impossible" by many teachers, who would often rather be working at the senior high school. The problem involves the curriculum of the junior high school, where students are given a booster shot of the same material covered in the elementary school. Since the main crisis in this Fifth Stage is the attempt to achieve a sense of identity, very different subject matter is called for.

This suggests the study of the self. It could be approached in a variety of ways, some of which are described more fully in later chapters. One productive way includes the study and practice of techniques of meditation, about which we have learned so much in recent years. When I suggest this to most junior high school principals, however, they tend to regard me suspiciously.

But this is a book about psychology, not curriculum. Nevertheless, if you teach or intend to teach at the junior high school, I hope Erikson's ideas will persuade you to consider revisions of curricula at this level.

Intimacy vs. Isolation: 18-25

The next three stages have to do with one's adult life. The sixth stage, Intimacy vs. Isolation, is closely intertwined with the Identity Stage. A person cannot dare to have an intimate and deeply honest relationship with others unless he has some sense of identity.

As Erich Fromm suggests, each of us is really alone, in that no one else can ever experience life exactly the way we do. We are prisoners in our bodies, never able to be certain that our senses are working properly. Most of us suspect at one time or another that something's "wrong" with us, a feeling we usually hide. This aloneness can only be relieved by sharing our innermost thoughts with someone else. This other person is in a position to *validate* our own experiences. Such validating "feedback" is essential to our sanity. Fromm suggests that our reaction to it is what we mean by "love."

Intimacy, then, provides us with chances to receive validation. Just as it takes some sense of identity in order to dare to be intimate with someone, it takes intimacy with others in order to dare to come to a fuller sense of identity through the vital information about ourselves that they give us. Each of these stages can facilitate the growth of the other.

On the negative side, when one suffers from identity confusion, there is a tendency toward self-absorption. The personality is not powerful because its strength is splintered among the person's many selves. During adolescence and young adulthood, indecision and alternation of roles frequently cause confusion between love and hate. A non-validating response ("You're nothing but a damned coward!") from a loved one causes rage in the lover. There is an intermingling of one's patterns of cooperation and competition, the untangling of which is the main "element of the social order" for this stage. This can only be achieved by honest, self-revealing conversation with an intimate.

When the young adult is able to achieve intimacy with another and has developed a strong sense of identity, he has great power for accomplishment. He is then able to successfully enter the seventh stage, Generativity.

Generativity vs. Stagnation: 25-65

Generativity refers to the process of being useful to society, thus repaying it for its care and protection of us as a child. As in the Industry Stage, the goal is to make things (products, beds, meals, paintings) in order to obtain the rewards they can bring. In the Generativity Stage, one's productivity is aimed not merely at material rewards but at generating a deep sense of well-being.

Several researchers have suggested that most adults never reach this stage: males become fixed in the Industry Stage, doing their work simply to obtain social symbols of success; females become fixed in the Identity Stage, confused and "untogether" psychologically—more mature than males, but able only rarely to become really intimate with them.

In generativity's opposite, stagnation, we see self-indulgent adults who are unable to contribute to society's goals. Indeed, they act as though they were their own only child.

Erikson makes tradition and education the social goals of the generative adult. Such a person wants to pass on the best of the past while helping others prepare for their future because it is satisfying and *re*generative, to do so.

Integrity vs. Despair: 65...

Finally, if one has been able to spend one's adult life being generative, then a sense of integrity is possible in this last stage. The adult who has a sense of integrity accepts his life as having been well spent and sees his life-long efforts as having been integrated in a useful way. He feels a kinship with people of different times and places who have helped create a more dignified life for mankind. Because of his integrity, he has wisdom.

When a person sees his life as lacking integration, he feels despair at the impossibility of "having just one more chance." He often tries to hide his terror of death by appearing contemptuous of mankind in general, and of his own kind (e.g., religion, race) in particular.

Table 2-1. Erik Erikson's Theory of Development

A Stages	B Psychosocial Crises	C Radius of Significant Others	D Related Elements of Social Order
1 Infancy 0-1 1/2	Trust vs. Mistrust	Maternal Person	Cosmic Order
2 Early Childhood 1 1/2-3	Autonomy vs. Shame, doubt	Parental Persons	"Law and Order"
3 Play Age 3-5	Initiative vs. Guilt	Basic Family	Ideal Prototypes
4 School Age 5-12	Industry vs. Inferiority	Neighborhood School	Technological Elements
5 Adolescence 12-18	Identity and Repudiation vs. Identity, Confusion	Peer Groups and Outgroups; Models of Leadership	Ideological Perspectives
6 Young Adult 18-25	Intimacy and Solidarity vs. Isolation	Partners in Friendship, sex, Competition, Cooperation	Patterns of Cooperation and Competition

Continued

7 Adulthood 25-65	Generativity vs. Self-Absorption	Divided Labor and Shared Household	Currents of Education and Tradition
8 Maturity 65 +	Integrity vs. Despair	"Mankind" "My Kind"	Wisdom

We are now working toward, and fighting for, a world in which the harvest of democracy may be reaped. But if we want to make the world safe for democracy, we must first make democracy safe for the healthy child. In order to ban autocracy, exploitation, and inequality in the world, we must realize that the first inequality in life is that of child and adult. Human childhood is long, so that parents and schools may have time to accept the child's personality in trust and to help it to be disciplined and human in the best sense known to us. This long childhood exposes the child to grave anxieties and to a lasting sense of insecurity which, if unduly and senselessly intensified persists in the adult in the form of vague anxiety—anxiety which, in turn, contributes specifically to the tension of personal, political, and even international life. This long childhood exposes adults to the temptation of thoughtlessly and often cruelly exploiting the child's dependence by making him pay for the psychological debts owed to us by others, by making him the victim of tensions which we will not, or dare not, correct in ourselves or in our surroundings. We have learned not to stunt a child's growing body with child labor; we must now learn not to break his growing spirit by making him the victim of our anxieties. If we will only learn to let live, the plan for growth is all there (Erikson, 1950).

Birth Order

Although studies of the effects of the order of a child's birth on personality are not unanimous, there is enough agreement to warrant a brief consideration of them.

First, investigators have found that the most significant differences are between first-born children and those born later (called "other-borns"). No reliable differences in personality can be discerned between second-and third-borns, middle-and last-borns, etc. This goes against popular beliefs (e.g., last-borns are usually more selfish).

When we consider possible reasons for differences between first-and other-borns, this finding is not surprising. The most widely held theory suggests that first-borns are the only children in a family who believe they are the center of their world, and then, with the birth of a sibling, perceive that they have lost that favored position. It is only natural that the first-born, the only child to experience the undivided attention of his parents and relatives, should become so egocentric. It is also natural that he should greatly resent the loss of his singular status. To the extent that this change is traumatic, the first-born child suffers an attack on his basic trust which will have strong effects on his personality development. By the way, children without siblings have the first-born's center-of-the-world status, but don't experience its loss. We would therefore expect findings on them to be conflicting, and we do. First-born twins apparently are like other-borns, which also fits the theory.

First-borns differ from other-borns in that they are:

1. More anxious. They worry a lot. There is some evidence that first-borns are more likely to become neurotic (e.g. develop phobias and obsessions), but *less* likely to become psychotic.

2. More interested in social approval. This may explain the relative absence of psychosis, in that psychotics are generally quite antisocial.

3. More sensitive to the feelings of others. They are more empathetic, but often less sympathetic, than other-borns.

4. More successful economically.

5. Less successful emotionally. For example, MacDonald (1965) found first-borns to be poorer marriage risks. He found happiness in marriage to be ordered, from high to low, as follows:

    a. Other-born male to other-born female.

    b. First-born male to other-born female.

    c. Other-born male to first-born female.

    d. First-born male to first-born female.

6. More creative.

7. More intelligent.This is probably due to the greater attention received in the first year of life. There is also some evidence that the mother's hormonal pattern is permanently altered by the birth of the first child, which might affect the intelligence of children born later.

8. More likely to be found in the ranks of eminent people.

9. Better achievers in school at all levels.

10. Are more reflective, less impulsive.

11. Have stronger consciences and behave more morally. This is explained by some researchers as the result of the stricter discipline first-borns receive, especially from the father.

Knowledge of these facts can lead to a greater understanding of the child's behavior, but there is also a real danger of the self-fulfilling prophesy. That is, if you know that a child is first-born, you expect him to be more anxious, and he becomes so as a result. I would suggest waiting at the start of a semester for a month or two before finding out each child's birth order. You can even make a prediction before finding out, an activity which will surely deepen your perception of your students.

Locus of Control

The idea that learning comes about when appropriate responses are reinforced is well-accepted. When the child acts appropriately, he is rewarded, making it more likely that he'll do the desired thing the next time. This applies not only to learning facts, skills, and concepts, but to the shaping of personality as well.

Psychologists have been interested recently in a concept called "locus of control." First investigated by Julian Rotter, this concept refers to the child's belief in his capability to obtain reinforcement. Some children almost never accept the credit or blame for their actions. Instead, they have a general belief that the world is a place of chance and luck. If good things happen to them, they believe it is because they were lucky or because sombody likes them. When bad things happen to them, they do not see the part played by their own behavior. They assume that they have had a bad break. These children are said to have an external locus of control. Judy, who is described in Chapter Nine, is a perfect example. When she was nine years old, she was an accomplished thief and liar. She easily adjusted the truth to fit her needs. For her, the main thing was whether or not she got caught; a matter of good or bad luck, rather than a consequence of her own behavior. Other children feel a strong sense of control over their environment, and as a result, realistically seek to influence it. They are said to have an internal locus of control.

Many educators believe that an internal locus of control is the better personaltiy trait since the person with faith in his own sense of control is more likely to try to influence the world around him. He has a greater interest in learning, is more curious about new situations, and more easily enters into personal relationships with others. He is also more teachable, because he is more responsive to the reinforcements teachers offer.

It is possible to be too internal, however. In this case, the person believes that everything that happens to him is his own fault, or to his credit. Nevertheless, it is usually considered desirable to be more toward the internal end of the locus of control continuum. Diagrammatically, that looks like this:

High Internal |————|————|————|————| High external
          1   2   3   4   5

Measures of locus of control are numerous; unfortunately, most are not yet adequate for use in schools. Much research remains to be done here. The one measure which I have found to work rather well, especially at the third to seventh grade levels, is the Nowicki-Strickland Test of Locus Control (Table 2-2). A score for internality is obtained by giving one point for every "no" answer, with the exception of nos. 4 and 18.

Table 2-2. Nowicki-Strickland Test Of Locus Of Control

· This is not a test, we just want to know what girls and boys your age think about certain things. Circle the yes or no in front of the questions below. There are no right or wrong answers. You should circle the one that most often is true for you.

yes	no	1. Are some kids just born lucky?
yes	no	2. Do you feel that most of the time it doesn't pay to try hard because things never turn out right anyway?
yes	no	3. Do you believe that wishing can make good things happen?
yes	no	4. Do you feel that most of the time parents listen to what their children have to say?
yes	no	5. Do you feel that it's nearly impossible to change your parents' mind about anything?

yes	no	6. Do you feel that when you do something wrong there's very little you can do to make it right?
yes	no	7. Do you believe that most kids are just born good at sports?
yes	no	8. Are most of the other kids your age stronger than you are?
yes	no	9. Do you feel that one of the best ways to handle most problems is just not to think about them?
yes	no	10. Do you feel that when a kid your age decides to hit you, there's little you can do to stop him or her?
yes	no	11. Have you felt that when people were mean to you it was usually for no reason at all?
yes	no	12. Do you believe that when bad things are going to happen they just are going to happen no matter what you try to do to stop them.
yes	no	13. Most of the time do you find it useless to try to get your own way at home?
yes	no	14. Do you feel that when somebody your age wants to be your enemy there's little you can do to change matters?
yes	no	15. Do you usually feel that you have little to say about what you get to eat at home?
yes	no	16. Do you feel that when someone doesn't like you there's little you can do about it?
yes	no	17. Do you usually feel that it's almost useless to try in school because most other children are just plain smarter than you are?
yes	no	18. Are you the kind of person who believes that planning ahead makes things turn out better?
yes	no	19. Most of the time, do you feel that you have little to say about what your family decides to do?

The Hierarchy of Needs

One of the best ways to understand personality growth is to look at basic human needs. The late psychologist Abraham Maslow spent most of his illustrious career examining the development of needs. Maslow argued that man has basic instincts, to which he pays far too little attention. These instincts are not like those of animals—loud voices telling us precisely what to do and when. But the voices are there, and a person who is psychologically healthy is one who is able to listen to and heed these commands.

Maslow believed that we have six basic instincts. These instincts operate similarly to Erikson's life crises. That is, they are manifested in a sequential order, with the basic needs present at birth and higher order needs showing up as maturation proceeds. Furthermore, successful fulfillment of later needs requires that earlier, more basic needs be met first.

Maslow named the six needs as follows:

1. Physiological needs. These are the needs we have for basic creature comforts: food, water, warmth, air.

2. Safety needs. These refer to our requirement to be free from threat to our lives. These needs also include our desires for familiarity and regularity.

3. Belongingness and love needs. All people want to feel that they belong somewhere and that at least one other person feels a sense of love and caring for them.

4. Esteem needs. We need to feel that we are worthwhile and capable, and that the society we live in values our contribution to it.

5. Self-actualization needs. We also need to be in touch with those resources that lie deep within us. These include imagination and creativity, our ability to experience great joy, and to make total use of our potential. Maslow suggests that we carry not only our past inside us but also our future, in the sense that the direction of our growth lies within us and needs to be fulfilled.

6. Aesthetic needs. Very few people actually are aware of having an aesthetic need. This is the need to make an important contribution to mankind. It is the desire to have a deep understanding of the world around us and the purpose of life. This need exists on a high level, and only a few (e.g., Einstein, Keller, Lincoln) experience it.

The insight of Maslow's hierarchy can readily be seen. Clearly, if we are suffering from severe hunger pains, it is unlikely that we will be concerned with whether or not people respect us. In fact, we may be quite willing to steal, even if this brings us the condemnation of our community. It is usually the case, therefore, that when a person's needs in one particular level are unfulfilled, those needs must be preeminent. He is not likely to be concerned with higher level needs.

Maslow also made a distinction between deficiency needs and being needs. Deficiency needs are those needs which can be satisfied. Being needs, on the other hand, increase as they are fulfilled (they are also termed "growth needs"). Examples of deficiency needs would be thirst and hunger. When we have enough, we no longer want any more. An example of a being need would be the ability to understand and appreciate music. The more we come to like music, the more we desire the joys it can provide.

Maslow believed that earlier psychologists, such as Freud, over- emphasized deficiency needs. They saw motivation as the drive to eliminate needs. The ultimate goal of human beings is to return to *nirvana*, a needless state. Maslow felt that this theory explained only part of our behavior. It applied, he suggested, more to sick individuals and those whose low level needs are unmet, than to most people in civilized countries today. He argued that we should pay more attention to man's being needs, now that his deficiency needs are normally well taken care of.

Although the hierarchy of needs is sequential, there are some notable exceptions to the sequence. Some individuals become so involved with taking care of their deficiency needs that they become incapable of experiencing any being needs. Some neurotic individuals, for example, seem to be so threatened by their environment, that they must constantly take care of their safety needs. Drug addicts, alcoholics, and compulsive eaters are other examples of people fixated on deficiency needs. On the other hand, some individuals seem so involved with being needs that they neglect their deficiency needs. Great artists and martyrs are examples of this type.

Another of Maslow's important ideas is his definition of normality. For him, normality is essentially a question of self-fulfillment. Thus, what is normal is the inner ability to make oneself the best and fullest possible personality that one is able to create. This concept, which Maslow calls self-actualization (level 5), is the one for which he is best known.

The self-actualized person is one whose personality is free from the deficiency problems of youth and the neurotic problems of adult life. This is a person who is able to concentrate on the essential problems of life because he accepts his inner self. There is a high correlation between the way he presents himself to the world and the way he knows he really is.

Persons who are self-actualized are more likely to have what Maslow called "peak" experiences. The peak experience is a momentary flash of insight which brings with it great joy and gratitude at being alive. The perception at this time is ego-transcending and self-forgetful. People during and after a peak experience characteristically feel fortunate and grateful. They feel that they have a new understanding of their lives and their relationship to the world around them. A peak experience is a "moment of ecstasy."

Unlike most of his fellow psychologists, Maslow spent the majority of his time studying individuals who were notable healthy and gifted. On the basis of these lengthy studies, he suggested that the self-actualized person:

1. Is realistically oriented toward the world.
2. Is more accepting of himself and others..
3. Has a high degree of spontaneity.
4. Is problem-centered rather than self-centered.
5. Is inclined to be detached, meditative, contemplative.
6. Is likely to come up with a fresh appreciation of people.
7. Tends to be mystical.
8. Identifies strongly with his fellow man.
9. Has a deep and intimate relation with a few others.
10. Has strong democratically oriented values.
11. Is highly ethical and moral.
12. Tends to see humor in everyday things.
13. Has a great deal of creativity.
14. Is resistant to conformity, though not a radical.
15. Is able to give love without making demands in return.
16. Has a high tolerance of ambiguity.

Maslow suggested that most of these characteristics are the very ones that our education system should promote. They are the values we discover, he believed, when we look at the free choices of healthy individuals.

Summary

There are numerous other aspects of personality growth (e.g., sex role identification, body image), but those most relevant to teachers are covered here. If you are tempted to apply the ideas of Erikson, Maslow, and Rotter to your acquaintances, give in to the temptation, by all means.

In fact, you may want to try using the theories in a more formal way. If you do, start by making the following tables, which I have filled in with hypothetical data:

Table 2-3. Erikson's Crises

Name	5 -10	10 - 15	Age 15 - 20	20 - 30	30 - 60	60 +
Jim			Identity			
Mary					Generativity	
Sue				Intimacy		
Ann		Identity				
Hal		Industry				

As you can see, in the column representing each person's age, I have put the Eriksonian stage with which I think that person is dealing. Clearly, age and stage don't always match. If you classify enough people on the chart, interesting patterns begin to emerge. The same is true for Maslow's hierarchy of needs and Rotter's locus of control:

Table 2-4. The Hierachy Of Needs

Name	5 - 10	10 - 15	Age 15 - 20	20 - 30	30 - 60	60 +
Ralph					Self-Act	
Nancy	Safety					
Linda				Self-Act		
George				Love		
Greg			Esteem				

Table 2-5 Locus Of Control

Name	5 - 10	10 - 15	Age 15 - 20	20 - 30	30 - 60	60 +
Fran-cois			2*				
Hank						4
Darlene					5	

Continued

Lucy	2
Pat 5	
Louise	2

*1 = most internal, 5 = most external

Although this exercise will enhance your understanding of personality development, there is the danger of forming rigid attitudes about the personalities of others. As each of the psychologists represented in this chapter would agree, the human personality is always in process, and is continuously capable of dynamic growth. The teacher's role is to understand the directions of personality growth, discover where each child is on these continua, and foster his advancement to the next higher level. Means for encouraging this progress are explained in later chapters.

References

Coleman, James C. *Abnormal Psychology and Modern Life.*. (fifth ed.). Glenview, Ill.: Scott, Foresman, 1976.

Erikson, Erik H., *Childhood and Society.* New York: Norton, 1950.

Erikson, Erik H., *Identity: Youth and Crisis.* New York, Norton, 1968.

Evans, Richard I. *Dialogue with Erik Erikson.* New York: Dutton, 1969.

Kilpatrick, W.K. *Identity and Intimacy.* New York: Delta, 1975.

Maslow, Abraham H. *Farther Reaches of Human Nature.* New York: Viking Press, 1971.

Maslow, Abraham H. *Toward a Psychology of Being.* New York: Van Nostrand, 1962.

Nowicki, S., and B.R. Strickland. "A Locus of Control Scale for Children," in *Journal of Consulting and Clinical Psychology,* Vol. 40. 1973.

Chapter 3

Understanding
Intellectual Growth

What do we mean when we say a person is "intelligent"?
Why do children think so differently from adults?
How can a helpless infant become an Einstein?

Although our answers to these questions today are far from perfect, the answers given by scientists at the beginning of this century were amazingly naive. It was widely believed that, mentally, the child is a little adult, and it is only necessary to pour information into him in order for him to reach mental maturity.

Jean Piaget's Search for the Intellect

In the fifty-five years since Jean Piaget began answering these questions, we have come to realize that the development of the intellect is incredibly complicated. Happily, Piaget himself was unusually well qualified to seek answers to these questions. A friend of Einstein's and a student of Freud's, he also possesses more than his share of that evasive characteristic, intelligence. By the age of eleven, the precocious Swiss was demonstrating his scientific gift. He wrote a paper on the behavior of the Albino sparrow which was accepted in the French Journal of Ornithology. His scientific activities continued, and at fifteen he was offered the post of curator at the Geneva Natural History Museum. He turned it down, however, in order to finish high school. He received his Ph.D. in biology at the age of eighteen. By the 1920's he had started a family, and his observation of the mental development of his three children soon led him into an interest in psychology. From 1920 through the present he has written over fifty books on cognitive development, most of which are considered classics in this field.

Piaget's ideas were not well accepted in the United States until very recently, however. Psychologists here had rejected his thinking because it was not based on experiments, as are most of the theories in the United States. Piaget does not subscribe to carefully controlled studies. He prefers to informally interview children of various ages and ask about their approaches to various problems. This method caused American scientists to be wary of his conclusions. In addition, he has publicly criticized both the psychoanalytic and behavioristic schools of

psychology, which did not help his popularity here. Although not strictly a humanist, this is the school to which he is most closely associated.

However, systematic experimental studies of his ideas have so
uniformly confirmed his thinking that now Piaget is well accepted
throughout the world. At eighty years old, he continues his research as
Director of the Jean-Jacques Rousseau Institute in Geneva, Switzerland.

Those many years of study have produced a magnificent vision of
human intellectual functioning. More and more, we see Piaget's concepts
creating an impact on American education. It is essential that the student
of education achieve a solid understanding of those concepts.

The General Theory

Piaget's first major insight was the recognition that children don't
merely think less well than adults; they think in a different fashion.
Rather than using logic, he discovered, they use what he calls
"psychologic." Two examples of psychologic are "animism," and "artificialism." Animism is the belief that inanimate things are alive and
have a will of their own. As one child Piaget interviewed suggested, 'The
sun started because it found out people were alive." Another child said,
"You shouldn't step on a rake because you will make it mad and it will
jump up and hit you." Artificialism is the idea that natural processes
which happen of themselves are controlled by outside agents. As one
child put it, "A great man lit the sun up with a match, that's how it got
started." How is it that children grow from this stage to a stage in which
they routinely employ complex thinking? Piaget suggests that this comes
about through the gradual attainment of increasingly effective mental
structures. The process is actually a special case of overall biological
functioning. No matter how simple the level of the organism, be it a frog,
an amoeba, or the simplest cell, the process of biological functioning is
always the same. There is constantly an adaptation to an everchanging
environment through the reorganization of the organism's structures.
These two concepts, organization and adaptation, are central to Piaget's
theory. Both have proven to be extremely useful concepts to educators;
let's look at adaptation first.

Adaptation

Adaptation is itself made up of two interdependent processes;
"assimilation" and "accommodation." Every action which we undertake,
whether mental or physical, is composed of both these processes. We
assimilate when we change our perception of the environment to fit the
concepts we have in our minds. We *accommodate* when we change the
concepts in our mind to fit what we preceive in the environment. Some
examples will make the distinction clearer.

Because we have the natural tendency to conserve energy, we try to
do as much assimilation as possible. All organisms attempt to assimilate
the surrounding environment. It is simply easier to see the environment
around us as something that we already understand and can handle. It is
harder when we have to change ourselves in order to adapt to it.

A good definition of "meaningfulness" has to do with assimilation. A thing is meaningful to the extent that we are able to assimilate it, that is, to the extent that it is similar to what we already know. If we cannot fit our perception of an object or a problem to our already existing structures, then for the time being it has no meaning for us.

Let us look at the word "recognition." Think for a moment what the word really means. When an object which we are perceiving is very familiar to us, we have no trouble knowing what it is. We "cognize"it, that is, we are able to perceive and understand it with very little mental activity. When it is not so familiar, it is necessary to re-cognize it, that is, to rearrange what we are seeing in order to comprehend it. Let me give you an example. Turn this book upsidedown for a moment. I am sure that you still know that it's a book, and you can probably even read it in the upsidedown position. It takes you longer, though, because you have to rearrange what you're perceiving before you're able to do any thinking about it. This book is obviously the same book as it was when it was right side up, but your brain doesn't know that at first. You have to reorder your perception so that you can assimilate the information into your mind.

Children are constantly faced with the need for assimilation. Consider a child that has learned to lift a heavy green book. When he comes across a lighter red paperback, does he know whether or not he can lift it? Most children will quite readily reach over and lift up the red book the way they had learned to lift the green one. When they do this, Piaget tells us, they are failing to notice that the two books are different. To their mind's eye, the two books are perceptually the same. Thus we can see that the data is modified so that it can be assimilated into the mind's existing storage.

Sometimes when a new object or problem cannot be assimilated, it is simply filtered out or altered. We literally "don't believe our eyes." This is known as "selective perception." Many studies have been done on this. Harvard psychologist, Jerome Bruner, for example, found that when asked to draw pictures of various coins, poor children draw them considerably larger than do wealthy children. Bruner believes this indicates that the poor child actually sees a coin as bigger, because he has so few of them.

Piaget compares mental assimilation to the assimilation of food. All food is different in some way. Our digestive system changes it chemically until it is all the same, however. In this way it can be assimilated into our body structure (our cells).

Our mental structures are comparable to cells. Piaget calls these structures "schema." Schema are the concepts or abilities which we have stored in our mind which make us able to interact with our world. Piaget calls combinations of schema "schemata."

We are born with some schema, the sucking response, for example. The eye blink and the knee-jerk reflexes are other examples. MIT's celebrated linguist Noam Chomsky has suggested that we are even born with some language schema. He divides language into surface structures and deep structures. Surface structures have to do with cultural differences: for example, French children learn French, Eskimo children have twelve different words for snow. The deep structure, however, causes us to use nouns, verbs, and other parts of language consistent in all languages. These, Chomsky suggests, are the result of genetic schema, which we *must* follow. Language consists of these parts of speech because of the way our brains have evolved, and not necessarily because our environment is so organized that only nouns, verbs, and the like can describe it.

When assimilation won't work (an object is too strange, an idea is too different), but action must be taken, than the organism must accommodate itself to the environment. It must change existing schema or add new schema in order to be able to adapt itself to the environment.

Suppose the child mentioned above who has learned to pick up books uses the same technique to pick up a heavy chair. He quickly learns that his lifting-carrying schema will not solve his problem. Perhaps in his struggle to lift the chair, he accidently shoves it six inches across the floor. After several trials he may realize that another way to move objects is to push them across a surface rather than carrying them. He has discovered a new moving schema and has therefore accommodated his internal structures to fit the external problem. Learning new responses is the essence of intellectual growth, according to Piaget.

It should be pointed out that even when the child lifted the second book, some accommodation occurred. When the child realized that he could lift this new object (it could have been a brick, a lamp, or a doll), he now has a larger schema for "moving small, light things." Even in the example of eating, where food is assimilated, our cells are slightly different as a result of having eaten, so there was some accommodation in that, too.

Another major contribution of Piaget's is the realization that mental adaptation always begins with the manipulation of things. As the child manipulates things, he gradually incorporates more and more understandings, concepts, skills, and abilities. He increases the number and variety of schema with which he can work. But more important, as he incorporates these ideas, he also learns the process of adaptation itself. This will be used in the highest levels of abstract thinking. Thus human beings progress from reflex actions to habits to high level intelligence by going from sensory and motor activity to concrete to abstract thinking. This process will become clearer when the stages of development are described.

Equilibration

The balance between assimilation and accommodation in any activity is extremely important. Sometimes we already know how to do something and should assimilate it, but we don't realize that we know how to do it and must learn it anew. This would be a case of accommodating when we should be assimilating. On the other hand, sometimes we try too long to use our old techniques when we should be less rigid and more willing to learn a new approach.

This balance between the two Piaget calls equilibration. A critical aspect of intelligence is knowing when to assimilate and when to accommodate, that is, the ability to maintain one's equilibrium. Mentally retarded children are an example of people who excessively use accommodation. They do not recognize that they've already learned a similar behavior. Schizophrenics, on the other hand, who tend to be very rigid, are an example of people who assimilate when they should accommodate.

The Development of the Intellect

Historically, psychologists have looked at human development in one of two ways. Some have seen development as a continuous flow of even growth. Others have recognized stages of development, in each of which some specific goal is sought. Today almost all psychologists find the stage approach of development more helpful than the continuous approach.

There are two kinds of stage theories; discreet and overlapping. Freud's stages of personality development are an example of discreet stages. Most development theorists today, however, argue that while there are stages in human development, when we look closely at them we definitely see considerable overlap. Piaget subscribes to this position.

The essential factor about stages is that they always follow a particular sequence. The ages at which individuals go through stages may vary, but the sequence of stages does not vary. Piaget has discovered four such stages of intellectual development. The ages given for each stage are approximations for the rural Swiss children Piaget has studied. These age ranges are even more approximate for American children, who apparently go through the stages somewhat earlier.

The following is the order of the stages;

1. The Sensorimotor Stage—birth to two years.
2. The Preoperational Stage—two to seven years.
3. The Concrete Operational Stage—seven to eleven years.
4. The Formal Operational Stage—eleven and up.

Before considering the characteristics of each stage, two processes that occur as children develop intellectually should be pointed out. First, children are *egocentric*. For infants, egocentricism means that they do not separate themselves from the outside world. In young children, egocentricism refers to their inability to take anyone else's point-of-view.

Watch little children. They assume everyone understands what they are saying. They usually don't bother to prove things, and they don't recognize contradictions in their thinking. Little children rarely have conversations with each other. They talk at one another, or engage in what Piaget calls "collective monologues." As children develop intellectually, they become less and less egocentric.

A second process which occurs as children progress is called *decentration*. Initially, young children cannot attend to different aspects of an object at once. They *center* on one aspect of it. If you line up a row of ten buttons and below it put another row of ten buttons, but space these buttons wider apart, young children will say the the second row has more.

O O O O O O O O O O

O O O O O O O O O O

They are centering on the length of the row, and cannot attend to the number of buttons. As with egocentrism children decenter as they develop intellectually.

The Sensorimotor Stage — birth to two years

During this stage, the infant's thinking depends upon his senses and his ability to manipulate things. There is no mental manipulation of objects. At this stage, a child's knowledge of, say, a table, depends on his perception and touching of it. The child's perceptual and physical activity are the origin of later intelligence.

Piaget assumes that newborn infants begin life with basic inherited structures, for example, the knee-jerk and sucking. During the Sensorimotor Stage, these basic structures are quickly modified and expanded through assimilation and accommodation, so that near the end of this stage very young children have the beginnings of symbolic representation, or thought as we commonly know it.

An extemely important change that takes place during the Sensorimotor period is the infant's development of *object constancy*. Infants have no sense that an object that has left their field of vision still exists. When a toy rolls out of sight, the infant does not search for it. Over time, though, infants develop a sense that objects do exist even if not in their vision. Infants' endless fascination with peek-a-boo is an example of the lack of object constancy.

The Sensorimotor Stage has great importance for later intellectual development. On the basis of careful observations of infants, Piaget has specified six substages.

*Substage I—Reflex Actions—*Birth to 1 month

During the first substage of the Sensorimotor Stage, infants exhibit inborn reflexes such as sucking. The sucking reflex becomes a sucking schemata by repeatedly exercising the reflex. The infant is assimilating his reality into existing structures; thus, the infant will suck anything that touches his lips. Later, he will engage in sucking actions where no food or objects are present. The point is that inborn reflexes, and later the schemata, need to be exercised and repeated. The infant actively seeks to exercise schema. Thus, a behavior such as thumbsucking results from the gradual modification (through assimilation) of the sucking schema.

*Substage 2—Primary Circular Reactions-*One to four months

The second substage involves the development of habits. The infant tries to re-establish or rediscover a behavior that had a pleasurable result. By trial and error, and without apparent intention, the infant succeeds in doing so. Thereafter, the child repeats the behavior or series of behaviors. A habit is established. Piaget refers to the process as a primary circular reaction. The infant repeats a behavior, originally an accidental discovery, in order to rediscover the novelty or pleasure it aroused in him. The behavior has no goal or purpose other than recapturing the original pleasure.

Substage 3—Secondary Circular Reactions—Four to ten months

In the third substage, however, the infant begins to engage in secondary circular reactions. He now performs behaviors in order to procure results in the external environment. There is intention on the child's part. Piaget gives the example of his son, Laurent, who by chance moved his arm so that a string attached to his hand caused some toys to rattle. Laurent, over a period of time, learned the arm movements necessary to cause the interesting noise to happen again. Laurent was engaging in a secondary circular reaction. His concern was more with changes in the external environment than with his own bodily states.

*Substage 4—Coordination of Secondary Schema—*Ten to twelve months

Substage Four continues the development of intentionality. The child is capable of setting a goal (finding a hidden object), and of finding a means to obtain the object. His activities, though, are still dependent on his ability to see part of the object. He will remove obstacles (a pillow hiding a watch) to get at the object. It is during this substage that the infant develops an awareness of object constancy. He will actively search for an object that has been removed from his field of vision.

*Substage 5—Tertiary Circular Reactions—*Twelve to eighteen months

Tertiary circular reactions dominate the fifth substage of the sensorimotor period. The infant repeats behaviors in order to procure effects on the environment (secondary circular reactions), but he varies the behaviors to get different results. Piaget suggests that at this stage the infant seems to be interested in novelty for its own sake. The infant is also capable of discovering new means to accomplish an end. Piaget describes how his daughter, Lucienne, tried to obtain a toy he had placed in a small, closed box. At first, she tried to pinch the box between her fingers (she had recently done this in obtaining a handkerchief). She then struck the box so that it swung around. She was then able to grab the toy. In Piagetian terms, she first tried to apply an existing schema (assimilation) to the problem, but eventually she accommodated to a new "retrieval" schema and retrieved the toy.

*Substage 6—Beginning of Thought—*Eighteen to twenty-four months

The last substage is important because it marks the beginning of symbolic thinking. During this substage the child develops internal representations of reality. Piaget notes how Lucienne, in an attempt to get a watch chain out of a matchbox, looked at the problem, tried previous schema which failed, opened and closed her mouth, then pulled open the match box and obtained the chain. In this example, Lucienne's mouthing movements represented how she had thought out the problem.

She formulated a solution in this way and did not have to manually solve the problem by trial and error. She used *rudimentary thought* instead of sensorimotor movements.

The Preoperational Stage—2 to 7 years

As we have seen, near the end of the Sensorimotor Stage the infant has begun to use mental representations in dealing with his environment. The preoperational stage expands upon symbolic manipulation. The child becomes freed, to some extent, of a direct motoric and sensory interaction with his world. For Piaget, the preoperational period is dominated by the development of language and of mental symbols such as numbers and arrows.

Although we might say that the child from two to seven has begun to think, his thinking is not logical in the way we adults (should) think. Children's thinking during these years is, in fact, illogical. They live in another world. Piaget, again after careful observation of how children in this age group think, has identified several characteristics of preoperational thinking, some of which will be briefly described.

Children's thinking is "transductive" as opposed to deductive or inductive. Instead of reasoning from the general to the particular (deductive) or the particular to the general (inductive), the preoperational child reasons from particular to particular. Piaget gives the example of his daughter, Jacqueline, who didn't have her afternoon nap. She proceeded to conclude that it was not afternoon. Jacqueline proceeded from one particular, her nap, to another particular, afternoon. Closely related to transductive reasoning is the preoperational child's use of *juxtaposition*. Here, the child explains one event by another event close to it. He might, for example, explain the sun's presence by the presence of clouds. In his mind, the closeness of the sun (up there) and the clouds (up there) has explanatory worth. Have a conversation with a five-year-old in which you ask him to explain things. You will undoubtedly notice numerous examples of transductive reasoning and juxtaposition. It is important to remember, though, that the child *thinks* he is giving you an explanation, and may in fact be completely unable to understand his contradictions even when you point them out.

The Concrete Operations Stage—7 to 11 years

The preoperational child also lacks other processes necessary for logical thinking; reversibility, conservation, and classification, all of which develop during the concrete operational stage. To understand what happens to children's thinking in this stage, we need to consider these three operations in some detail.

As an illustration of Piaget's concept of *reversibility*, consider his beaker experiment (Fig. 3-1). In it, a child is shown two identical beakers—both are tall and thin (beakers A and B), and contain an equal amount of water. The child is asked "Which has more water?" He will usually say they are the same. The water in beaker B is then poured into a short, wide beaker (beaker C).

Fig. 3-1

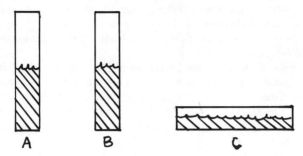

The child is then asked which beaker has more water, beaker A or C. He will usually say that A now has *more*. The preoperational child lacks reversibility, the ability to mentally reverse a series of steps. He cannot backtrack and remember that the volume of water in beaker B was the same as the volume of water in the first beaker. The concrete operational child can mentally pour the water from C back into B. He knows that beakers A and C have equal amounts of water.

This same experiment also illustrates *conservation*. Conservation means that objects retain their basic properties no matter what form they take. In the above example, the preoperational child's response, that the tall thin beaker has more water than the short wide one, results from his attention to only one aspect of the problem. The same child might also say that the short wide one has more water, again for the same reason. He does not have a sense of relationship between height and width with respect to volume. (This is also an example of decentration.)

Piaget uses another classic example to determine whether or not a child has reached the Concrete Operational Stage. He takes a ball of clay and rolls it out to form a long snake. He then asks the child which has more clay, the ball or the snake. The concrete operational child, having reversibility and conservation, knows that the amount of clay has remained the same. He is able to see that as the clay gets thinner, it also gets longer, or that the volume is conserved. Preoperational children, who cannot comprehend the relationship, are likely to say that the snake has more clay.

In addition to conservation and reversibility, the concrete operational child also develops the ability to *classify* objects. He is able to "organize" reality. One test involves showing a child 20 wooden beads; 16 of which are brown, and 4 are white. Piaget asks the child, "Are there more wooden beads or more brown beads?" The preoperational child will say there are more brown beads, whereas the concrete operational child will say there are more wooden beads. The point here is that the concrete operational child has the general classification of wooden beads.

In another noted experiment, the child is shown a picture of a group of flowers; 6 roses, 6 tulips, and 6 daffodils. The experimenter says to the child "All of the roses have died; are there any flowers left?" A child at the preoperational stage will often respond that no flowers are left, indicating his lack of the general class of flowers. The concrete operational child will respond that some flowers still exist; he has learned the principle of classification.

The child in the Concrete Operational Stage is able to solve mental problems, but he has to do so in a *very concrete way*. For example, the beaker experiment has to be performed in front of the child. It would be unlikely that he could solve this problem if you explained it to him verbally. He can only manipulate reality mentally when he has real objects to work with.

Formal Operations Stage — 11 to 15

In the Formal Operations Stage, which begins in early adolescence, children first begin to think abstractly. Formal operational thinking is distinguished by the adolescent's ability to formulate hypotheses, to generate alternative solutions to them, and to devise a method of verifying these solutions. The following two problems reveal how adolescents think.

Problem I (which is presented verbally):

There are three girls—Mary, Jenny, and Sally. Mary is taller than Sally. Mary is shorter than Jenny. Who is the tallest? Most 12 or 13-year-olds will be able to solve this problem because they can think abstractly and in verbal terms. The average 9-year-old will have a great deal of trouble in correctly answering the question.

Problem II

The subject is given two dice and told to throw them on the table several times and keep track of the results. The table is constructed so that the outer portion is wood and the inner portion is metal. One of the dice has a magnet imbedded opposite "1".

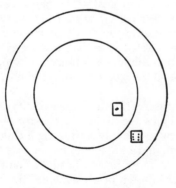

On repeated throws of the dice, the number "1" turns up more often than would be expected. A fourteen-year-old might initially conclude that one of the dice is weighted. He then repeats throwing the dice to verify the hypothesis that he has formulated that one die is weighted. Then he notices that "1" only turns up when the supposedly weighted die lands on the metal portion of the table. He wonders if it could be magnetized. He throws the suspicious die again to verify this hypothesis. He eventually verifies his second hypothesis that "1" shows more often because of a magnet in the die that is activated by the metal portion of the table. In terms of formal operational thinking, what is significant here is that the adolescent systematically approached the problem by setting up two hypotheses, and then devised means of testing them.

In the ability to think hypothetically, we see the fruition of intellectual growth. Although adults certainly go on building new and more complicated schemata, there will be no more changes in cognitive style. The development of basic mental structures and operations has been completed.

In summary, Piaget sees the development of intellect as beginning with very few mental structures, and no mental operations at all. Through physical interaction with the environment, for example, playing with blocks, the child begins to develop mental schemata. In the preoperational stage, the child begins to learn a language and with it, the ability to categorize his environment. While he cannot yet perform true mental operations, the process of internalizing events in his environment so that he can manipulate them in his mind now gets its start. In the concrete operation stage, he becomes able to imagine how his surroundings can be changed without actual manipulation. Finally, in the formal operations stage, he is able to hypothesize ideas as well as concrete objects.

While Piaget's picture of the development of the intellect is the most widely accepted view, there is one major competing theory, that of Harvard psychologist Jerome Bruner.

Bruner's Three Stages of Intellectual Growth

During many of the years that Piaget was studying children's thinking in Switzerland, Bruner was doing the same in America. Though Bruner's description of intellectual growth is similar to Piaget's, it differs in some important ways.

The primary differences are that Bruner finds there are three, rather than four, stages of change in cognitive activity, and the onset of each stage is far less tied to age than in Piaget's view. Each has to do with the primary way in which thoughts about the world are represented in the child's mind. These are:

Enactive Representation

Thinking here is mainly in terms of actions, not symbols or words. To learn to shovel, a child must dig. The child learns by doing and by imitating others, not by being told what to do. This coincides with the fact that most of what the young child needs to learn is of a physical nature. Bruner's description of this stage matches well with Piaget's ideas about sensori-motor thinking.

Iconic Representation

When children reach this stage, they can think about objects without acting upon them. They can imagine a shovel just lying on the ground—they don't need to actually use it for digging. They are able to understand the use of pictures to represent objects, and can begin to use diagrams.

Symbolic Representation

Now language comes into prominent use. The operation of a steam shovel can be described to the child, even if he's never seen one. He no longer depends on the object itself or a picture of it; words will suffice. Because the child can now think in symbols, he is able to make logical derivations. His mental operations become more compact, and much more powerful.

Bruner assigns no ages to his stages. He believes that the sequence in which the three types of thinking develop does not vary. However, he argues that once they have developed, each continues to have a place in the thinking patterns of older children and adults. Thus, when an adult learns to ski, he must be taught enactively. Iconic or symbolic representations of skiing will not help much.

Bruner's first two stages correspond rather closely to Piaget's. Contrary to Piaget, however, he sees the development of logical and hypothetical thinking developing far sooner.

Another more important difference between the two theorists is the emphasis placed on genetic vs. instructional aspects of learning. For Piaget, the genes play the major role. Bruner sees instructional techniques as vital, although he would not deny the importance of genes. He once said that "Any idea or problem or body of knowledge can be taught to anyone at any time, in some intellectually honest form." By this, he means that if the material is presented in a mode that corresponds to the child's current intellectual stage, he can learn advanced concepts. These concepts are then re-presented later in a mode commensurate with the later mental stage, to deepen his understanding.

For example, we can teach a first-grader economics, if we go about it correctly. The common approach, teaching about a grocery store, is all wrong. Grocery stores are complex systems, encompassing most of the principles of economic theory. Symbolic thinking is required to fully understand such a system. It is far better to demonstrate a manufacturing firm, and allow the class to actually make something and sell it. Children who are only able to think enactively can comprehend this simpler system.

Because Piaget's account of intellectual growth is much more detailed than Bruner's, it is a more testable theory, and as such is receiving more attention by psychological researchers. But unlike Piaget, Bruner has used his theory to build a psychology of instruction which has proven considerably useful to educators. It is described in detail in Chapter Ten.

Intelligence

The discoveries of Piaget and Bruner have only recently affected American education. Historically, our main approach to understanding the intellect has been through research on the Intelligence Quotient (IQ).

One of the best known investigations of intelligence is Louis Terman's famous study of 1,500 California children whose IQ's were over 140. This study, which followed the children's progress for over thirty years starting in 1925, dispelled the myth that very bright people tend to be inferior in other ways. Terman found that on the average, the children turned out to be:

1. above average in height, weight, physical ability and general health.
2. significantly higher in school achievement.
3. earlier to walk and talk.
4. earlier to reach adolescence.
5. more likely to skip a grade or two.
6. better adjusted socially and more often chosen as group leaders.
7. less likely to get divorced.
8. less likely to be criminals or alcoholics.
9. had a total of 2,000 scientific papers and 33 novels to their credit in 1959, and had taken out 230 patents.
10. had a death rate 33 percent lower than average.

Does this study prove that children with high IQ's are *genetically* superior? Not really. Several children were included in the study whose homeroom numbers were accidentally entered in place of their IQ scores. The ten statements above generally applied to these children too! Perhaps being *treated* as someone with a high IQ makes the difference.

The mountain of research that has been done on IQ started at the turn of this century with the efforts of Alfred Binet, working for the French minister of public education in Paris. The minister had decided that children with really low mental ability, the "mentally retarded", were in need of instructional techniques different from those of other children. To learn who these retarded children were, he commissioned Binet to devise a test of mental ability. The test he developed is the great-grandparent of today's IQ tests. Everybody knows about IQ, but not many understand how the test works, and this is one of its many problems.

The IQ test is really a series of tests. Some have as few as five subtests, some quite a few more. Each subtest purports to measure some aspect of mental functioning. Arithmetic reasoning and verbal associations are examples. Significantly, social and perceptual abilities are not included, even though they are mental functions. IQ tests only try to measure the so-called "cognitive" abilities, the kinds of things typically taught in school. They do not try to measure school learning, but rather to predict it. The tests attempt to measure genetic ability only, but clearly previous learning is involved. The failure of some parents and teachers to understand the limitations of the test constitutes a second major problem.

More specifically, the test can only predict "ability to do well in a white, middle-class, American school." If that sort of prediction is required, then IQ tests are highly reliable and valid, but they cannot be used to compare the *intelligence* of white, middle-class Americans with others.

A third problem stems from the use of a single score. Let's take the popular *Wechsler Adult Intelligence Scale*. Suppose we give this test to two sixteen-year-olds, and find that they get these subscores:

Verbal Subtests	*John*	*Karen*
A. Information	10	25
B. Comprehension	10	0
C. Arithmetic	5	0
D. Digit Span	10	25
E. Similarities	5	0
F. Vocabulary	10	0
	50	50

They each got a total "raw" score (the number of answers they got right) of 50. We now look at a table of raw scores to get their "mental age", which is the average age of children who get 50 on the test. These averages are based on many thousands of scores. We find that 50 yields a mental age of 16. The formula for computing IQ is:

$$IQ = \frac{Mental\ Age}{Chronological\ Age} \times 100$$

(Multiplication of all scores by 100 gets rid of decimal points.) Thus both John's and Karen's IQ = 16/16 × 100 = 100. Their IQ of 100 is exactly average— mentally they are seen to be like the typical sixteen-year-old. The problem is that they aren't at all like each other!

John is average in all six areas tested. Karen is a genius at Information and Digit Span, and severely retarded in Comprehension, Arithmetic, Similarities, and Vocabulary. Of course, this example is an exaggeration, but children who have the same IQ frequently can be quite different from each other.

One researcher, J.P. Guilford, whose life's work has been spent trying to learn how many distinct mental traits there are, believes there are actually 120! He comes to this conclusion by analyzing the results of hundreds of mental tests, using complicated statistical procedures. He says there are three main features of what he calls the "structure of the intellect": operations, contents, and products. There are five types of operations: memory, evaluation, cognition, and convergent and divergent thinking. Convergent thinking would tackle a problem such as "how much is 291 times 352", for which there is only one right answer. A problem for divergent thinking would be "what would change if it rained up instead of down?" There are four kinds of contents: figural, symbolic, semantic (note the similarity to the stages of Piaget and Bruner) and behavioral. There are six types of products: units, classes, relations, systems, transformations, and implications. For each operation, there is a separate content and product possible; for example, convergent thinking about figural classes, or memory of semantic implications.

Guilford's investigations are the most thorough to date, but they have had little influence in the classroom. This is probably because it is so unwieldy to deal with so many variables. Unfortunately we tend to be content with just one, the ambiguous IQ.

A fourth problem with the IQ score is that it is intended to be a measure of innate ability, and therefore should not change over time. However, individual scores do vary over the lifetime of the person being measured, and we now know some facts about how this variation occurs. The most significant data come from a study by Benjamin Bloom, in which he found that IQ begins to stabilize quite early in life. By four years old, fifty percent of the variation in IQ has become stable, and by eight years old, eighty percent has become fixed. That is to say, the chances of improving a person's IQ, while not very great at birth, decrease rapidly in childhood. By the time a person has reached his teens, his intelligence, especially his verbal intelligence, is pretty well determined. New learning experiences and environments are not likely to have an impact on it.

Bloom's data appear to indicate that IQ is largely determined by our genes, as òpposed to our environment. A recent study by Arthur Jensen backs this up. Seeking to understand why the average IQ of whites is fifteen points higher than blacks, he reviewed a large number of investigations on the relationships of IQ's between twins raised apart and together, between adopted children and their parents, and other such correlations. He concluded that genes account for four-fifths of intelligence. Therefore, Jensen argued, the IQ difference between whites and blacks is basically a fixed difference, and little can be done about it. "Compensatory education," he said, "has been tried, and failed." If Jensen were right, then much of our current educational philosophy on equal opportunity would no doubt change. His study has already affected government policy. However, there are several reasons for educators to reject his conclusions, at least at present.

The methods of the study are controversial. For example, the only available studies of twins have been of white twins. Conclusions based on these studies might be different for black twins. The correlations between IQs of parents and their children appear to represent a genetic factor. However, the effects of parents' training of their children, which they then pass on to their children, cannot be separated from genetic effects.

Probably the most serious problem for Jensen's position is that compensatory education, for example, Head Start, doesn't start until age four. There is compelling evidence to indicate, however, that the most important influence of the environment on IQ ends at one and a half! We know from excellent animal studies and from beginning research on humans that the development of our nervous system itself is affected by interaction with the environment. The main nervous pathways (macroneurons) are fixed at conception, but the tiny interconnections between these pathways (microneurons) go on growing in humans for a year and a half. It appears that orderly variety (remember Erikson's basic trust stage?) stimulates the number and extent of growth of microneurons. If this is the case, then IQ scores are in large part the result of one's *early* environment. Compensatory education of infants has never been attempted.

An approximation of such an effort was reported in a very recent study by Scarr-Salapatek and Weinberg. They looked at IQ's of black children adopted during the mid-60's by middle-class white parents. The researchers did not contend that white parents are "better" than blacks, but only that the whites had higher IQ's and socio-economic status. Given the level of education and occupation of the biological parents, the predicted IQ score of the black children would have been 90. Instead, they averaged 106. More revealing, the researchers found that the... "earlier a child was placed, the fewer disruptions in his life, and the better his care in the first few years of life, the higher his later IQ score was likely to be." This is strong evidence that intellectual ability *is* responsive to stimulation if it comes early enough.

Although many have called Arthur Jensen a racist, it seems clear that he is a highly competent researcher who was trying to shed more light on the nature vs. nurture controversy. However, his conclusion that we should no longer try to compensate minority children for the effects of centuries of oppression is not at present supportable.

The investigations of the researchers mentioned in this section have served to improve the accuracy with which we measure the intelligence quotient. Their avowed purpose in this research has been to help us individualize instruction for students at various intelligence levels. Unfortunately the use of the IQ has sometimes led to just the opposite effect. Children were labeled according to their level of IQ. Then all the children at that particular level were given instruction presumed to be appropriate for that level. This approach is too rigid and categorical for many of today's educators, who prefer the more dynamic approach of Piaget. With the exception of the controversy stirred up by Jensen's research, the interest of American educators in IQ has been declining rapidly in recent years.

Non-Linear Thinking

The conceptions of intellectual growth presented in this chapter are based on the study of several generations of children. If the speculations of futurist Marshall McLuhan prove accurate, however, these conceptions may need to be revised. He suggests that the thinking patterns of the latest generation differ markedly from those of earlier generations.

As McLuhan has demonstrated so insightfully, the means by which we take in information determines to a great degree the way in which we learn, and more important, what we learn. More than we ever dreamed, the medium which gives us our information controls our very thinking styles.

McLuhan has defined three stages in the history of media. The first started with the beginning of man and lasted until about 1459 when the Gutenberg press was invented. Media were virtually nonexistent during this first period. People got their information face-to-face in a verbal fashion. Only after the invention of the printing press did people begin to get information in a different way.

This second period he calls the "age of print-oriented man." The main thinking style during this stage is referred to as "linear." We see the extreme of this kind of thinking in the late Eighteenth and early Nineteenth Centuries with the so-called Age of Reason. One's emotions were suppressed in order to put one's logical mind in charge of all decision-making. It was this repression of feelings which Freud was to combat so successfully in the early Twentieth Century, by offering a powerful explanation of the importance of our emotional nature.

Print-oriented man remained emotionally aloof from the events of his time. He was able to avoid emotional involvement because he got most of his information about the world in the form of print, usually some considerable time after the event had occurred. National and international news reached him so late that he seldom felt any sense of involvement with it. He could therefore read with detachment about bloody wars and hideous famines. It is in the Nineteenth Century that we see the "rugged individual" and the "self-made man" so admired. This is a person who rises above the masses through his total self-interest and disregard for the misfortunes of his fellows.

This emotional atrophy seems to have been the result of emphasizing one sense, vision, to the exclusion of the others. By using mostly the eyes, and mostly for reading, it was possible to view the world in a sequential, categorical way. Anything which did not fit logically was excluded. Intuitive insights, which occur in the unconscious and rely for information from all the senses, were thus severely limited. Hence, the circumstances were right for self-centered individualism.

This second period in man's information history ends around the turn of this century with the advent of electronic media: the telephone, the telegraph, the phonograph, radio, movies, television, and satellite communication. McLuhan argues that these inventions have moved us into a third stage, in which the whole world is becoming a gigantic global village. He names this period the "neo-tribal stage." People are once again coming into frequent and immediate personal contact through technology. We are being forced into a new concern for the well-being of others.

Today's young adults are the first generation to have known television all their lives. They are used to having information bombard them in a non-sequential form, as it does on television news programs. Although older adults watch television, too, they react to it differently. In their childhoods, they were used to the linear inputs of information like newspapers, magazines, and books. Children today simply are not as concerned about order and logic. Many movies which are popular today tend to disregard time sequence and logical development; they seldom have a beginning, middle, and end. Rather, they attempt to create sense impressions. Consider, for instance, the movies of Fellini, Truffaut, and Wertmuller. You don't try to understand such movies, you just *feel* them. It is therefore hard to reason with today's youth—they just don't think the same way their parents do. As Norden puts it:

> The generation gap is actually a chasm, separating not two age groups, but two vastly divergent cultures. I can understand the ferment in our schools, because our educational system is totally rearview mirror. It's a dying and outdated system founded on literature values and fragmented and classified data totally unsuited to the needs of the first television generation.

Table 3-1 summarizes McLuhan's ideas.

Table 3-1

Marshall McLuhan's Media Theory

I. Tribal Villages	II. Print-Oriented Man	III. Neo-Tribal Man—Non-Linear Thinking
A. ?-1451	1451-1900's	1900-?
B. Media non-existent	Printed media	Electronic media
C. Face-to-face contact	Contact through reading	Personal contact through technology
D. Non-linear thinking, arational	Linear thinking, rational	Non-linear thinking, rational-arational
E. Sensual, use of all senses	Anti-sensual, emphasis on eyes	Sensual, use of all senses
F. Non-sequential info. input	Sequential info. input	Non-sequential info. input
G. Group-oriented, "other-directed"	Self-oriented, "inner-directed"	Group-oriented "inner-other directed"
H. Home manufacture-man as craftsman	Assembly lines-man as automation	Computor automation-man as inventor

Summary

Some analysts believe that McLuhan has been insightful in calling attention to the numerous effects of media on thinking style, but argue that he has exaggerated the extent of these effects. They suggest that though his ideas seem to fit well with the rebellious attitudes of youth in the late 1960's, the return to "normalcy" among today's young people, probably because of their greater concern over job prospects, appears to contradict his theory.

Whether right or wrong, McLuhan's ideas pertain primarily to styles of thinking rather than to the developmental patterns of mental structures. The latter are of a deeper and more permanent nature. Especially to a theorist like Piaget, the genetically supervised unfolding of mental structures is unlikely to be affected in any crucial way by cultural customs, innovations in media, or any other environmental force.

I think that we in education would be wise to consider the advice of McLuhan, Bruner, and other researchers in determining how we go about educating, but I think we will do best, at least for the present, to pay most attention to Piaget's description of the course of intellectual growth. His is the most dynamic view of the process, the accuracy of his theory has received substantial support from recent research, and its implications are proving most helpful to educators.

The author wishes to thank Phillip Churchill for his contribution to this chapter.

References

Bruner, Jerome S. *On Knowing*. New York: Atheneum, 1973.

Bruner, Jerome S. *The Process of Education*. New York: Vintage, 1963.

Bruner, Jerome S. *The Relevance of Education*. New York: Norton, 1973.

Bruner, Jerome S. *Toward a Theory of Instruction*. Cambridge, MA: Harvard U. Press, 1966.

Ginsburg, Herbert, and Sylvia Opper. *Piaget's Theory of Intellectual Development*. Englewood Cliffs, N.J.: Prentice-Hall, 1969.

McLuhan, Marshall, and Quentin Fiore. *The Medium is the Massage*. New York: Bantam Books, 1967.

Piaget, Jean. *The Child's Conception of Physical Causality*. Totowa, N.J.: Littlefield, Adams & Co., 1969.

Piaget, Jean. *The Language and Thought of the Child*. New York: World Publishing, 1973.

Piaget, Jean. *Play, Dreams, and Imitation in Childhood*. New York: Norton 1962.

Piaget, Jean. *The Psychology of the Child*. New York: Basic Books, 1969.

Piaget, Jean. *The Psychology of Intelligence*. Totowa, N.J.: Littlefield, Adams, & Co., 1973.

Stearn, Gerald E., McLuham. *Hot and Cool*. New York: Signet, 1967.

Part II

Chapter 4

Encouraging Learning

When a child takes the chair to begin learning, another radio receiver senses his presence through his EID (Electronic Identification Device) and signals the central learning computer to plug in that particular child's learning history. The child puts on his combination earphones and brainwave sensors, so that OBA (Ongoing Brainwave Analysis) can become an element in the dialogue. (Some schools use the brainwave pattern, much in the manner of a fingerprint, to identify the learner.) Once the computer picks up the child's ongoing brainwaves, it immediately begins reiterating (in drastically foreshortened form) his last learning session. The child watches his most recent lesson reeling by on his display. If he wants to continue where he left off last time, he holds down his "yes" key until the reiteration is finished. If not, he presses down his "no" button, and the computer begins searching for other material appropriate to the child's level of learning, material which is flashed onto the display until the child presses "yes". The "select" process generally takes less than two minutes. The dialogue then begins (Leonard, *Education and Ectasy*. 1968, p. 148).

For most of the educators I know, the phrase "learning theory" has unpleasant associations. It conjures up a nightmare of complex, twisted relationships between countless concepts, all expressed in undecipherable jargon. Theoretically, learning theories should lead to a better understanding of teaching, but in the past their contributions have been limited indeed.

Lately, however, important innovations and specific instructional strategies have resulted from the earlier work of several theorists. In this chapter three of these new teaching techniques are described: behavior therapy, behavior modification, and modeling. Each is preceded by a description of the learning theory on which it is based.

Pavlov's Stimulus Association Theory

The first formal theory of learning was devised by the Russian psychologist, Ivan Pavlov, in the late 1800's. Famed for his experiments with dogs at the beginning of this century, Pavlov attempted to develop an explanation for the learning of all animals, including humans. His efforts were so successful that until recently any psychologist in Russia who attempted an alternative explanation was in serious trouble. During Stalin's regime, some psychologists who insisted on non-Pavlovian approaches to psychology were sent to Siberia.

Pavlov decided that since salivation at the smell of food was a highly regular and measurable response in dogs, it would make an ideal behavior to study in order to understand more about learning. He reasoned that if he could teach a dog to salivate at the ringing of a bell as well as at the smell of food, and if he were to observe closely how the dog learned this, he could gain insights into the learning process. This simple approach led to the discovery of a number of important learning principles.

Pavlov's experiment began with a dog held stationary in a comfortable harness. A tube led from under his tongue to a calibrated vial which showed precisely how much he salivated. He was presented with some meat. Naturally the amount of salivation differed depending upon a number of factors; such as the type of dog, the number of hours since he had eaten, etc. Pavlov made certain that the circumstances were constant in each test. He then rang a bell before presenting meat to the dog. After a number of presentations, it was found that the mere ringing of the bell, without presentation of any meat at all, caused the dog to salivate. It was clear that the dog had learned to salivate to a stimulus (the bell) linked to the original stimulus (meat). Pavlov called this linking of the two stimuli "first order conditioning."

He then went on to discover a number of principles which govern learning in this simple case. First, he tried sounding a buzzer before sounding the bell. In this case again, no meat at all was presented. After a number of repetitions of the buzzer-bell combination, he found that the dog would salivate at the sound of the buzzer, even though the bell was not sounded. The salivation to the buzzer was never quite as much as it was for the bell, but clearly new learning had taken place. Pavlov referred to this as "higher order conditioning." He suggested that this is the way in which most learning in life actually takes place.

Pavlov found that not only can a new stimulus be substituted for a previous one if enough repetitions occur; he also found that stimuli *similar* to that used in the learning experiment would cause salivation. If he rang a bell of a different tone from the original bell, some salivation would occur (but never as much as for the tone that was originally used). This phenomenon, which he called "stimulus generalization", follows a very orderly pattern. Thus if you teach a dog to salivate by sounding the tone of C, he will also salivate, but to a lesser amount, to the tones of B and D. He will salivate, but to an even lesser degree, to the tones of A and E, and so on.

Stimuli which automatically elicit a certain response in the absence of any learning are called "unconditioned stimuli." Examples are salivation to the smell of food, crying when stuck with a pin, and pulling one's hand away from a hot stove. Pavlov demonstrated that much of our learning comes about from the association between these unconditioned stimuli and stimuli which later in life come to be paired with them. These later stimuli are called "conditioned stimuli." An example of a conditioned stimulus would be a mother's cry of "Hot!" when a child starts to touch a stove. If the child gets burned a couple of times, he will jerk his hand away from any object when his mother cries "Hot!" Another example of a conditioned stimulus is the feeling of hunger we suddenly notice when we look up at the clock and see that it is ten minutes before noon. Clocks do not elicit hunger pangs, but since most people are accustomed to eating around noon, the sight of the clock at mealtime reminds them that they should feel hungry.

I had a teacher in junior high school who used this principle to great advantage. Very early in the year, whenever anyone was talking while she was trying to teach, she would tap lightly on the blackboard with a piece of chalk. At first, of course, this brought about no result. After tapping for a moment, she would tell the offenders to go to the principal's office. From that point the mere tapping of the chalk caused such nervousness that there was no need for further discipline. Our frightened response to that chalk sound had been deeply conditioned.

Pavlov's theory of learning, called the "classical theory", explains rather well how we learn our emotional reactions. It does not seem to be so helpful in understanding school learning, however. Most unconditioned stimuli, such as presenting food or sticking with the pin, are not available for use in the classroom. Therefore, this theory is proving to be much more useful in explaining the learning of emotional responses. Behavior therapy is an example of how learning theory can help people learn more effective responses to deal with their own emotions.

Wolpe's Behavior Therapy

As you grow you learn many emotional reactions, such as attitudes, opinions, beliefs, and values. With most of these, you are probably reasonably happy. However, you may also have learned some emotional reactions with which you are less happy. Prejudices and phobias would be among these. Building on Pavlov's theory of learning, psychiatrist Joseph Wolpe has developed a technique for reversing the effects of prejudices and phobias. This is one of the most useful applications of Pavlovian psychology.

Let us suppose, to pick a fairly common example, that you are terrified of snakes. Let us further imagine that you would like very much to get rid of this phobia, since you're aware that nearly all snakes you are likely to come in contact with are perfectly harmless. If you were to go to Dr. Wolpe, your treatment for this phobia would go something like this:

In the beginning, your therapy would have little to do with snakes. You would first need to learn Wolpe's relaxation technique. This technique involves easing muscle tension, deep breathing exercises, and the like. When you have become capable of relaxing your body, quickly and at will, the therapy moves into the second stage.

The whole method is based on this critical point: two competing responses cannot occur at the same time. You are presented with a stick, and you are told to think about snakes and, at the same time, employ your relaxation techniques. Thus a totally relaxed reaction competes with the regular anxiety reaction and since you are only holding a stick, the relaxation technique wins out.

The therapy moves along in stages. Having become completely comfortable holding the stick, you hold it while you look at a picture of a snake. Next a length of rubber hose is substituted for the stick, and then you are given a rubber replica of a snake.

When you are completely relaxed with these artifacts, you are taken to a room in which a snake is living in a glassed-in terrarium. At this point in the therapy your anxiety would be strongly aroused, so a considerable amount of time is spent practising relaxation under these circumstances. Next you are requested to cross the room toward the snake, and move as close as you can. Finally you stand in front of the terrarium until you are able to gaze at the snake without undue fear. At this point you will be given a rubber snake to handle while you look at the live snake in front of you.

The final point of the therapy involves handling the snake itself. At first you reach into the cage without touching the snake; you just hold your hand there until you are relaxed. Then you touch the snake, and finally you are able to pick it up. Almost everybody who has a strong fear of snakes is able to go through these steps and wind up handling the snake. The conditioned response of fear to the snake stimulus has been reconditioned to a response of relaxation. It may be hard to imagine that you would actually be able to do this since you have not gone through each of the steps. This treatment and other examples of behavior therapy usually take a considerable amount of time. Only when you have experienced the intermediate steps is it possible for you to achieve the desired results.

Wolpe and his associates have been quite successful in relieving a considerable number of phobias with this technique. Another example is the treatment of acrophobia: the fear of heights. A group of people with this phobia meet on the first floor of a tall building, and its members have dinner together. They are taught the relaxation technique and soon find themselves quite comfortable with each other. The next week exactly the same process takes place, except that the meeting is held on the second floor. Gradually they move up through the building, from time to time skipping floors, until they have finally reached the top floor of the building.

In the past, many psychologists suggested that if we simply relieve the symptoms of a phobia we will have done little good, because there are deep underlying causes of these symptoms. It was suggested that when a person eliminates one kind of phobia, a new one will emerge, since the underlying problem has not been relieved. Research undertaken during the past fifteen years does not support this assertion. In most cases, when the phobia was cured, no other symptoms emerged. It may be that the elimination of the phobia so improves the person's self-concept that the underlying cause is alleviated.

The Pavlovian model has been highly useful with emotional distresses. However, its usefulness to us in the classroom is limited to such problems as stage fright and school phobia. A more useful classroom learning theory is that of B.F. Skinner.

Skinner's Theory of Learning

When B.F. Skinner began to study learning in the late 1920's, his interest had nothing to do with improving teaching. In those days, he wanted only to satisfy his curiosity about how organisms change when they interact with the environment. He believed that scientists should start studying simpler organisms, and work up to investigating the complexity of humans. Pigeons and rats were chosen for study because their nervous systems are reasonably similar to those of humans, and because manipulating their learning did not pose the ethical problems that arise with human experimentation. Skinner also felt that knowledge gained about those animals would provide better clues to the study of humans. If so, this would save the researcher time, effort, and costly mistakes.

Skinner makes two basic assumptions about the learning of all organisms, whether an amoeba or a human being. First he assumes that all learning is determined by forces outside the control of the organism. What we learn and how we learn it is determined completely by genetic inheritance and by the influences that come to bear on us from our environment, past and present. Thus he does away with the concept of free will, which would otherwise be a complicating factor in any theory of learning.

He further believes that behavior, rather than thought, is the only appropriate subject for the study of learning. Thus he is known as a behaviorist psychologist. Skinner argues that the study of learning is analagous to a training technique used in engineering schools called the "black box method." In this technique, engineering students are given a black box with two terminals. They vary the voltage, amperage, and wattage of the electricity put in one side, and then meter the results coming out the other side. They are not allowed to know what is inside the black box; it is their job to infer what is in there by watching responses of the black box to the electrical stimuli. This is analagous to the study of learning, as there is no way for us to know what is going on inside the human head. Thus Skinner is opposed to theorists such as Freud, Erikson, and Piaget. He feels that they are presumptuous to make guesses about the mechanisms of the mind at this early stage of study.

Having made these assumptions, Skinner studied the relationship between three variables: stimuli, responses, and the reactions of the environment to responses. Like Pavlov, Skinner's formula for learning is simple. It follows these three steps:

1. Some stimulus occurs in the environment. This might be a question from the teacher to the student.
2. A response is made in the presence of that stimulus. An example might be a correct answer on the part of the student.

3. One of three things happens as a result of this response: the response is reinforced; the response is punished; or the response is ignored.

Skinner argues that if the response is reinforced, it is more likely to result the next time that stimulus occurs. Thus if the teacher were to ask that question again, the student is more likely to give the right answer, because that response was reinforced. If the response is punished, the response is less likely to result in the future. If the response is simply ignored, it also becomes less likely to result in the future. Each of these three concepts: reinforcement, punishment, and no response (which Skinner called "extinction") needs further explanation.

Notice that Skinner does not use the word "reward." He feels that this is distinctly different from reinforcement. The idea of reward includes some notion about what makes a person feel good for having made a response. There is a problem with this for Skinner: it assumes that we know what is going on in the mind of another person. We know what is rewarding to us, but we can only guess as to what is rewarding to someone else. Skinner prefers to define reinforcement as anything that makes a response more likely to happen in the future, without making any reference to how it makes the individual feel.

There are two kinds of reinforcement, and the difference between them is important. Positive reinforcement refers to any event which, when it *starts* to occur after a response, makes that response more likely to occur in the future. Negative reinforcement is any event which, when it *ceases* to occur after a response, makes that response more likely to occur in the future. Thus both types of reinforcement make the response *more* likely to occur. Postive reinforcement might be giving a child candy for doing the right thing. Negative reinforcement might be ceasing to twist someone's arm when he gives you back your pen.

Numerous experiments have shown that both types of reinforcement can work equally well in the short run. However, the association between the person doing the reinforcement and the type of reinforcer used can make a big difference in long-term learning. If a person regularly uses positive reinforcement, the learner tends to have positive feelings toward that person. If the person regularly uses negative reinforcement, learning will occur, but the negative associations will build up toward the person doing the reinforcing and also toward what is being learned.

In my own life, a memorable example was my study of the Latin language. Our teacher held us under the constant threat of her sneering disdain if we did not do our assignments well. We would spend the whole class period hoping to make the right response so that the threat of her disapproval would be removed. When we did make the right response, she did not congratulate us; she merely said that we may sit down. We knew that we would not be under that threat for the rest of the class. Hence, we were negatively reinforced. I got very high grades on the citywide exams in Latin, as did most of the members in that class. However, my attitude toward Latin today is one of great distaste, and I cannot translate even the simplest sentences. Teachers like her not only disaffect our attitudes toward their subject matter; they also sour our attitudes toward reading and learning in general.

Skinner defines punishment as any occurrence that follows a response and causes that response to be *less* likely to happen in the presence of that stimulus the next time. Punishment is not nearly as good a teaching technique as either kind of reinforcement, for two reasons. For one thing, punishment tells us what not to do, but usually does not tell us what to do. Also, like negative reinforcement, it creates an unpleasant association with the stimulus. Skinner therefore recommends that punishment be used as little as possible.

To reduce the likelihood of inappropriate responses, Skinner recommends the use of extinction techniques. Extinction simply means that when an undesirable response occurs, it is disregarded. It is true that in some ways this could be regarded as punishment, but certainly it is not nearly as severe as a tongue lashing, ridicule, or some other kind of aversive punishment. When a response is unreinforced for a long enough time, it is discontinued.

One of the discoveries that Skinner made about the use of extinction was that it is frequently followed by "spontaneous recovery." After a period of extinction, the supposedly extinguished response is likely to reappear spontaneously. The response recovers its previous strength even though not reinforced. This recovery is temporary, however, and if reinforcement is continuously withheld, the behavior will become permanently extinguished.

Skinner discovered a number of characteristics of reinforcement that are of considerable importance to teachers. One of these is that reinforcement is more effective the more quickly it follows the response. He also found that the frequency of reinforcement can have very differential effects, and these will be described in greater detail.

Referred to as the "schedule of reinforcement," there are two basic types of frequency: continuous and partial reinforcement. Continuous reinforcement, as the term implies, means that reinforcement is given every time the correct response is made. Partial reinforcement is given something less than every time. Skinner discovered there are four basic categories of partial reinforcement.

Fixed ratio reinforcement. Under this schedule, some specific ratio is established between the reinforcement and the number of responses necessary to achieve it. This ratio does not change over time. An example of fixed ratio reinforcement would be "piecework", which used to take place in almost all factories. Under piecework conditions, the worker, let us say in a shoe factory, would get paid five dollars for every ten pairs of shoes that he sewed, rather than fifty cents per pair. If he sewed thirty-nine pairs before quitting, he would receive no payment for the last nine pairs. This has the psychological effect of making most workers work faster, because they realize when they start a series of ten pairs of shoes, they will receive no money until they finish the tenth pair. Unions fought against this for years, and have almost succeeded in outlawing the practice.

Fixed interval reinforcement. In this type of reinforcement, the time elapsed, or interval between responses, rather than the number of responses is the critical variable. Thus a certain amount of time must have elapsed since the last reinforcement before the next reinforcement can be delivered, regardless of how many responses are made by the organism in between. An example of this would be a television news program, which only comes on at certain times of the day. You can turn the television on as frequently as you like between news programs, but you won't be reinforced for doing it unless you wait until the program is scheduled. Another example would be the weekly paycheck. Here you must make the response of being on the job. If you put in the required number of hours, you receive the reinforcement of a paycheck.

Variable ratio reinforcement. Variable ratio reinforcement is similar to fixed ratio; the only difference is that the ratio itself changes over the course of the learning. An example of this would be a slot machine, the notorious "one-armed bandit." Years ago, these machines were on a fixed ratio schedule, which repeated itself over a number of uses. For example, it would pay off the thirty-sixth time that someone put a coin in, then the twenty-second, the eighty-fifth, then the twenty-second and then back to the thirty-sixth, and so on. Smart gamblers detected this, and would watch a particular slot machine. When they had figured out the schedule of the machine, they would wait until just before the machine was to pay off. Having learned the player's name, they would have the loud speaker system in the casino call the person away from the machine. They would then deposit the remaining coins in the machine, and reap the rewards of the previous gambler's efforts. Machines are now on a variable ratio schedule. A mechanism inside the slot machine varies the actual ratio so that it works out in favor of the casino over the long run. No one is able to predict precisely what the ratio will be because it changes all the time, only approximating a specific ratio over the long run. Another example of the variable ratio schedule might involve a child who begs his mother to go out and play, only to be told "no." If he continues to whine and harass his mother, she may finally give in. This would be reinforcing the child on a variable ratio schedule. He will have discovered that he can go out if he asks enough times. This has the powerful effect of making the child think that perhaps the next attempt will be the one that will win; his behavior will be markedly persistent under this schedule.

Variable interval reinforcement. The example of the whining child might also fit this schedule. It doesn't matter how frequently the child requests to go out, but how long he's willing to keep making the requests. Time would be the critical variable rather than the number of responses. The slot machine example would not fit here; it doesn't matter how fast you put the coins into the machine, but only how many. Another example of the variable interval schedule would be what happens when we sit quietly in the woods. At first, nothing happens. Slowly, we begin to enjoy the soothing silence. Then we become aware that we are being watched by a rabbit, and share a moment of mutual curiosity. Reinforcing events like these (that is, if you find them reinforcing) continue to occur unpredictably as time passes. Usually, the longer we stay, the more we are rewarded for our patience. Thus we are reinforced on a variable interval schedule.

Which schedule of reinforcement is best? A continuous schedule promotes the quickest learning. However, it is the least "resistant to extinction", that is, responses learned under continuous reinforcement quickly become weaker and drop out of use after the reinforcement has been stopped. Variable schedules are much slower to bring about learning, but they are much more resistant to extinction. This is because the person's expectations are different in each of these reinforcement situations.

The best sequence to use for most types of learning is:
1. Introduce the learning with continuous reinforcement, following this path until the response is reasonably well established.
2. Switch to one of the fixed reinforcement schedules to firmly establish the response.
3. As soon as possible, switch to variable reinforcement.

Skinner used this sequence to teach pigeons to peck at a disk in order to obtain some grain. Pigeons tend not to like to peck at disks; possibly it is irritating to their beaks. Skinner used a variable ratio schedule to train some pigeons in disk-pecking, then ceased reinforcing them. One pigeon continued to peck at the disk over ten thousand times without a single reinforcement. This is an example of how resistant the variable schedules are to extinction.

Another principle in Skinner's theory is discrimination. When a response is well-learned, it is made not only to the original stimulus, but to all stimuli like it. Sometimes responding to stimuli similar to the original can be quite inappropriate. Then the organism must learn to discriminate the appropriate stimulus from similar but inappropriate ones. For example: an infant is lying gurgling in her crib, emitting all manner of meaningless sounds. Her mother and father bend over the crib, smiling at their daughter's efforts. Then, quite coincidentally, she utters the syllable, "da." Both parents rejoice, especially the father. Soon she makes the sound again, and is even more excitedly reinforced by smiles and hugs. In the days to come, the child emits a "da" whenever any adult, her grandmother or the plumber, comes into her vision. She receives no reinforcement for the response in the presence of these stimuli, though, and so "da" becomes extinguished for all stimuli but her father. Discrimination has occurred.

This model of learning has been expanded in a variety of ways to meet the needs of classroom learning. Most of these techniques are variations of "behavior modification," which will now be described.

How to Use Behavior Modification

The most common concern of beginning teachers is misbehavior in the classroom. Ask any new teacher what he is most worried about, and he will usually tell you in one word: discipline! A second problem that has concerned experienced as well as beginning teachers is how to get students to study material that they don't seem to care about. Any instructional technique that helps solve these problems would naturally receive a hearty welcome. It appears that behavior modification is just such a technique.

Behavior modification is a precise prescription for handling specific classroom situations. Its proponents ridicule generalizations such as "be yourself," or "seize the moment of intellectual curiosity." While these mottos may have some underlying merit, they are too general to be of any real use to the classroom teacher. Behavior modification concerns itself with only one thing: changing behavior. It does this by following three specific steps: define the behavior to be changed; establish a level of current behavior; and modify that behavior.

The key to defining behavior lies in picking an action which is completely observable. "Understanding" would not be such a behavior because we cannot see it in operation. Behavior modifiers believe that all worthwhile educational goals can be observed, and therefore measured. Only when we have clearly specified the behavioral objective can we be sure that we will be able to modify it.

This aspect of behavior modification has been much criticized. Opponents argue that while "appreciation of music" is not stated behaviorally, "identifying twenty composers," although stated behaviorally, is not what they mean by appreciation. Math teachers who see the subject as a way of improving problem-solving skills are not satisfied with simply measuring the student's ability to compute as an index of his math ability. They argue that behavior modification is only able to deal with external behaviors, that are usually of less importance than internal thought processes. They believe this leads to a superficial view of the goals of education. This disagreement is unresolved at present. Here we see clearly that although the psychologist wants to deal with education scientifically, questions of values are ever-present.

Before behavior can be modified, it must be known at what level a behavior is being exhibited. This tells us whether or not the reinforcement techniques we are using are actually increasing the number or strength of the responses we are attempting to modify. The teacher must observe carefully the frequency of the behavior. It is important that a behavior be observed in the setting in which it is going to be modified. Behavior exhibited in a classroom may be quite different from that exhibited in the principal's office. Of course this level must be stated behaviorally. Some examples would be: "misspells five words per page"; "talks out approximately every eight minutes"; or "refuses to participate in class discussions."

When the level of behavior has been established, attempts to modify it can begin. In the example of the student who refuses to participate in a discussion, it is not enough to wait for the desired behavior to occur so that we can reinforce it. It will be necessary to get the student to perform the behavior first. One approach to this is to use the modeling technique, which will be discussed in the next section of this chapter. Another approach is to set up a reinforcement schedule, which will usually call for moving from continuous to fixed to variable schedules of reinforcement. Behavior modifiers insist that the consistency with which the modification is followed is of extreme importance. They claim that most failures in behavior modification come about when teachers are inconsistent. Often the very behavior that the teacher is trying to get rid of is performed as a result of inconsistency. Suppose a student is told he must do all his homework to get a reinforcement. Then the teacher says that just this once it would be alright not to do it. This puts the student on variable ratio reinforcement for *not* doing the behavior. He will continue to try to get out of doing his homework. Therefore, reinforcement must always come after the appropriate behavior, never before.

An important aspect of behavior modification is what Skinner calls "shaping." Teachers, he argues, often expect too much at one time. It is usually necessary to accept some small vestige of the desired behavior at the start of a behavior modification program. At first, the teacher reinforces any small step toward the goal. After this improvement has been reinforced for a while, the teacher then withdraws the reinforcement, and only reinforces additional progress toward the goal. For example, in the case of a child who has trouble talking in class, the teacher at first will be willing to reinforce even one-word statements. After a while, however, the teacher refuses to reinforce only one word, and withholds reinforcement until whole sentences are used. When this has been established, then the teacher will demand even more intensive participation. In this way, the teacher gradually shapes the behavior toward the final goal. It is important not to over-reinforce behavior at any one step. Each step must be reinforced just enough so that it can be readily extinguished when the behavior of the next step starts to occur.

The process of shaping is so important that I would like to give you a further example from my own experience. I was a student in a psychology laboratory, and my assignment was to teach a rat to perform an unusual behavior. The final goal I chose was to teach the rat to sit in front of its food tray and bow ceremoniously twice before the tray before taking any food. You may be sure that this is not a common behavior in rats. I started by teaching the rat to go to the tray to get food, and then stopped putting any food into the tray. The rat naturally sat in front of the tray with a puzzled look on his face, apparently waiting for some food to come. After it had sat quietly for a few moments, I then fed it. The rat soon learned that it must sit quietly in front of the tray in order to be fed. Then I waited until the rat, still sitting there, began to wash its face, which is a typical behavior. I then quickly reinforced this. Soon the rat learned to wash its face before eating. Again I withheld reinforcement until the rat made a forward motion with its head while his paws were on his face. I quickly reinforced this. From then on it was easy to teach the rat that to get food, he must place his paws together, and bow deeply twice before the tray in order to get any food from it. To the observer who had not seen my teaching technique, it would look like I had a Japanese rat performing a tea ceremony!

There are several types of behavior modification being explored today. The two of most use to teachers are the token system and programmed instruction. The token system is a means of encouraging behavior considered appropriate that simultaneously allows the teacher to attempt to modify different kinds of behavior with different students. In this system, tokens are given to students immediately after they have performed the behavior that the teacher has specified. The tokens can be just about anything: little disks, pieces of paper, or checkmarks on a chart. When the student has earned a pre-specified number of tokens, he is given a prize.

In conjunction with the token system used to increase appropriate behavior, teachers often attempt to decrease bad behavior through the use of extinction, punishment, and negative reinforcement. Extinction usually involves giving the child the silent treatment when he's behaving inappropriately. Negative reinforcement usually means sending him to a "time-out" space, in which he is forced to sit and not participate in classroom activities until he can agree to change his behavior. When the offensive behavior stops he is allowed to leave the time-out space. Although punishment is considered to be almost always inappropriate, in some severe cases it seems necessary. For example, autistic children are usually severely withdrawn and hostile. It has been found that slapping is often the only way to get them to come out of their withdrawal and begin to interact with their environment, an action that can be reinforced.

Oponents of the token system list a number of criticisms:

1. Giving children prizes for appropriate behavior in the classroom teaches them to be "extrinsically" motivated. Thus they come to believe that learning should only be done when one is paid for it. It is better, critics feel, to try to teach children to be "intrinsically" motivated so that they see learning as a rewarding experience in itself. Proponents of behavior modification reply that there is no reason why the token system cannot be set up so that it gradually leads from extrinsic to intrinsic reinforcement.

2. Children whose behavior is appropriate in the classroom don't participate in the token system. They feel cheated because they don't get any prizes for their good behavior and learning skills. This is a difficult problem, and one for which no real solution has been found. It is possible to put every child in a classroom on a token system, but this often carries the system to a ridiculous extreme.

3. Some opponents argue that the system works too well. They say that because it is so effective, teachers are tempted to use it to change behaviors that should not be changed. The rights of the student remain a tangled and unresolved question here.

4. Behavior modification is just as powerful in the hands of the bad teacher as in the hands of the good one. As one observer put it, "It allows the cruel teacher to feel scientific and objective about his cruelty."

Too often the token system has been used haphazardly or in other ways injurious to students. It is a very effective means of helping students move toward intrinsic motivation, but teachers must plan carefully before setting up such a system in their classroom.

The second type of behavior modification, programmed instruction, can also be used effectively in the classroom. It is a method of organizing academic material into a logical sequence of small inputs, leading to overall mastery of that material. In reading the material, students are frequently asked questions that they must answer in order to continue. They are then quickly told whether or not they are right. A basic assumption of the system is that immediate feedback on the correctness of the student's response is itself reinforcing, and helps the student learn the material better. The system is organized so that the average student gets the answers right approximately ninety percent of the time. Proponents of this method feel that this achievement percentage assures deeper and more lasting mastery.

Programmed instruction usually comes in one of two forms: the programmed book, and the teaching machine. The programmed book presents a question on one page, the student answers the question, and then turns the page to find the correct answer. If he got the correct answer, he is asked to go to page X. On page X his instruction goes forward in the prescribed sequence. If he answered incorrectly, he has to go to either page Y or page Z, depending on which wrong answer he chose. On pages Y and Z, he is told why he got the wrong answer and what it was he should have understood. The reader is then allowed to go on to page X. The material is easy at first, and almost all students get the answers right. As students become accustomed to the technique, the material gets harder.

The teaching machine also presents information in the sequential manner of the programmed book. Instead of using pages, however, it uses "frames." Frames are paragraphs of information presented in a window on the machine. On one type of teaching machine, the student reads the frame, is then asked a question, and figures out his answer. He writes his answer in another little window, then pulls a lever that uncovers the correct answer. On other machines he is asked a question and given up to four answer choices. The choices have buttons beside them, and if the student pushes the wrong one, the machine will not continue. He must push buttons until he gets the correct answer.

Teaching machines may be "linear," in which all students follow the same sequence, or they may be "branched." In this approach, when the student presses the wrong button, the machine presents him with an additional series, a "loop" of material designed to clear up his misunderstanding of the original frame. When he has mastered the material on the loop, he comes back to the main sequence. If he makes more mistakes, he will be led through additional loops to insure that he understands each step before going on to the next one.

Supporters of programmed instruction have argued in favor of its use for the following reasons:

1. It forces the student to attend to what he is reading. We are all familiar with having read a chapter in a book and not really remembering very much of it. This is less likely to happen in programmed instruction.
2. Programs can be designed for various levels of difficulty so that all students can reach mastery of the material to be learned.
3. Students may work at their own speed rather than waiting for the slower students or trying to catch up with the faster ones.
4. No one but the student sees his mistakes, so the embarrassment of answering incorrectly in a classroom is avoided.
5. The material tends to be better organized than teacher lectures or discussions.
6. Because students make few errors, they seldom experience feelings of failure.
7. The instruction is self-supervised so that teachers are freed to help other students in the class.
8. The students get immediate feedback rather than having to wait for test results.
9. The machines can be set to keep track of errors. Teachers have a running record of how students are doing in any particular program and can give them advice as to how they can improve their work.

Critics of programmed instruction list the following complaints about it:

1. It is quite impersonal.
2. Misunderstandings are not corrected because the teacher is not aware of them.
3. Bright students are often bored because they always know the answers.
4. Slow students are frequently frustrated because they have a considerably higher error rate.
5. When programmed instruction was first introduced some years ago, many educational firms rushed programs into production, seeing a chance for large profits. Thus, the early programs were generally poor, a difficulty which has not yet been completely rectified.
6. Programmed instruction can be rather dull when answering questions over and over again becomes monotonous.
7. The machines and some books are too costly.
8. Many students don't care to know about correctness, especially when they don't care about the material they're studying, so immediate feedback is not reinforcing for them.
9. Usually the program does not allow for discussion or critical reaction to ideas.

10. There is some evidence that excessive programmed instruction may suppress creativity and individual judgment.

A technological advance in programmed instruction, one that may be able to alleviate many of these difficulties, is computer-assisted instruction. In this approach, teaching programs are designed for the computer's incredible speed and flexibility.

A proposal which combines behavior modification and humanistic teaching through the flexibility of computer-assisted instruction has been made by George Leonard. In his best-selling book, *Education and Ecstacy,* he describes an "education fair" called the Kennedy School. The year is 2001. This school has two main components; knowledge and skills mastery, and their applications in life situations.

Knowledge and skills mastery is accomplished in learning booths which are controlled by the computer. Each student must spend a certain amount of time in the activity, but he decides what areas he studies. Suppose he chooses to study Nineteenth Century American History. He enters the appropriate booth and inserts his plastic identification card in a slot. The computer checks his profile, and almost instantly learns his age, IQ, past performance, and other lessons, interests, etc. The computer then selects the appropriate program for him from several programs that teach Nineteenth Century American History.

He sits at a console before a television screen, with a pair of earphones on his head. An electronic bracelet on his wrist monitors his vital signs, giving the computer on-going information on his interest level, alertness, etc. He holds a cathode ray pen with which he can write directly on the television screen, in order to ask and answer questions, draw pictures, trace diagrams, etc. He proceeds through the program, branching when he makes mistakes. Motivational side-tracks (for example, five minutes of his favorite music) occur when he does well, needs a rest, etc.

When he completes his lesson, he is free to join one of the small groups interacting throughout the fairgrounds. Each with a teacher, the groups of students discuss problems, act in plays, and otherwise experience the application of their computer lessons.

Some teachers specialize in direct contact with students. Others spend all their time creating and improving computer lessons. A few do both.

Leonard suggests that there is no reason why his Kennedy School could not exist today, since all the technology needed to implement it is available now.

Computer-assisted instruction now has the following advantages over teaching machines:

1. The computer's ability to provide branching is virtually unlimited.
2. The computer can be hooked up to a television screen, slide machines, tape recorders, and other equipment to add more variety and interest.
3. The computer can be used with many students at the same time. It can thus gather information on many reactions to the

same program and use this information to improve the ways in which it asks and responds to questions. And it can be used to do almost instant statistical analyses on the types and numbers of various responses.

At present, the promised advantages of computer-assisted instruction have not been realized. The problem is not merely that the costs of the computer are enormous, but also that the immense compelxity of programs written for a well-designed computer program necessitates long-term use of these programs. Constant change in factual subject matter, our philosophical values, and professional techniques, make it difficult to be sure such programs will be usuable for a long enough period to justify the cost of their design.

Now let us consider a third aspect of learning, modeling.

Bandura's Theory of Modeling

Alfred Bandura, a social learning theorist, believes that there are actually two types of learning. One type of learning results from an individual's direct experience with his environment. Pavlovian and Skinnerian conditioning are examples.

A second type of learning described by Bandura, which also has great practical value for teachers, is "imitative" learning. Unlike Pavlovian and Skinnerian conditioning, the individual need not interact directly with his environment. Individuals learn by observing behaviors of others, and then modeling their own behavior accordingly. Very often, when we encounter new situations, we try to recall how some esteemed person in our lives handled or might have handled it. For example, it is common for new teachers to model their teaching style after a teacher whom they particularly admired.

Imitative learning is not merely random observation and copying of behaviors. Bandura notes that the role of the model is of central importance for immediate learning. The effectiveness of a model in influencing someone else's behavior depends upon the model's status, power, and competence. The model has to be attractive in some way to the learner. For example, a nine-year old boy is more likely to imitate Bobby Orr's hockey techniques than he is one of his peers, since Orr possesses higher status and competence as a hockey player. Obviously, there are situations imaginable in which the boy would be more likely to imitate a peer instead of a hockey star. The point is that the learner has to perceive the model as being worth imitating.

Bandura indicates two ways in which modeling influences behavior of others. The first way is simply that one individual may acquire new behaviors as a result of observing someone else. Second, modeling may strengthen or weaken an individual's inhibitions to act. If a child sees someone receive praise for stealing, the child's inhibitions against stealing may be weakened. It is highly possible that if the child sees stealing reinforced often enough, he eventually will steal himself. Conversely, a child who sees stealing punished has his inhibitions to steal strengthened.

Bandura has also made a distinction between the *learning* of a behavior and its *performance*. Children are exposed to many models who supply dozens of behaviors that can be learned through imitation. However, learning a behavior does not necessarily mean that the child will perform it. The performance of a behavior learned through imitation depends upon the child's expectations about the consequences of the behavior. If he expects a positive reinforcement, he probably will perform the behavior. Anticipated punishment reduces the likelihood of the child performing the behavior.

Most of Bandura's theorizing about imitative learning, and particularly his valuable distinction between learning and performance, is derived from his fascinating research on aggression. Bandura subscribes to the notion that aggression is a learned behavior. Aggression, according to him, is not instinctive to man—a position advanced by ethologists Konrad Lorenz and Robert Ardery; nor is its rechanneling of instinctual urges from the id, as Freud suggests. Children learn aggressive acts by being exposed to models who act aggressively. When a child anticipates a positive reward for acting aggressively (he sees a TV or movie character praised by peers for killing, stealing, or fighting), the chances of imitation increase. Consider one of Bandura's experiments on aggression.

The experiment was done with nursery school-aged children divided into three groups (A, B, & C). Each group watched a film of a woman (the model in this case) perform a series of aggressive acts on a five-foot tall plastic doll. The model purposefully performed aggressive acts such as slapping, which four-year-olds normally wouldn't do. In the film shown to group A, the model received positive reinforcement from another adult after acting aggressively; for group B, the model was punished. Nothing happened to the model in the film shown to group C.

Bandura next put each group into a separate room exactly like the room in the film to determine which group would act most aggressively. The children were rated on the basis of how closely their aggressiveness approximated the model's aggressiveness. Consistent with his theory, Bandura found that group A acted most aggressively, group C next, and group B (who watched the punished model) acted the least aggressively.

But Bandura also wanted to know how much aggression was *learned* through imitation (the first part of the experiment only revealed how much aggression was *performed*). He offered the children in each group a reward (candy) to act like the model. It turned out that children in each of the groups performed nearly as many aggressive acts as group A had at first. These results were also found when television rather than film was used.

It is interesting to note that in the first part of the experiment, girls performed fewer aggressive acts than boys in all three groups. But in the second part of the experiment, when rewards were offered, the girls were just as aggressive as the boys. Bandura explains this phenonmenon by noting how our society generally encourages boys to act more aggressively. Girls presently have greater restrictions with respect to aggression.

Bandura's experiments have important significance for teachers. Children learn aggression from models (parents, friends, teachers, television), and will act aggressively if they anticipate positive reinforcements for doing so. When a child behaves aggressively, it's necessary to understand what the child expects to receive. Is it attention, even if in the form of shouting? Is it praise and esteem from classmates? Is it a "tough guy" self-concept that needs preserving?

Bandura's position is quite like Skinner's: learn what the reinforcement is, and attempt to change it. In the case of imitation, we need to try to make inappropriate models less reinforcing, and substitute more appropriate models which are reinforcing.

Usually, the single most important model in the classroom is the teacher. And what are the teacher's primary behaviors upon which students model themselves? Not the ones we most often think of, according to University of Chicago psychologist Phillip Jackson. He spent nearly a year quietly sitting in the back of classrooms trying to observe the situation with as few presumptions as possible. The common perception of the teacher as a source of information is not what it's really all about, he learned. In the course of their instruction, teachers teach three other lessons of far greater importance to children. Jackson argues in his classic book, *Life in Classrooms* (1968), that teachers, especially in elementary schools, serve as powerful models for these student behaviors and self-concepts:

1. How to become a member of a group, and learn all the rules which that entails. The main focus of these rules is self-inhibition (don't talk, walk around, or go to the bathroom whenever you feel like it).

2. How to react to constant evaluation. Teachers continuously mete out judgments, and children watch closely how this is done.

3. How to deal with different levels of power (mostly, how to react to someone with more power and sanctions than you—the teacher).

Jackson believes that these three learning situations are really more central to the student's learning than the course content. That is, they have a deeper and more lasting impact than most of the curriculum learned in class. Thus, it matters more *how* a teacher presents information and runs the classroom than *what* the instruction is about (Marshall McLuhan would surely agree).

Teachers need to examine how they perform these roles. Although Bandura would have the teacher look carefully at his role as model, he also cautions that it shouldn't be overdone. It can be like watching yourself dance: if you study your behavior too closely, you won't be able to do anything right. You can get valuable feedback from videotape recordings and from colleagues, but you must avoid becoming too self-

Table 4-1. Summary of Learning Techniques

Learning Technique	Reinforcing Method	Size of Group	Procedure	Main Application
Behavior Therapy (Pavlov, Wolpe)	None	Individual	Repeated Pairing of S-R, Relaxation, Desensitization	Reducing fears and anxieties
Behavior Modification (Skinner)	Tokens, Prizes	Individual, small group, whole class	Reinforcement of appropriate response, Extinction of inappropriate	Altering classroom behavior
Programmed, Computer Assisted Instruction (Skinner)	Knowledge of Results	Individual	Reinforcement of appropriate response, Extinction of inappropriate	Mastering skills and knowledge
Modeling (Bandura)	Power of Model, Consequences of Model's Behavior	Small group, whole class	Exposure to model	Altering classroom behavior

conscious about the whole thing. Chapter Eleven gives suggestions for achieving this.

Summary

Behavior therapy, behavior modification, and modeling behavior; each is a complex instructional strategy. The three are summarized in Table 4-1. For each, I have indicated a number of problems. Teachers should understand each strategy and know when to refrain from the use of one when the problems involved outweigh anticipated benefits. At the same time, the problems should not make teachers overly fearful of using one or more of the strategies in the classroom. In my experience, there have been many cases in which one of these approaches seemed to be the only possible solution. I think that they may turn out to be the most important innovations in education ever, but only if we are willing to take a hard look at the values questions, such as bribery, overly-powerful teachers, and indoctrination, that underlie their use.

References

Atkinson, Richard C., and H.A. Wilson. *Computor-assisted Instruction.* N.Y.: Academic Press, 1969.

Bandura, Albert. *Principles of Behavior Modification.* N.Y.: Holt, Rinehart, and Winston, 1969.

Skinner, B.F. *Beyond Freedom and Dignity.* New York: Bantam/Vintage, 1971.

Skinner, B.F. *About Behaviorism.* New York: Knopf, 1974.

Chapter 5

Fostering Creative Problem-Solving

How Kuriosity Killed the Kat

This is the story about a very curious cat named Kat. One day Kat was wandering in the woods where he came upon a big house made of fish. Without thinking he ate much of that house. The next morning when he woke up he had grown considerably larger. Even as he walked down the street he was getting bigger. Finally he got bigger than any building ever made. He walked up to the Empire State Building in N.Y.C. and he accidentally crushed it. The people had to think of a way to stop him so they made this great iron box which made the cat curious. He finally got inside it but it was too heavy to get him out of again. There he lived for the rest of his life. But he was still curious until his death, which was 6,820,000 years later. They buried him in the state of Rhode Island, and I mean the whole state.

by Jerry Hilgard, a seventh-grade student

Most people reading this little story might consider it cute, but not many would realize the creative potential it shows. The restless imagination darting from place to place, the daring exaggeration, the disdain for triteness; these are early signs that this boy's mind has great creative possibilities. With appropriate encouragement, he will become a tremendous asset to society. As was documented in Chapter One, such encouragement is increasingly essential.

Research on creativity began only in 1950, and much remains to be discovered. This chapter describes the various schools of thought related to creative problem-solving. Definitive answers cannot yet be given, but consideration of the following ideas can greatly help teachers foster the creative problem-solving abilities of their students.

Defining Creativity

Attempts to define creativity have been numerous. In 1960, one researcher listed 26 definitions of the concept, and a number of new definitions have been offered since then. Most of these definitions can be classified into one of three categories: the *product* resulting from the creative effort, the mental *process* which produces it, and the *personality traits* of the creative problem-solver.

The Creative Product

Virtually all assessments of the creative product note that it cannot be produced by logical, routine, or mechanical processes. The criteria used by the United States Patent Office demonstrate this. These criteria may be summarized as follows:

The product must have come about as a result of qualified intellectual activity, but it should be clear that it has resulted from something more than logic.

The product must be useful, and provide a stride forward.

It must overcome special difficulties.

The amount of experimentation before the achievement of the novelty is considered relevant.

Also relevant is the existence of a history of failure prior to the invention.

The product is considered particularly creative if experts had been skeptical about its success.

A major problem in judging the creative product has been *how* to judge it. Critics and experts often disagree about the creativity of a product. In addition, history is replete with misjudgments made at the time the creative product was offered. The search for objective, unbiased criteria has been elusive.

Phillip Jackson and Sam Messick, both of the University of Chicago, have attempted to overcome this problem by specifying the emotional reactions that people should make to a creative product (see Table 5-1). They offer four basic criteria for judging creative products: unusualness, appropriateness, transformation and condensation.

Table 5-1. Criteria For Judging Creative Products

Product Properties	Judgmental Standards	Emotional Responses of Judges
unusualness	norms	surprise
appropriateness	context	satisfaction
transformation	constraints	stimulation
condensation	summary power	savoring

(From Jackson, P.W. and S. Messick. "The person, the product and the response: Conceptual problems in the assessment of creativity," in *Journal of Personality*. 1965, 33 (3), p. 309-329.)

The first criterion, unusualness, always appears in definitions of the creative product. This criterion is judged by a comparison to the existing norms. Jackson and Messick suggest that if a product is really unusual, the almost instantaneous response of the judging person should be one of surprise. Salvador Dali's painting of the crucifixion as viewed from *above* the cross surely meets this criterion. People frequently gasp on first seeing it.

In the case of the second criterion, appropriateness, they argue that it is necessary to make a judgment as to how useful, helpful, or relevant a product is. When a product is particularly appropriate in terms of its context, they believe that judges will respond with a feeling of intense satisfaction. Many people find Handel's *Messiah* to be unusually satisfying music because of its ability to uplift them spiritually.

The third criterion, transformation, asks whether or not the product overcomes conventional constraints and rules which usually exist in a particular area. Jackson and Messick suggest that transformation be judged in terms of the constraints within which the creator is working. For example, Beethoven is considered an unusually creative composer because of his inventiveness within the stringent constraints placed on the composition of classical music. When a product offers a unique transformation, Jackson and Messick believe that judges will react to the product by feeling unusually stimulated.

The final criterion, condensation, is typified by the simplicity of the product. The product has great summary power and condenses complex elements into a simple, pure unity. This pertains to poetry and other literary efforts, of course, but it may also have to do with the sciences, as in the case of the mathematical or physical formulae (for example, $E=MC^2$). It may even be true of an exquisitely prepared meal. Jackson and Messick observed that people judging a product which demonstrates great condensation will want to savor the product, as when we want to hear our favorite piece of music over and over, or return to look at a great painting.

J.E. Drevdahl demonstrates this power of condensation in his excellent summary definition of creative products. For him creativity is:

> ....the capacity of persons to produce compositions, products or ideas of any sort which are essentially new or novel, and previously unknown to the producer. It can be imaginative activity or thought synthesis where the product is not a mere summation. It may involve the forming of new patterns and combinations of information derived from past experience or the transplanting of old relationships to new situations, and may involve the generation of new correlates. It must be purposeful or goal-directed, not mere idle fantasy, although it need not have immediate practical applications or be a perfect, complete production.

Although there is more agreement today on the definition of creativity, judging the creativity of a product by looking only at the product itself is usually quite difficult. Often it helps to know something of the creator's state of mind (the mental processes which caused the act of creation) and his personality (his ways of viewing and dealing with life).

The Mental Processes of Creative Problem-Solving

As with attempts to define creative products, we also find that there are several explanations of creative mental processes. These definitions form two schools of thought; the first emphasizes the association of parts of problems; the second emphasizes the restructuring of wholes.

Associationism

The first school is known as associationism, in which all thinking is conceived of as a chain of ideas. The three theories of learning presented in the previous chapter are examples. These ideas are sometimes linked together through "associative play" in which the thinker is just fooling around with ideas. This is the most frequent cause of creative ideas. Thus new ideas are thought to be produced by the trial-and-error association of old ideas. Numerous pairings of ideas are made randomly until a pairing of ideas occurs that remedies a problem, generates a new use, or the like.

Psychologist Sarnoff Mednick is a strong supporter of this school of thought. He argues that creativity is simply the process by which ideas already in the mind are associated in original, unusual and useful combinations. He believes that every idea we have in our mind is associated with other ideas in our mind. These associations are arranged in lists, with one list for each idea we have. Those associations at the top of the list are closely associated to the particular idea; as we move down the list, the associations to that idea become weaker and weaker. For example, if you were asked for the first thing that comes to your mind when someone says "black," you would probably say "white." That is because "white" is a close associate of the concept "black" for most of us. "Magic" might also be an association, but it would come to mind less quickly. It is therefore somewhat lower on the list of associations to "black." "Black Forest" would probably be lower still. Mednick argues that creativity is the pairing of ideas which are less likely to be associated in people's minds, that is, those lowest on the list. It is the association of these so-called "remote" ideas that produces creative products. An example of this kind of remote association would be a phrase from a poem by Marianne Moore, which demonstrates how putting unusual ideas together can result in a pleasing new idea: "The lion's ferocious chrysanthemum head." No one associates this billowy flower with ferocity, but somehow the apparent contradiction is appealing; it makes us see the lion in a refreshingly new way.

Word Association Test

This is an exercise to discover how well you are able to see the relationship between things. In each example, there is a set of three words. You are supposed to think of a word which has something to do with each of these words.

For example, if the three words were : limburger, cheddar, and cottage—a good answer would be cheese, because each is a kind of cheese. A more difficult example would be: rat, blue, and cottage—but again, a good answer would be cheese. A rat likes cheese, and blue cheese and cottage cheese are kinds of cheese.

Now try these sets of words. If you can't think of a good word in a minute or so, skip that example and go on to the next.

1. flap   tire   beanstalk   _____

2. mountain   up   school   _____

Continued

3. package	cardboard	fist	_____
4. surprise	line	birthday	_____
5. madman	acorn	bolt	_____
6. telephone	high	electric	_____
7. hair	income	fish	_____
8. cream	bulb	heavy	_____
9. up	knife	band-aid	_____
10. snow	wash	skin	_____
11. out	home	jail	_____
12. slugger	belfry	ball	_____
13. stage	game	actor	_____
14. Roman	arithmetic	one	_____
15. cat	color	dark	_____

The correct answers, and an explanation of this test, will be found on page 72.

Mednick believes that people differ in the way in which associations exist in their minds. Some people tend to have very short lists of very strongly associated ideas, and they can produce only a few associations. These people usually have very rigid personalities and are dogmatic in their beliefs. Other people have long lists of less tightly associated ideas. Their self-concept is not so closely tied to getting the one right answer. They are not so threatened by being wrong. Thus they have the freedom to do the mental search for remote associations, which might turn out to be "silly," but which also might be a really creative combination.

Mednick suggests that there are three basic ways in which remote associations are produced:

Serendipity. Trial-and-error associations of ideas accidentally produce useful, new ideas. The invention of the X-ray would be an example. Mednick tells of a physicist friend of his who places slips of paper with physical concepts on them in a fish bowl. When he has time, he randomly draws out slips of paper in pairs and looks at the two ideas to see if together they produce a new and creative idea.

Similarity. Sometimes new ideas come about because of the supposedly irrelevant similarity of the two ideas. For example, a creative association between words might occur because they happen to be homonyms. The fact that they sound alike is itself irrelevant, but might associate the words in a new and useful way. For example, thinking about "beat" and "beet" might produce a creative recipe for cooking beets by beating them into a fluffy consistency as in a spinach souffle.

Mediation. In this case, two words that seem to have nothing to do with each other may be brought into association because they are both linked with a third thing. For example, "rat" and "blue" might be associated by "cheese."

Mednick feels that "familiarity breeds rigidity." If one comes to know a great deal about a particular subject, he gradually becomes less able to be creative about it. This is because he assumes that the laws and principles in that particular area of knowledge must be so, and he no longer questions them. Therefore, it is the person who is relatively new in the field who is more likely to come up with remote and unusual associations. This may be the reason that theoretical physicists and master chess players are said to have passed their prime by the age of twenty-five. It is also true that many of the world's great inventors develop their best ideas in the early years of their thinking. Einstein was only nineteen when he developed his theory of relativity. This is not to say that no one is able to resist the growing rigidity of age. Stravinsky, Picasso, and Maugham made exceptional contributions in their later years, but such highly creative elderly people are extremely rare.

Explanation of the Word Association Test

The WAT is a facsimile of Seymour Mednick's more extensive test called the Remote Associates Test. Here are the correct answers to it.

1. flap	tire	beanstalk	JACK
2. mountain	up	school	HIGH
3. package	cardboard	fist	BOX
4. surprise	line	birthday	PARTY
5. madman	acorn	bolt	NUT
6. telephone	high	electric	WIRE
7. hair	income	fish	NET
8. cream	bulb	heavy	LIGHT
9. up	knife	band-aid	CUT
10. snow	wash	skin	WHITE
11. out	home	jail	HOUSE
12. slugger	belfry	ball	BAT

Continued

13. stage	game	actor	PLAY
14. Roman	arithmetic	one	NUMERAL
15. cat	color	dark	BLACK

In his Remote Association Test, of which this test is an adaptation for younger children, Mednick is trying to achieve a format that can be scored easily and accurately. That is why he has designed a test for which there are correct answers. Some people argue that this contradicts the nature of creativity. However, if Mednick's theory is correct, it is certainly more helpful to have a test for which there are right answers than one for which the answers are a matter of opinion. Educators have tried for some time to find an objectively scored test of creativity, both because we want to be able to identify a child's creativity level and gear our educational efforts to his level, and because we want to be able to evaluate the effectiveness of those methods.

Mednick's idea is that creativity is the bringing together of concepts that seem to have little to do with each other. The goal is to join the concepts in new and meaningful ways. An example would be Edison's combining the concept of vacuum with making a wire glow with electricity to produce the light bulb. Mednick believes that this is an adequate description of all types of creativity, whether verbal or non-verbal. He believes that his test gets at the very basis of creativity and is not merely verbal. Because the ideas and concepts of his test are known to everyone, a high level of verbal sophistication is not necessary to do well on it.

To select items for the test, Mednick first determines what associations people have for a variety of words. There have been many studies of people's associations to various words and there are many lists of associations from which to choose. Three words are selected that all have a fairly close association with a fourth word but have little or no association with each other. Very few people will say "cottage" when you say "blue" and very few people will say "rat" when you say "blue." However, when you say "cheese," people may say "rat," or "cottage," or "blue."

Therefore, Mednick argues that though these three words have little association with each other, they have a high level association with the word "cheese." The person who can regularly figure out what fourth word will associate the three unrelated words on his test is likely to be a creative person.

Once a person suggested to me that a good word with which to associate "rat," "blue," and "cottage" would be "lake," because the word "cottage" made you think of a lake and there are sometimes rats in the cottage and sometimes the lake is blue. Mednick would argue that it is not as good an answer as "cheese" because it needs to be explained.

Whether or not Mednick's theory is correct is debatable. However, the effectiveness of his test has been demonstrated. When people known to be highly creative by their productivity take the test, they tend to score considerably higher than people who have no such record. If the test can distinguish highly creative persons from those who are not, then its use may be preferable to judging a lot of "creative products." Most likely, it's also useful for predicting creativity in children before they have become able to prove their creativity through their own efforts.

J.P. Guilford, another leading theorist of the associationist school, argues that there are two kinds of associations involved in creativity. He calls these convergent and divergent thinking. In convergent thinking, we are expected to produce an answer to a question for which there is only one right answer. If we are asked, "How much is 27 times 493," we may not know the answer, but we know there is only one correct answer, which is computed by following a series of mathematical operations. Divergent thinking involves questions for which a variety of answers might be appropriate. "What would happen if it rained up instead of down?" is an example of a question calling for divergent thinking. Guilford argues that creativity involves divergent thinking in the early stages of the creative process. After a variety of possible mental associations have been produced, convergent thinking takes over the task of selecting the best alternative.

Structuralism

The second school of thought has a variety of names, but it might be called structuralism. One of its leaders, Michael Wertheimer, argues that the creative musician does not write notes on a page in hope of composing something. Rather he gets a half-formed idea of the finished whole of the musical work, then works backward to complete it. He is not merely associating ideas in a chain as the associationist would suggest. Rather, he sees an entire structure and then rearranges its parts in order to form a new structure. For Wertheimer, creativity is the operation of dividing a problem into sub-wholes and still seeing these sub-wholes with clear reference to the whole. Creative solutions are often obtained by changing one's point of reference. For example, when we look at a scene, certain things stand out and others are in the background. If we change our point of looking at the scene, the background sometimes becomes the foreground. Thus, the whole picture is restructured in such a way as to bring about a whole new concept. Wertheimer believes that this is a better way to look at creative activity than to see it merely as the linking up of associations.

A rather different structural view of creativity is the psychoanalytic concept of Sigmund Freud. In his opinion, conflict gives birth to creativity. Furthermore, although conflict accounts for creativity in some, it motivates neurotic behavior in others. The difference is that the creative person resolves his conflicts fruitfully and brings to the world new resolutions of old problems, while the neurotic maintains his delusions. This view of creativity places little emphasis on reasonng, but instead emphasizes symdols, dreams and mental fantasies.

Another view of creativity, that of psychoanalyst E.G. Schachtel, emphasizes perception. He believes that there are two basic ways of looking at the world: the autocentric and the allocentric. We begin life in the autocentric mode. The child views his world with little or no objectivity, relating to objects only in terms of their effect on his own pleasure. He perceives objects only when they have a particular importance to his present state of mind. Gradually the child's thinking develops into the allocentric mode, in which an object is perceived as it really is; that is, without specific regard to its effect on the perceiver. The older child is less subjective. He is the manipulator of objects, rather than being manipulated by them, as in the autocentric mode.

Often, however, people slip back into the autocentric mode. Objects are again perceived in terms of how they may be used by the perceiver, or avoided if they are likely to produce pain. Also the person perceives objects in terms of their newness and strangeness and, consequently, as possible threats to him. Therefore, he tends to try to avoid new and strange objects and ideas. Schachtel believes that the creative process involves *resisting* this latter stage in order to remain perceptually open to the world.

The associationist and structuralist schools appear to contradict each other; it seems they cannot both be right. I find that the associationist explanation fits best when we are examining children's creative efforts. When it comes to adult creativity and to the complex products of a person like Einstein, I think the structuralist view serves best. No doubt our understanding of creativity will be advanced when we see in what ways both schools contribute to a third explanation of the mental processes of creativity.

Personality Traits and Creativity

One of the most fruitful approaches to the study of creative problem-solving has been the investigation of personality traits apparently related to creativity. As our knowledge of the personality of the creative person increases, it becomes possible for us to determine which techniques can be used to encourage the related personality traits. It is hoped that this will, in turn, promote creativity itself.

One of the most comprehensive studies of creative personality traits was done by research psychologist Donald MacKinnon. He asked thousands of architects to name the most creative architects in the U.S. Having identified the one-hundred most creative architects by this method, Mac Kinnon brought them together and administered a number of well-known personality tests to them.

He found clear evidence that the creative architects had a greater tendency toward mental illness than the average person, but that they also had more adequate self-control to keep this in check. Another test used in the study measured the person's preference for neutrally perceiving objects, as opposed to judging whether the objects were good or bad. The creative group showed a strong preference toward neutral perception. This indicates more openness to experience, and a greater flexibility than would be indicated by a high judgment preference.

Another of MacKinnon's interesting findings resulted from the use of the Allport-Vernon-Lindzey Study of Values. The creative group scored highest in two apparently opposing values, theoretical and aesthetic values. The difference between these two values is probably better described in the terms used by Jackson and Messick. They suggest that creative people are able to be *both* analytical (similar to theoretical) and intuitive (similar to aesthetics) in their thinking, two approaches which in most people compete with each other. For example, logical thinkers perceive intuitive thinkers as those who "jump to conclusions." Contrarily, intuitive thinkers accuse analytical thinkers of being "cautious traditionalists". Most creative problem-solving calls for the rare ability to do both. It starts with an intuitive flight of fantasy, and is followed up by a careful analysis of the appropriateness of the new idea. This is what associationist J.P. Guilford is saying. Thomas Edison suggested that the balance between the two is "one part inspiration and ninety-nine parts perspiration." A similar disparity seems to exist between the aesthetic (or intuitive) value that is interested only in "what?" and the theoretical (or analytical) value that always insists on knowing "how?" and "why?" MacKinnon suggests that the creative person is one who can handle the tension between the two, and who is better able to bring about a productive reconciliation between them.

Mednick's *Word Association Test* showed the creative group giving far more correct answers than the average individual. Several instruments showed the all-male creative group to be higher in their identification with female attitudes and interests than were other architects. Finally, MacKinnon used the Terman *Concept Mastery Test* to measure intelligence and found that it has no relationship to creativity.

Psychotherapist Frank Barron argues that creative individuals prefer complexity and imbalance in their environment. This suggests that creative people have a *need* for disorder. He believes that the situation is similar to one in which an animal deprived of food for a long time will learn more quickly when finally rewarded. The creative individual is one who seeks the more complicated and disorganized problems of life. Creative people are more likely to search for situations that seem to defy one's reason. They have the confidence that after they have worked hard and have had a great deal of tension and pain, a superior form of pleasure will be attained with success. This finding has also been indicated in several studies with younger people.

Carl Rogers has contributed a great deal of research on creativity, and has summarized three characteristics of the creative personality which other authors have also discovered:

Extensionality. This refers to the individual's openness to experience and his lack of defensiveness about his own personality. A number of theorists have cited this ability to confront reality starkly and without self-delusion as a critical component of the creative personality.

Internal locus of evaluation. It is frequently the case that in order to preserve one's picture of one's self, experiences that conflict with this image must be blocked from awareness. This is done through the use of "defense mechanisms." Some common ones are presented in Table 5-2.

The creative person is typically self-confident to the point that he feels little need to block conflicts from awareness. He can therefore be more objective. This is probably due to the fact that the creative person is more interested in pleasing himself than in pleasing others. This concept is quite similar to Rotter's idea of locus of control described in Chapter Two, and to Schachtel's allocentric mode of perception.

Table 5-2
Common Defense Mechanisms

Compensation	The attempt to make up for a perceived inadequacy by excelling at something else.
Introjection	Adopting the standards and values of someone with whom you are afraid to disagree.
Rationalization	Coming to believe that a condition which is contrary to your desires is actually what you wanted all along.
Projection	Ascribing to another the feelings you actually have about him.
Regression	Reverting to behaviors which were previously successful when current behavior is unsuccessful.
Reaction formation	Adopting feelings toward someone which are exactly opposite to one's real feelings.
Identification	Adopting the standards and values of someone whom you wish you were like.
Repression	Unconsciously forgetting experiences which are unpleasant to remember.
Sublimation	When unable to fulfill one's sex drives, this need is made up for by being creative in another area (e.g., becoming a great artist).
Displacement	When unable to express one's emotions to one person (e.g., angry at the boss), you express them to someone else (e.g., yell at your wife).

Continued

| Isolation-compartmentalization | Holding two mutually exclusive beliefs at the same time. |

The ability to toy with elements and concepts. Creation, by definition, requires a departure from the norm. Therefore, a playful attitude toward life and the ability to do things differently from others is necessary to being a creative person.

Psychologist Herbert Stein studied creative scientists and found that, compared to less creative scientists, they were more distant from their parents and from adults in general. The creative scientists tended to engage more frequently in solitary activities in their early lives. They also tended to strive for more remote goals, and were more consistent in their desires for reward.

Educational researcher Paul Torrance gave some toys to first and third graders and studied their creative ability to improve them. The toys he gave the children were a fire truck (considered a masculine toy), a nurse's kit (feminine), and a toy dog (neutral). As would be expected, first grade girls suggested more creative improvements to the nurse's kit, the boys excelled with the fire truck, and both groups did equally well with the toy dog. However, third grade boys did much better than third grade girls on all three toys. Torrance suggests that this surprising finding may result from the growing pressure on girls in these grades to accept the *status quo*. Thus, girls become less the challengers of authority than boys. The task presented to them requires a sensitivity to defects as well as an ability to suggest improvement (as is probably the case with all creative tasks). This in turn requires an ability to doubt the *status quo*, which girls appear to exhibit less and less from the first to third grade.

Several researchers have found that creative women are usually more masculine than ordinary women. This is probably because the traits of independence and dominance, thought to be masculine, are part of being creative. Conversely, creative men are usually more feminine than ordinary men. This is probably because the trait of sensitivity, thought to be feminine, is also part of being creative.

Abraham Maslow, whose theory of needs was presented in Chapter Two, spent years of study on the creative personality. He adds the following traits to our picture of creativity:

Creative people are more spontaneous, expressive, natural, and less inhibited than others. They are less afraid of ridicule.

They are relatively unfrightened by the unknown, the mysterious, the puzzling, and are often positively attracted to it.

They have less need of other people and tend to be less afraid of them and less hostile toward them.

They are also less afraid of their own impulses and hidden emotions. The "civil war within the average person between the forces of their inner depths and the forces of defense and control seems to have been resolved" in creative people.

Creative persons often have competing personality traits within themselves. For example, they seem to be highly selfish, but also giving, depending on the circumstance. They can be intellectual in one situation, emotional in another. They make much less of a distinction between working and playing than other people. They tend to be more mature than the average person, but are also quite able to be child-like when they feel like it.

As Maslow points out:

> But this is precisely what the great artist does. He is able to put together clashing colors, forms that fight each other, dissonances of all kinds into a unity. And this is also what the great theorist does when he puts puzzling and inconsistent facts together so that we can see that they really belong together. And so also for the great statesman, the great therapist, the great philosopher, the great parent, the great lover, the great inventor. They are all integrators, able to put separates and even opposites together into unity.

Summary Description of the Creative Child

In general, creative children:

Like to do their own planning, make their own decisions, and need the least training and experience in self-guidance.

Do not like to work with others, and prefer their own judgment of their work to the judgment of others. They therefore seldom ask other students (or their teachers) for their opinions in this respect.

Take a hopeful outlook when presented with complex difficult tasks.

Have the most ideas when a chance to express individual opinion is presented. These ideas frequently invoke the ridicule of the class.

Are much more likely to stand their ground in the face of criticism.

Are the most resourceful when unusual circumstances arise.

Can tolerate uncertainty and ambiguity better than others.

Are not necessarily the "smartest" or "best" students.

In their compositions, creative students typically:

Show an imaginative use of many different words.

Are more flexible, e.g., in a narrative, they use more situations, characters, and settings. Rather than taking one clearly defined train of thought and pursuing it to its logical conclusion, creative students tend to switch the main focus quickly and easily, and often go off on tangents.

Tend to elaborate on the topic assigned, taking a much broader connotation of it to begin with, and then proceeding to embellish even that.

Are more original. (This is the *most important* characteristic. The others need not be evidenced, but this one must be.) This student's ideas are simply different from the average student's response. Perhaps you might react to the creative child's work in this way: "I know what most of the kids will do with the topic, but I never know what to expect from this one."

The Critical Period Theory

I have argued that there is a mental process and a set of personality traits which together make up the human capacity for creativity. I have also strongly urged that we need to do what we can to nurture our children's creative powers. The question remains as to whether these creative powers *can* be affected by an educational process.

Pro-Critical Period

There are a number of psychologists who believe that there is a critical period during the first five years of life, in which creative potential is determined. After that, efforts to foster creativity are doomed to failure. Qualities such as creativity become fixed and can no longer be influenced. Coincidentally or not, theorists of this view are also followers of Sigmund Freud.

The "guilt-will" theory of Freud's student, Otto Rank, is an example of this school of thought. Rank suggests that the determinant of creativity is the parent's positive reaction to the child's developing will in its first few years of life. If the parents react negatively, the child feels guilty about his desires, suppresses his will in order to maintain their love, and grows up acquiescent and unimaginative.

A position quite similar to Rank's is held by Weisberg and Springer. On the basis of their in-depth studies of children, they conclude that parental influences are critical to the development of creativity. They hypothesized that only the child from a "non-anxiety producing" early environment has any likelihood of becoming a creative adult.

Another neo-Freudian position is that of Deutsch, who believes that creativity is an unconscious defense against the commission of a neurotic act. Fantasies which occur in the preliminary stages of mental illness are thought to be similar to the fantasies of the creative person. But while the neurotic merely imagines that the changes he so desperately desires have occurred, the creative individual actually brings about the desired change. Because this process occurs in the unconscious (to a large extent, the product of early childhood experiences), the process is considered extremely resistant to conscious manipulation. Thus, school programs to develop creativity, according to this theoretical position, would be of little value.

A third (and even more deterministic) position in support of the critical period hypothesis is Alfred Adler's "compensatory theory of creativity." Adler, another of Freud's students, hypothesized that creativity is generally the result of overcoming a severe personal difficulty in childhood. The difficulty typically lies either in a neurotic character, or an organic disorder:

> Often (geniuses) started with gravely imperfect organs. In almost all outstanding people, we find some organ imperfection. We gather the impression that they were sorely confronted at the beginning of life but struggled and overcame their difficulties. We can notice how early they fixed their interests and how hard they trained themselves in their childhood. They sharpened their senses so that they could make contact with the problems of the world and understand them.

Clearly, therefore, if no serious personal difficulty is faced and overcome during childhood, most individuals are not very likely to be outstanding-

ly creative in later life. If this extreme position is accepted, school programs to develop creativity will probably be of little avail.

Anti-Critical Period

Opposed to the critical period hypothesis are a group of theorists
who agree that an individual's creative potential can be realized at any
age.

Abraham Maslow "...tends to see more or less creativity in every
person, if only as a suppressed potential, and asks the questions, 'Why
was it lost?' 'How much is left?' 'How much can be recovered?'" Suppressed creative potential can be released, he argues, through a clearer
understanding of the self. Creative persons are comparatively unfrightened by the unknown and often are attracted by it. This unknown
element includes the self: self-actualizing persons typically seek to know
themselves, accept what they find, and are adept at integrating this new
knowledge with their prevalent self-concept. Maslow claims most people
have had this type of experience and can become proficient at achieving
it.

Seymour Kubie, a well-known psychiatrist, has argued that the
typical situation in American classrooms has been so stultifying that
students are not merely conformists, but actually semi-neurotic, and that
educators do not recognize the situation because they tend to regard the
typical as the normal. Viewing creativity as a "preconscious" activity
(operating between the conscious and unconscious processes), he feels
that teachers need to provide freedom for students to engage in
preconscious activity. This is done by assisting students to acquire
divergent thinking skills and attitudes, which in turn leads to creativity
and frees the student from his masked neuroses.

Eric Fromm, famous author of *The Art of Loving*, argues that
creativity is largely a matter of having the right set of attitudes. He says
there are five relevant attitudes that can be fostered at any point in life:

The capacity to be puzzled or surprised.
The ability to concentrate.
An objective knowledge of self.
The ability to accept conflict and tension resulting from polarity.
The willingness to let go of securities such as parental support.

J.P. Guilford, former president of the American Psychological
Association, suggests that:

> Education in this country has unfortunately been too much dominated by the learning
> theory based on the stimulus-response model of Thorndike, Hull and Skinner. People,
> after all, are not rats (with a few exceptions) and they are not pigeons (with similar ex-
> ceptions). Let us make full use of the human brains that have been granted us. Let us
> apply a psychology that recognizes the full range of human intellectual qualities. We
> must make more complete use of our most precious natural resource—the intellectual
> abilities of our people, including their creative potentialities (Guilford, 1962).

Probably the most adamant advocate of education for creativity is
Paul Torrance, whose many studies and reviews of research on the sub-

ject have convinced him that many useful instructional techniques exist. He categorically states that "We now know that (school-aged) children can be taught in ways that bring their creative thinking abilities into use in acquiring even the traditional educational skills..."

The position of this second group of theorists, therefore, is that creativity does not become fixed in early childhood, but is a characteristic which can and does change in later life. It is argued accordingly that if instruction is effectively designed, it is likely that *all* students will benefit from it, commensurate with their existing levels of performance.

My own experiences as a classroom teacher and consultant to teachers have made me a strong proponent of the second school of thought. I believe the Freudian school has mainly to do with those children who develop emotional disturbances. The latter group of theorists offer the best description of the creative abilities of the vast majority of people.

The Two String Test

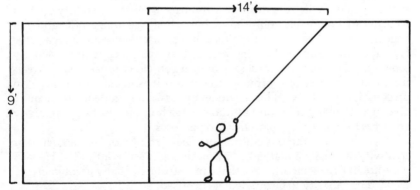

How can the child in the picture tie these two strings together? You see he can't reach the other string. The two strings are of equal length. Each is almost nine feet long. They are permanently attached to the ceiling of the room at 14 feet from each other. To help him solve this problem, the child may use any *one* of the following objects: a mouse trap, a wooden spring-type clothes pin, *or* a pair of vice-grip pliers. None of these is long enough so that he could use it to reach the other string. The explanation follows.

The Two-string Test

The correct answer to Maier's *Two String Test* is that any object can be used to solve the problem. One simply needs to attach one of the objects to the string, swing it away from him, run over and grab the other string, then return to the center and catch the weighted string as it swings back to you. The strings can then be easily tied together.

I have never heard of any other solution to this test. As you can see from looking at the picture carefully, you can only walk about eight feet toward the other string holding one string in your hand. Since the distance between the strings is fourteen feet, you still have six feet to go. No one is tall enough to reach out with one hand, one foot, or any of the objects to be able to reach the other string.

One of my students did have a unique reaction to the test. I asked for volunteers to solve the problem which I had set up in the classroom. A nun came forward. After studying the problem for a moment, she decided that none of the pieces of equipment would work. She reached into the apron of her habit and took out an enormous set of rosary beads. Holding one string in her hand, she walked out as far as she could towards the other one, swung the rosary beads over her head, managed to catch the other string and bring it to her. Since that time, I have never allowed a nun to attempt to solve this problem.

I have administered this test under many different circumstances and a number of interesting results have regularly occurred. I found that sixth graders are almost always able to solve the problem within the fifteen minutes allowed. Of the eighth graders tested, about 80 percent are able to solve it. I have given it many times to undergraduates and find that about 50 percent of them can solve it. Virtually no graduate students are able to solve it. Other researchers have reported similar findings.

Apparently, the reason is that the more education one has, the less capable he is of handling creative problem-solving situations. Researchers have suggested that there is the difficulty of "functional fixity," which increases with education. The longer we are in school, the more we come to accept the specific use that a thing has, the more rigid are our ideas about objects, and the less we are able to use them in a variety of different ways. This has a tendency to stultify our creative imagination.

An example of functional fixity is the case of a graduate student who suggested that the rat trap was the right answer. He decided that he would catch a large number of rats with a rat trap until he got one which was not seriously injured. He would then make a pet of it and train it to run over to the other piece of string and bring it to him so that he could attach it to the other. This is an imaginative idea, but it would not solve the problem since a rat would never be able to bring the string very far because it would lift off the ground. It does show, however, how rigid our attitudes can become toward the specific use of an object. Sixth graders have no trouble at all thinking of a rat trap as a weight.

Another difference that I found was between males and females. Many times women have told me they are incapable of handling this type of problem before I completed one-fourth of the explanation. I usually urged them to listen to the rest of the problem and then try to solve it. However, though most were polite enough to do this, it was quite clear that they had given up on the problem. I found that females were no more than one-half as successful as males in solving the problem at any age level.

One student suggested that the problem is basically one in mechanics, that since women have less training in mechanics, naturally they do less well. Another student, a married woman, suggested that this was not at all the case. She said that she frequently encountered problems in her daily housework which required using things in ways other than they were normally intended. She felt that many women got training in this. She argued that her husband, on the contrary, was very reluctant to do a job unless he had all the tools that were appropriate for doing it. She suggested that this is typical with men and their work, and they get much less practice in using things in alternative ways.

I agreed with her, and believe that the reason women do less well is because of the anti-creative attitudes they get from their mothers and fathers and their female elementary school teachers. The study by Torrance which I described earlier demonstrates this. Of course female children today are less rigidly molded than previously; it is doubtful that Torrance's experiment would yield the same results now. To the extent that real changes in sex role are coming about, we can happily anticipate a much larger creative contribution from women.

> In my dream I saw the world
> in a frame of imitation gold.
> I heard fear pounding in my ears
> And in the white light
> I could only see black.
> Blinded by the sound of darkness:
> I saw invisible fingers
> and heard non-existent sounds
> I was a non-existent person
> in a non-existent world.
>
> God help me
> as I stab myself with a
> rubber knife.
>
> By "Sam," an eleventh grade girl

Promoting Creativity

Even if we can agree that creativity is a valuable trait and should be fostered, there remains the complicated question, "How?" In his ground-breaking article, educator Ralph Hallman has listed a number of obstacles and aids to creativity. The more significant of these are summarized here.

Creativity appears to be a rather delicate capacity. Being creative involves the danger of sticking one's neck out; therefore, it is rather easily inhibited. Several prominent obstacles to creativity are:

Pressures to conform. Probably the major inhibitor, this involves standardized routines and inflexible rules. Authoritarian parents and teachers who place emphasis on following orders are responsible for the demise of a great deal of creative talent.

Ridicule of unusual ideas. This destroys one's feelings of worth, and makes one defensive and compulsive.

An excessive quest for success and the rewards it brings. In most cases, this means trying to meet the standards and demands of others in order to obtain the rewards they have to give. In the long run, this distorts one's view of reality, and robs one of the strength of character required in a creative act.

Intolerance of a playful attitude. Innovation calls for playing around with ideas, a willingness to fantasize and make-believe, and a healthy disrespect for accepted concepts. Here the creative person is seen as childlike and silly, and his activity as wasteful, but these are only appearances. As Hallman remarks, "Creativity is profound fun."

Parents and teachers can teach children to be more creative, but not with traditional authoritarian methods. While specific techniques can now be described, thanks to some imaginative research, the attitude of the teacher remains the most important factor. Hallman suggests these approaches as aids to creative teaching:

Provide for self-initiated learning. Most teachers find it hard to encourage children to initiate and direct their own learning. After all, this is certainly not the way most of them were taught. Teachers fear that if children are given greater freedom to explore reality on their own, the students will learn wrong things, and/or will not learn the right things in the proper sequence. We must put less emphasis on learning "the right facts," and more on learning how to learn. Even if our children do temporarily mis-learn a few things, in the long run the practice in experimentation and imagination will be greatly to their benefit.

Encourage pupils to over-learn. Only when a child makes himself fully familiar with a particular situation can he detach himself enough to get an original view of it.

Defer judgment. The teacher encourages the child to make wild guesses, to juggle improbable relationships, to take intellectual risks, to take a chance on appearing ridiculous. He does not block unusual ideas by over-stating what is required, or by providing correct answers too quickly.

Promote intellectual flexibility. Children are encouraged to shift their point-of-view, to dream up new ideas for things, to imagine as many possible solutions to a particular problem as possible.

Encourage self-evaluation. When a person comes up with a creative idea, at this time he is always a minority of one. History is replete with examples of ideas that were rejected to years before people began to realize their worth. Therefore, the creative person must be one who knows his own mind and is relatively independent of the judgment of others. In order for him to become a good judge of his own thinking, the child must be given ample opportunity to practive such judgments.

Use lots of open-ended questions. One extensive study showed that 90 percent of the time the average teacher asks questions to which there can be only one right answer, which the teacher already knows. Questions that pique curiosity and allow many possible right answers were asked only 10 percent of the time.

Assist the child to cope with frustration and failure. Thomas Edison tried more than 2,000 combinations of metal before he found just the right kind for the electric element in his first light bulb.

Guidelines for Creative Problem-solving

Here are some suggestions that should make *you and your students* more creative problem-solvers:

Avoid the "filtering out" process which blocks problems from awareness. Become more sensitive to problems by practicing looking for them.

Never accept the first solution you think of. Generate a number of possible solutions, then select the best from among them.

Be aware of your own defensiveness concerning the problem. When we feel threatened by a problem, we are less likely to think of creative solutions to it.

Get feedback on the solution you decide on from others who are less personally involved.

Try to think of what solutions someone else might think of to your problem.

Think of opposites to your solutions. When a group tried to think of ways to dispose of smashed auto glass, someone suggested trying to find uses for it, and fiberglass was invented!

Give your ideas a chance to "incubate." Successful problem-solvers report that they frequently put a problem away for a while and later on the solution comes to them full blown. It is clear that they have been thinking about the problem on a subconscious level, which is often superior to a conscious, more logical approach.

Sometimes ideas seem to fork, like the branches on a tree; one idea produces two more, each of which produces two more, and so on. It is often useful to diagram your thinking, so that you can follow each possible branch to its completion.

Be self-confident. Many ideas die because their owner thinks they *might* be silly. Females are especially vulnerable here, according to research.

Think about the general aspects of a problem before getting to its specifics.

Restate the problem several different ways.

Become an "idea jotter." A notebook of ideas can prove surprisingly useful.

Divide a problem, then solve its various parts.

"Weird" ideas often spark great ones.

Really good ideas frequently require some personal risk on the part of the creative problem-solver. In this, we are like the turtle, who can never move forward until he sticks his neck out.

Classroom Activities that Foster Creativity

Several programs are available that are designed to foster creativity. The best of these are:

The *Purdue Creativity Training Program*

Its authors, Feldhusen, Treffinger, and Bahlke, say that:

"...(PCTP) consists of twenty-eight audio-taped presentations and stories, each accompanied by printed exercises for development of creative thinking and problem-solving abilities. The presentations convey a brief message concerning effective thinking, followed by stories which focus on historical persons (inventors, discoverers, and nationwide world leaders) and famous events in history. The exercises provide opportunities for the use of fluency, flexibility, and originality in writing and drawing. Research had shown that PCTP and its specific components have been effective in fostering creative thinking and related attitudes among elementary school pupils" (1974, p. 21).

The *Productive Thinking Program*

Designed by Covington, Crutchfield, Davies, and Olton, they say it is:

"...a programmed instructional sequence, consisting of sixteen units designed to foster creative problem-solving abilities and related attitudes among fifth and sixth-grade students. The subject is presented with a series of mystery or detective problems which are used as a vehicle to introduce a number of guide posts for creative thinking and problem-solving...Research studies have...supported the effectiveness...of PTP" (1974, p. 21).

The *Reading 720 Program*

Its author, Clymer, says:

"...it is designed to develop creative reading skills by encouraging the reader to become sensitive to disharmonies, deficiencies, ambiguities, puzzling problems, etc. encountered in the text and to build and test hypotheses about these phenomena. Since awareness of incompleteness in knowledge is a powerful motivating force, the teacher is provided certain strategies for creating that condition before, during, and after the reading experience" (1974, p. 15).

Some of the best activities for promoting creativity are designed by teachers. The following suggestions come from an imaginative teacher in Dover, Massachusetts, Karen Zikoras:

Rephrasing the question. When a question is asked, I often ask students to rephrase the question orally, or on paper. This enables me to see if they really know what they are searching for, and if they understand the problem.

Artificial problems. Each day I give the students an artificial problem for which they must discuss the possible solutions with other students and come up with a number of solutions. An example of this would be: "You are separated from a group of hikers and you get lost in the wilderness in a remote section of Canada. It is late spring and the only provisions you have with you are your sleeping bag, a fish hook, and a knife. What do you do to survive, and how do you attract the rescue party?" Students can think up any solution just so long as they can give logical reasons for their actions. Another problem could be: "You are riding the escalator in a big department store, and an old woman, who is in front of you, falls and gets her coat caught in the stair grating. What do you do in order to help this women?"

Mix-a-story. This is an activity that gives the students a variety of components they must tie together in a logical format. Five envelopes (color coded) are given to the students and in each envelope there are cards that correspond to a major component of a story. Students pick cards from each envelope and then try to make a logical format and story out of the components. Here is an example. The envelopes are marked setting, plot, main character, theme, and outcome. The student may pick the following: setting—on an island; plot—to rob a bank; main character—an orchestra conductor; theme—sportsmanship is just as important as winning; and outcome—the invention explodes. Now the student must take all of these diverse components and try to form a logical, well-integrated story.

Future city. After a unit on cities, the students can build their own city of the future. They must decide on what problems they will face, and how they will solve their problems. (Problems such as waste disposal and transportation can be discussed.)

Scrambled sentences. Given sentences that are cut up into separate words, the students must try to arrange the words so that the sentence makes sense. More advanced students can have more than one sentence, and must place them into a readable paragraph. The sentences can also be scrambled riddles.

Decoding. Students make their own codes which follow a systematic format. They write a paragraph and transfer it into the code. Other classmates are then asked to try to decode the paragraph.

Number patterning. Given a sequence of numbers such as 1, 3, 6, 10, 15, 21, the students are asked to figure out the pattern and then write the next two numbers (28, 36).

Object descriptions. Have students bring in a common household object. They then must list adjectives which describe the object and the list must become more specific toward the end. Then the next day, students read their list, and other students try to deduce the object from the clues given.

Creative dramatics. Ask volunteers to come forward and describe to them a specific problem, such as, "upon reaching the checkout counter you find that you don't have your wallet. What do you do?" The children act out the problem silently, and then two other members of the class must try to decide the nature of the problem. They then silently act out an appropriate solution. Finally, the whole class tries to state the original problem and the solution.

Daffynitions. Students begin by giving precise definitions to words. Then a silly variation is introduced. Read the words below, and their new "daffynitions." See if students can create new "daffynitions" of this same type:

1. AFTERMATH: That which follows the arithmetic.
2. CONCUR: with a dog.
3. PORTENT: Low quality camping gear.
4. CAUTERIZE: That which attracts, as in "The diamond bracelet cauterize (caught her eyes)".
5. LOGOTYPE: That which is written on the trees.
6. HERFORD: Mother's car.
7. MYTH: A female moth.
8. INCREASED: Pleated or folded.
9. TRIPLET: A very short voyage.
10. PARAPETS: Two poodles.

Finally, *The Journal of Creative Behavior* is a rich source of ideas for teachers. In one of its first issues in 1967, it published an extensive list of "Methods and Educational Programs for Stimulating Creativity." Four times a year since then, the *Journal* has presented useful articles along these lines.

Summary

I believe that the most important factor in creativity, one which plays a part in virtually all of the aspects suggested by Hallman, is *tolerance of ambiguity.* It is fear of the unknown which makes cowards of us all. As the world changes at a faster and faster rate, it seems stranger. We feel more alienated from each other and even from ourselves. Intolerance of ambiguity is at the base of most of our problems. It is the real cause of all war. It is what is driving so many of us to the psychiatrist's couch. We must be taught to tolerate uncertainty and the anxiety it causes. The single most effective way I know is to foster the growth of our children's creative abilities.

References

Barron, Frank. *Creativity and Psychological Health.* New Jersey: D. Van Nostrand Company, Inc., 1963.

Cattell, R.B., and H.J. Butcher. *The Prediction of Achievement and Creativity.* New York: Bobbs-Merrill, 1968.

Dacey, J.S., and Richard E. Ripple. "The Facilitation of Problem Solving and Verbal Creativity by Exposure to Programmed Instruction," in *Psychology in the Schools,* July, 1967, IV (3), 240-245.

Dacey, J.S., and George Madaus. "Creativity: Definitions, Explanations, and Facilitation," in *Irish Journal of Education,* Summer, 1969.

Dacey, J.S.; George Madaus; and Anthony Allen. "The Relationship Between Creativity and Intelligence in Irish Adolescents," in *British Journal of Educational Psychology.* 1969, *39* (3), 261-266.

Dacey, J.S., and George Madaus. "An Analysis of Two Hypotheses Concerning the Relationship Between Creativity and Intelligence," in *The Journal of Educational Research.* Jan. 1971, *64* (5), 213-216.

Flescher, Irwin. "Anxiety and Achievement of Intellectually Gifted and Creatively Gifted Children," in *The Journal of Psychology,* V. 56, 1963, 251-268.

Hallman, Ralph J. "Techniques of Creative Teaching," in *Journal of Creative Behavior,* July, 1967, 1 (3), 325-330.

Gowan, J.C.; G.D. Demos; and E.P. Torrance, eds. *Creativity: Its Educational Implications.* New York: Wiley, 1967.

Guilford, J.P. "Factors That Aid and Hinder Creativity," in *Teachers College Record*. 1962, *63*, 391.

Kagan, Jerome, ed. *Creativity and Learning*. Boston: Beacon Press, 1970.

Klausmier, Herbert J.; Chester W. Harris; and Zackaria Ethnathios. "Relationships Between Divergent Thinking Abilities and Teacher Ratings of High School Students," in *Journal of Educational Psychology*. 1962, Vol. 53, No. 2, 72-75.

Kneller, George F. *The Art and Science of Creativity*. New York: Holt, Rinehart, and Winston, 1965.

Marksberry, Mary Lee. *Foundation of Creativity*. New York: Harper and Row, Publishers, 1963.

Maslow, Abraham. "Creativity and Self-actualizing People," in *Creativity and its Cultivation*. Edited by H.H. Anderson. New York: Harper and Row, 1959.

Mednick, Martha T. "Research Creativity in Psychology Graduate Students", in *Journal of Consulting Psychology*. 1963, V. 27, No. 3, 265-66.

Merrifield, Phillip R. "Trends in the Measurement of Special Abilities," in *Review of Educational Research*, Vol. XXXV, No. 1. Feb. 1965, 25-33.

Moustakas, Clark. *Creativity and Conformity*. Princeton, New Jersey: Van Nostrand, 1967.

Ripple, R.E., and J.S. Dacey. "Relationships of Some Adolescent Characteristics and Verbal Creativity," in *Psychology in the Schools*. July, 1969, VI (3), 321-324.

Speedie, S.M.; D.J. Treffinger; and J.C. Houtz. "Classification and Evaluation of Problem-Solving Tasks," in *Contemporary Educational Psychology, 1*. 1976, 52-75.

Stein, Morris I., and Shirley J. Heinze. *Creativity and the Individual: Summaries of Selected Literature in Psychology and Psychiatry*. Free Press of Glencoe, Ill. 1960.

Taylor, Calvin W., ed. *Creativity: Progress and Potential*. New York: McGraw-Hill, 1964.

Torrance, E. Paul. *Creativity*. Belmont, California: Fearon Publishers, 1969.

Treffinger, D.; R.E. Ripple; and J.S. Dacey. "Teachers' Attitudes About Creativity," in *Journal of Creative Behavior*. 1968, II (4), 242-248.

Treffinger, Donald J. "Methods, Techniques, and Educational Programs for Stimulating Creativity: 1975 Revision," in *Guide to Creative Action*. Edited by Parnes, S.J., R.B. Noller and A.M. Biondi. New York: Scribner, 1976.

Treffinger, D.J., and J.R. Huber. "Designing Instruction in Problem-Solving: Preliminary Objectives and Learning Hierarchies," in *Journal of Creative Behavior*. In press.

Treffinger, D.J.; S.B. Borgers; G.F. Render; and R.M. Hoffman. "Encouraging Affective Development: A Compendium of Techniques and Resources," in *Gifted Child Quarterly*. Spring, 1976.

Chapter 6

Moral Education

In a small village, a woman lay near death from cancer. One drug might save her, a form of radium which a druggist in the same town had recently discovered. The druggist was charging $2,000 for the drug, ten times what it cost him to make it. The sick woman's husband went to every one he knew to borrow the money, but he could only collect half of what the drug cost. He told the druggist that his wife was dying, and asked him to lower the price or let him pay later. The druggist refused, so late that night, the desparate man broke into the pharmacy and stole the drug. Should the man have done that?

The moral development of children was once the main goal of our schools. The first schools in America were closely tied to religious groups. The school marm and master were expected to inculcate good character in their students by any means they could. There was little question as to the definition of morality in the rural towns of seventeenth, eighteenth, and nineteenth century America. True, there were theological differences, but almost all adults in the town embraced the same ethical beliefs and helped reinforce these beliefs in the young.

At the turn of the century, this unanimity began to disintegrate. The causes of this discord are hard to pinpoint, but the waves of immigrants, together with the rush to cities and industrialization, surely played a major part. The so-called "melting pot" created growing disagreement on ethical principles.

The role of the schools in character development shrank smaller and smaller. Teachers were told to avoid moralizing, propagandizing, indoctrinating. Democracy was seen as guaranteeing each person's right to his own set of values, which schools were forbidden to mold. The last vestige of religious doctrine was removed in the 1950's when Madeleine Murray won her Supreme Court case against praying in public schools.

It is interesting to note that the situation in the Soviet Union over the past seventy-five years has been just the opposite. Soviet educators have increasingly refined their techniques for conditioning morality. In fact, the most important aspect of Soviet education, *vospitania*, translates "moral education." The soviet approach consists mainly of conditioning *habits* of morality. "Moral education should begin very early, before the child completes his first year, and before he can understand the nature of adult explanation," wrote T.A. Repin, in *From Zero to Seven (Ot Nolya Do Semi*, 1967, p. 154). If conditioning is done well, the Russian child psychologist argues, understanding will come later. Repin feels that a high level of accord between teachers and parents on ethical principles is absolutely essential in moral education. In terms of mutual agreement on a moral code, therefore, the Soviet Union appears to be where the United States was at the turn of the century.

Americans today are experiencing a rebirth of interest in moral education. This movement predominates at the elementary and junior high levels, but is rapidly gaining ground at the preschool level. Proponents say that Watergate, our high crime rate, and the "identity crises" of our disaffected youth indicate the need to assist the child toward a well thought-out value system that can guide his actions. This renewed interest is not based on a revival of religion, however. Its proponents argue that most Americans (and, indeed, most human beings) still subscribe to a unified moral code, which is not derived from any religion, but from our mutual need to interact fairly with each other. They believe that children tend to proceed through a series of stages to a full acceptance of this code, and that education should systematically promote this natural development.

They urge that teachers must no longer restrict their teaching efforts to a body of factual information and skills. As Niblett puts it: "A technical knowledge of, say, navigation can be immensely interesting in itself. But the course the ship is to take is chosen for quite other reasons than the navigator's skill in plotting it. The educated man needs to discuss his direction of progress and the 'whys' of conduct as well as to build up knowledge and skills." (Niblett, 1963, p. 27).

The research of several highly respected psychologists lends support to this point of view. This chapter will consider the theories of psychologists Jean Piaget and Lawrence Kohlberg on moral development, and the teaching methods of Kohlberg, Louis Raths, Sidney Simon and their associates for fostering improvement in the morality of children.

Piaget's Theory of Moral Development

Although best known for his theory of cognitive development, Piaget's ideas on the moral judgment of the child, first presented in 1932, have also received widespread acclaim. Piaget defines morality as "the understanding of and adherence to rules through one's own volition." He has studied the development of this process in a number of ways, but his main technique has been through watching children of various ages play the game of marbles. The game calls for each competitor to shoot a marble from behind a line into a circle of other marbles. Any marbles knocked out of the area then belong to the shooter. Piaget believes that this social situation offers a good opportunity for perceiving the development of morality, since children of most ages play marbles and can say something about their understanding of the rules.

His theory divides the development of morality into two categories: practice of the rules, and consciousness of the rules. He makes this distinction because often children are able to follow rules without knowing why. Practice of the rules develops in four stages:

Stage 1. The individual stage (ages 0-3). In this stage, the child is trying to understand the nature of the game of marbles. There are regularities in the play of the game. The child tends to ritualize these. He does this until the act is mastered, then he grows weary of it.

The rituals are not yet rules; there is no "oughtness" attached. The marbles are representative of this stage of morality in that they are symbols to be played with. They can stand for something else, for example, they can be cooked, they can be eggs in a nest, and so forth. These symbols are what Piaget calls "played" symbols. Only with the development of language and imagery can these symbols become objects of thought in themselves. Through practice and experience, one thing comes to stand for another.

The sense of obligation to follow rituals, which then become rules, comes only when some other person intervenes. If the intervener is respected and requests that a ritual be followed, then a sense of obligation comes into being.

Stage 2. The egocentric stage (ages 4-7). By now the older children have taught the younger ones the rules of marbles. Of course, just watching older kids, and sometimes receiving instructions from parents, lead to knowledge of the rules, too. Children at this age try hard to follow the rules, but make many mistakes. The importance of the game is that you play it with others.

In this stage, children not only misunderstand rules, but they often interpret them differently from each other. In other words, they play according to different sets of rules. The main aspect of this stage is that they don't seem to *mind* that there are different criteria for each player. It is perfectly all right with them if everybody wins. The goal is imitation of the older, more prestigious children.

Stage 3. Cooperation (ages 8-11). Now there is a general will to discover rules which are fixed and common for all players. Everyone must play the same. However, there are still considerable discrepancies in the child's information. The main point of this stage is no longer the manual dexterity of knocking a marble out of the circle. It has become winning out over another person, within the context of complicated rules. The game has now become truly social.

This cooperation is only a matter of intention. The child at this age tends to play according to the rules which seem reasonable to him. At best, he will give in to a rule which he doesn't like for the duration of one game only.

Stage 4. Codification of rules (age 12-plus). Previously, the child made many mistakes because he was incapable of reasoning abstractly. He may have noticed inconsistencies but he was unable to alleviate them. Consistency begins to prevail through the adolescent's new interest in the codification of the rules, a fact of great importance for teachers. Not only do adolescents seek to cooperate, and to sanction the behavior of anyone who doesn't; they also take great pleasure in anticipating *all possible cases* and in codifying them. This tendency has great motivating power and can be used to strengthen many kinds of instructional strategies.

Since there are at least ten known varieties of the game of marbles, and many options within each set of rules, the amount of information that the adolescent needs to store in his mind on this minor aspect of his life is astounding. Years ago, I spent several days with a group of my teenaged friends writing out the rules for the game of Black Jack, or "21." It never occurred to us to look them up in a book. We thoroughly enjoyed trying to decide what *we* thought was fair.

The thoroughness with which a child practices rules may or may not indicate his *consciousness* of them. The two are tied together, but not rigidly. Piaget argues that there are three stages in the development of consciousness of the rules:

Stage 1. Individualism (ages 0-5). At first rules are learned subconsciously as interesting examples rather than obligatory reality. When the child approaches any play, he knows that some things are allowed and some forbidden. He also knows that these warnings are not applicable from time to time only, but are meant to hold with great regularity (you must *never* rip a newspaper into shreds). At the end of this stage, the child develops a sense of "oughtness," but his specific understanding of the rules is limited.

Stage 2. Heteronomy (ages 6-9). To get at the consciousness of the rules here, Piaget asks three questions: "Can the rules be changed?" "Have the rules always been the same?" "How did the rules begin?"

In answering these questions, Piaget discovered that children become extremely rigid during this stage in terms of their respect for rules. The child believes that rules come from an authority figure, usually his father but sometimes the mayor of the town or the governor. He is willing to see the rules change occasionally, but he believes that if they do change it is because one of the authorities has changed them.

Thus if rules come from parental authority, they are in essence sacred and unchangeable. To children of this age, what few changes they make to the rules come not from them, but are the discovery of eternal truth.

These attitudes develop from the continuous union between the child's ego and the Elders. Just as a mystic cannot differentiate between his ideas and those of God, the child cannot distinguish between his own rule changes and the rules imposed upon him from above.

Stage 3. Autonomy (ages 10-12). Now the rules become the tools of the player, not the dictates of the adult or the older child. Any change of the rules is permitted so long as all agree on it. Among adolescents, democracy seems to be the natural extension of the earlier theocratic viewpoint. Now there is a natural equality of all participants. Of course, some ideas are more reasonable than others; the child counts on the group to recognize these. He also counts on the group not to allow unfair innovations, for these would make the game less a matter of work and skill than it is. An adolescent comes to realize that other generations have made changes in the rules. Marbles, for example, must have started with rounded pebbles with which children amused themselves. Originally, the rules of marbles were invented by the children themselves.

Piaget's theory of moral development is an admirable description of development *across* age groups, but it pays too little attention to differences *within* age groups. Lawrence Kohlberg has contributed significantly to an understanding of these differences.

Kohlberg's Theory of Moral Development

Kohlberg, Professor of Education and Social Psychology at Harvard, has studied the development of moral judgment for nearly 20 years. He suggests that three approaches to the study of moral development may be taken.

1. We can infer the individual's morality from observations of his behavior in situations calling for moral judgment. This is primarily what Piaget has studied.

2. We can attempt to determine the amount of guilt that accompanies the person's failure to resist temptation.

3. We can ask the person what he thinks should be done in a series of hypothetical situations, and why he thinks so. This has been Kohlberg's method.

Clearly, the three are not necessarily closely related. A person may act according to some standard but not realize it. Conversely, he may say he believes in that standard, but not actually behave that way. Kohlberg has found, however, that there is a fairly high correlation between the child's hypothetical judgment and his behavior. Kohlberg's technique has the advantage of being able to investigate many situations in a short period of time.

What determines our moral beliefs and behavior? Kohlberg lists three explanations:

1. Freud and his followers have argued that the young child develops a conscience, a set of beliefs about morality, based on the ideals presented to him by the adults responsible for him. They refer to this as his "superego." The strength of his superego is said to determine his behavior. However, research has given little credence to this theory.

2. Some religious groups have argued that the conscience is a combination of learned beliefs and innate knowledge of right and wrong. If the child's specific beliefs coincide with his inherited conscience, he will be "good." This theory suffers from the same problem as the psychoanalytic one above: ideals often fail to coincide with behavior.

3. Kohlberg's position is that morality is a matter of *decision-making ability* rather than of strength of conscience or superego. Thus moral behavior is determined mainly by intelligence, self-esteem, and ability to delay gratification (our so-called "will power"). Knowledge of consequences (the odds of getting caught) also plays a large part. Philosophical beliefs, especially those of children, tend to have a minor effect on the decision-making process.

However, Kohlberg believes (as does Piaget) that there is an innate aspect in human morality. It does not depend solely on what we have been taught. He calls this innate aspect the "principle of justice." It consists of our understanding that all humans are basically equal in value, and that fairness in our interrelations should be maintained. This principle is part of our nature and is universal. Rules ("stop at the red light") differ from culture to culture, but the principle of justice (the Golden Rule) transcends cultures. When conditions are appropriate, justice is the natural result of social existence. Adolescents of Piaget's codification stage often typify this strong need for fairness.

Kohlberg sees the development of moral judgment as an increasing willingness to act according to the principle of justice. He suggests that this happens in three stages:

1. Pre-conventional. The child is amoral; he acts on self-interest and fear of punishment.

2. Conventional. Concern for conventional rules of society begins, as does regard for authority and judgment of others; the child is group-oriented.

3. Post-conventional. Self-accepted principles come into primacy; emphasis is on having a sense of morality for its own sake, even if consequences are painful.

A comparison of Kohlberg's stages with Piaget's appears in Table 6-1. The comparison is between the kinds of reasoning used, not ages. Kohlberg's stages do not necessarily correspond to any age.

Table 6-1. A Comparison of Piaget's and Kohlberg's Stages of Morality

Piaget	Kohlberg
S1. Individual	S1. Pre-conventional
S2. Egocentric	S2. Conventional
S3. Cooperation	
S4. Codification	S3. Post-conventional

Each of Kohlberg's three stages is divided into two substages. These substages are presented in Table 6-2 (adapted from Kohlberg, 1968). With each is an example of the typical response a child at that substage might make to a hypothetical moral dilemma. In each example, it is *why* the child decides, not *what* that determines the stage he is in.

Table 6-2. Kohlberg's Stages of Moral Judgment

The dilemma: Al, age 14, sees his brother Jimmy, age 10, steal money from their mother's purse. Should Al tell Mom what Jimmy did?

Stage 1. Preconventional Morality

Substage 1. Obedience and punishment. Child is self-centered, has strict pleasure-pain orientation.

Al: "I wouldn't tell Mom — Jimmy would only get even with me later. It's better not to get involved.

Continued

Substage 2. Naive instrumental hedonism. Trade-offs and deals are made, but only if the child sees something in it for himself. Need satisfaction is still uppermost, but an awareness of the value of reciprocity has begun.
Al: "It's better if I don't tell. I do bad things sometimes and I wouldn't want Jimmy squealing on me."

Stage 2. Conventional Morality

Substage 3. Good-boy morality. Child is eager for approval of others. Wants to maintain good relations.
Al: "It's better to tell on him. Otherwise, Mom might think I was in on it."
Substage 4. Authority and social order. Child now seeks approval of society in general, but has rigid ideas as to what rules are; "law and order" mentality.
Al: "I have no choice but to tell. Stealing just isn't right."

Stage 3. Post-conventional morality.

Substage 5. Contractual legalistic. Child makes contracts and tries hard to keep them; attempts to keep from violating the will or rights of others, believes in the common good.
Al: "I'll try to persuade Jimmy to put the money back. If he won't, I'll tell. I hate to do it, but that money belongs to Mom, and he shouldn't have taken it."
Substage 6. Universal ethics, individual conscience. Obedience to social rules, except where they can be shown to contradict universal justice; the principles of pacifism, conscienctious objection and civil disobedience fall into this category.
Al: "The most important thing is that Jimmy comes to see he's being unfair to Mom. Telling on him won't help that. I'm going to try to show him why he's wrong, then I'll help him earn money to pay Mom back without her knowing."

Table 6-3 presents pro and con resolutions to the moral dilemma which introduced this chapter. Typical resolutions are given for each substage.

Table 6-3.
Ranked Resolutions to the Cancer Cure Problem

Pro	Con
Substages ranked 1-6:	**Substages ranked 1-6:**
If you let your wife die, you will get in trouble. You'll be blamed for not spending the money to save her and there'll be an in-	He may not get much of a jail term if he steals the drug, but his wife will probably die before he gets out so it won't do him much

Continued

vestigation of you and the druggist for your wife's death.

If you do happen to get caught you could give the drug back and you wouldn't get much of a sentence. It wouldn't bother you much to serve a little jail term if you have your wife when you get out.

No one will think you're bad if you steal the drug but your family will think you're an inhuman husband if you don't. If you let your wife die, you'll never be able to look anybody in the face again.

You'd lose other people's respect, not gain it, if you don't steal. If you let your wife die, it would be out of fear, not out of reasoning it out. So you'd just lose self-respect and probably the respect of others too.

If you have any sense of honor, you won't let you wife die because you're afraid to do the only thing that will save her. You'll always feel guilty that you caused her death if you don't do your duty to her.

If you don't steal the drug and let your wife die, you'd always condemn yourself for it afterward. You wouldn't be blamed and you would have lived up to the outside rule of the law but you wouldn't have lived up to your own standards of conscience.

good. If his wife dies, he shouldn't blame himself, it wasn't his fault she has cancer.

You shouldn't steal the drug because you'll be caught and sent to jail if you do. If you do get away, your conscience would bother you thinking how the police would catch up with you at any minute.

It isn't just the druggist who will think you're a criminal, everyone else will too. After you steal it, you'll feel bad thinking how you've brought dishonor on your family and yourself, you won't be able to face anyone again.

You're desperate and you may not know you're doing wrong when you steal the drug. But you'll know you did wrong after you're punished and sent to jail. You'll always feel guilty for your dishonesty and lawbreaking.

You would lose your standing and respect in the community and violate the law. You'd lose respect for yourself if you're carried away by emotion and forget the long-range point of view.

If you stole the drug, you wouldn't be blamed by other people but you'd condemn yourself because you wouldn't have lived up to your own conscience and standards of honesty.

Most young children and most delinquents are in Substages 1 and 2. Most adults are in Substages 3 and 4. Kohlberg estimates that 20 to 25 percent of American adults are in the post-conventional substages (5 and 6), and only five to 10 percent ever reach Substage 6.

At the lower substages, the person acts to avoid punishment; at the higher stages, he acts to avoid self-condemnation. Conduct, therefore, is correlated with beliefs, with the reasons for the conduct differing greatly at the various levels. Higher level subjects are much less likely to cheat, for example. It is clear that this is because they find cheating inconsistent with their life styles, rather than because they fear discovery.

One interesting experiment investigated the willingness of persons at the six substages to inflict pain on others. The setting for the study was the Milgram electric shock obedience test in which subjects think they are administering a shock of from 15 to 450 volts to a "learner" in order to get him to learn a task quickly. The "learner" is actually a collaborator who is not really shocked but who puts on a convincing performance. In this experiment, a majority of Stage Six subjects either refused to participate or quit when the victim expressed pain. The majority of the subjects at the other moral levels continued with the experiment. Many of the Stage Five subjects said they wanted to quit but felt they shouldn't because they had agreed to take part.

Kohlberg finds that about 50 percent of an individual's moral statements fall into one dominant substage, and the rest fall into the two adjacent substages. The substage of thinking remains fairly constant regardless of the content of the dilemma. The same substages are also found in other cultures; the sequence of development is the same, although the speed of development is faster and is more likely to proceed to higher levels in some cultures than in others.

In addition to his considerable research on moral development, Kohlberg and his associates have conducted numerous investigations in moral education. The next section describes this work.

Kohlberg's Approach to Moral Education

As was pointed out earlier in this chapter, moral education in the U.S. since the turn of the century has been limited. What there was had virtually ended by the 1930's. The goals then were to explain the American code of ethics to children, encourage them to follow the code, and provide them with activities aimed at practicing the code. These efforts were found to be almost entirely ineffective.

Kohlberg and his co-workers have designed a new approach to moral education which overcomes several important limitations of earlier methods. The Kohlberg technique relies on the universal principle of justice, rather than on cultural mores. It attempts to upgrade moral understanding and behavior through personal experiences rather than through the teacher's efforts. Finally, it depends on carefully researched psychological data, rather than on philosophical speculations.

The approach defines moral education as the stimulation of the next step of development rather than indoctrination of a specific moral code. It is a two-step process:

1. "Arousal of genuine moral conflict, uncertainty, and disagreement about genuinely problematic situations...(and)

2. The presentation of modes of thought one stage above the child's own."

Most children prefer to function at the highest level of moral reasoning they can comprehend. This is usually one level above the child's dominant level. Reasoning too far above the child's own level is not understood, and reasoning at lower stages, while understood, is rejected. Adults trying to reason with children often seem to alternate between appeals too advanced for the child to comprehend, or too childish to accept.

While there have been no systematic studies of efforts to upgrade moral reasoning in early childhood, an investigation by Kohlberg and a colleague illustrates the research being done with older children. They examined the reactions of three groups of students to their moral education technique: upper-middle-class 11 and 12 year old Jewish students in a religion class; sixth and tenth grade lower-middle-class whites and middle-lower-class blacks; and mixed socio-economic and racial background students in a high school law course. Some of the students in each of these groups were exposed to moral dilemmas, were made aware of different points of view, and were encouraged to argue and discuss each dilemma with students at adjacent stages of moral development. Other students in each group were exposed to lectures on the same material; still others spent their time on ordinary classroom activities. The investigators concluded that the much greater gain of the discussion group over the other two groups "...indicates an effect not due to time, re-testing, or participating in an experiment...Still more important, the change which occurred was genuine stimulation of development rather than the verbal learning of moral cliches." The change upward of approximately one full stage for the average member of the first group held constant one year later.

On the basis of this and several other studies they review, the authors take the position that "if brief periods of classroom discussion can have a substantial effect on moral development, a pervasive, enduring and psychologically sound concern for the school's influence upon moral development should have much deeper and more positive effects."

A second conclusion these authors draw from comparing studies across pre-adolescent and adolescent age groups is that the period from age ten to fourteen is critical in moral development. But this does not preclude the possibility of a similar critical period in the early childhood years. Studies indicate the importance of both early childhood and adolescent periods. We may find that younger children need to deal actively with problems more closely related to their daily lives. Furthermore, there is evidence that the amount and variety of social experience, and the opportunity to take a number of roles are important in moral development. Thus, middle-class and popular children progress farther and faster than do lower-class and social isolates. An approach to moral education specifically designed to promote seeing one's own experiences from the perspective of others is called "values clarification."

Raths and Simon's Theory of Values

Values clarification is the invention of a number of educational psychologists, primarily the late Louis Raths and Sidney Simon, of the University of Massachusetts. It is a less direct technique that Kohlberg's for helping people achieve moral attitudes and beliefs about life. Rather than telling the individual what a principled position would be, it emphasizes personal discovery through wide-ranging discussions with others. The teacher never criticizes a student's position; the method assumes that discussion itself will produce more highly principled values. It seems to work as well with young children as with adults.

This approach was initiated when Raths became convinced that unclear values, while a serious problem in their own right, were beginning to cause many related difficulties. Schools, he argued, have long been sensitive to the efforts on learning of physical handicaps, emotional disturbance, and more recently, of "learning disabilities." These three deterrents to productive learning are dealt with effectively in the schools today.

It has become apparent, however, that a fourth deterrent to learning, lack of motivation, is frequently caused by personal confusion about values. People who are unclear about their values tend to be flighty, indecisive, apathetic, inconsistent, over-conforming or over-dissenting, and superficial role players. This has been an increasingly serious problem.

Values can be likened to guidelines which give direction to life. When the guidelines are blurred or unclear, people are confused and have difficulty making decisions. People who have clear values, on the other hand, tend to be positive, purposeful, and enthusiastic about life.

How does this confusion come about? In large measure, it happens because of the bombardment of ideas from television, radio, and print, as well as the exposure to enormous numbers of friends and acquaintances that urban society and modern communication make possible. As Simon has put it:

> "The children and youth of today are confronted by many more choices than in previous generations...Modern society has made them less provincial and more sophisticated, but the complexity of these times has made the act of choosing infinitely more difficult." (Simon, *et al.*, 1972, p. 15)

More specifically, what is meant by the term "values"? Valuing is composed of seven processes:

1. *Prizing and cherishing.* If a value is truly a value to us, we have a sense of being glad about it. We are proud to be the kind of person who has such a value.

2. *Publicly affirming, when appropriate.* If we are really proud of a value we hold, we should be willing to let anyone else know that we feel that way.

3. *Choosing from alternatives.* A value which we hold because we have no choice is no value at all. There must have been alternatives

which we could have chosen, but decided not to.

4. *Choosing after consideration of consequences.* Obviously, a snap judgment about the importance of something does not really indicate a deep value. Only when we have given careful thought to the results of our decision can we be said to have a true value.

5. *Choosing freely.* If we are being forced by someone else to take a particular position, it cannot be said to really be our own value. As someone put it, "When we have to do something, we are not sure we want to, and we're pretty sure we don't."

6. *Acting.* Often we hear people say that they hold a particular value, but when called upon to do something about it, they are unwilling to act. A real value should be one on which we are willing to take action.

7. *Acting with pattern, consistency and repetition.* In the case of a true value, we should be willing not only to act but to act as part of our normal pattern. People can see this is the way we really feel about a particular issue because this is the way we regularly act about it.

Clearly, we should not expect these criteria to apply to the value system of most young children. These seven characteristics serve mainly as a description of the fully formed value.

There are four basic ways that we acquire values:

1. *Moralizing.* This is the most direct way that adults transmit their values to the young. It is traditionally the way we have taught children to believe what we think they should believe. It is harder and harder to use this method these days and it is becoming less effective. It really only works when everyone agrees which values are desirable. As was suggested earlier, this used to be the case in our country. It is no longer so. Today there are many different groups and individuals competing with each other to convince our young people what they should believe. This competition for the attention of young individuals is a major cause of values confusion.

2. *A laissez-faire attitude.* Some people feel that we should just leave children alone and they will come to their own attitudes and values by themselves. The Summerhill approach, described in Chapter Eight, is typical of this. A growing number of parents seem to have this attitude today. However, it, too, contributes to the many conflicts and confusions that young people are feeling.

3. *Modeling.* In this case, we do not tell the young person what to think, but by presenting a good example, by being an attractive model, we hope that they will imitate us. As with moralizing, however, the problem is that there are so many models for children to imitate. Modern communications techniques have increased the number of models a hundredfold. This method, therefore, doesn't seem to work very well either.

4. *Values clarification.* As Simon describes it:

> Thus, the values clarification approach does not aim to instill any particular set of values. The goal of the values clarification approach is to help students utilize the above seven processes of valuing in their own lives; to apply these value processes to already formed behavior patterns, and to those still emerging.

...The values clarification approach tries to help young people answer some of these questions and build their own value system. It is not a new approach. There have always been parents, teachers, and other educators who have sought ways to help young people think through values issues for themselves.

Many techniques for helping youngsters make decisions about their own value structures have been designed in the last decade. Simon, *et al.*, (1972) and Howe and Howe (1975) have suggested over 100 specific and highly practical strategies to help school-aged children build the values process into their lives. Several of these strategies will now be described.

Values Clarification Strategies

Values voting. The teacher reads questions to the class and asks "How many of you...(wish you were an only child?)" Those who do raise their hands, those who don't point thumbs down, and those undecided fold their arms. The teacher puts the vote for each question on the board. When the voting is completed, discussion starts. Some sample questions are:

How many of you...
> think black people are as nice as whites?
> would rather live some place else?
> like school?
> get enough sleep at night?
> have a best friend?
> like to be teased?
> are afraid of the dark?
> think it's all right for boys to play with dolls?

Forced Choice Ladder. The children must construct a ladder with three to eight steps (see Figure 6-1).

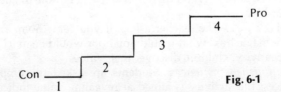

Fig. 6-1

The teacher suggests several ideas, objects, happenings, facts, names, etc., and makes a ladder with the same number of steps. Each child then writes his favorite on the top and so on. For example, four holidays could be suggested. When everyone has completed the task, one child at a time tells his choices.

Some examples are:
> a. doctor, lawyer, garbage man, salesman
> b. liar, cheater, bully, borrower
> c. mother, father, brother, sister
> d. Christmas, Easter, Thanksgiving, Halloween

Value Whips. This is a means by which children and teachers can see how others react to various issues. Someone poses a question to the class, then after a few minutes thinking time, "whips" around the room asking students to give their answers. Sample questions are:

    a. What is something you're proud of?
    b. What is a choice you made today?
    c. What is a favorite thing to do?
    d. What is something you're afraid of?

I Wonder Statements. This method is designed to stimulate probing, critical attitudes. After doing some other values clarification exercise, the teacher asks the students to complete such sentences as these:

    a. I wonder if...
    b. I wonder about...
    c. I wonder why...
    d. I wonder when...

Brainstorming. The idea here is to have the class generate as many imaginative reactions to a situation (attitudes, problems, solutions) as possible. Students are encouraged to respond quickly, avoiding criticism of their own ideas or those of the others. Quantity is encouraged, as it eventually breeds quality. Humorous and even silly ideas are also encouraged; even if such ideas are not useful, they often spark ones that are. Try to get everyone to contribute; timid students frequently have excellent ideas. Some questions might be:

    a. How can we make this class a happier place to be?
    b. What would be an interesting topic for discussion?
    c. Who are the finest people you know?
    d. What is the best thing to do when you're bored? Scared?

Three Characters. Designed to help the child become clearer about his own goals, this approach asks, "If you could be someone else, which three people would you be?" After each child has chosen, the teacher asks "Were your characters males or females?" "Would you be on anyone else's list?" "Would your best friend be able to guess who you put on your list?"

Magic Box. The teacher asks, "If you came home from school and found a magic box, what would you hope would be in it?" Through their own creativity, children discover their values.

Unfinished Sentences. Students are asked to complete unfinished sentences; this activity is aimed at revealing value indicators and often provokes useful discussion of them. For example:

    a. If I had my own car, I would...
    b. I like it best when people...
    c. If I had a thousand dollars...
    d. Secretly I wish...
    e. It makes me cry when...

Who Comes to your House? The children list all the people they can remember who have come to their house during the past year. Next to the list of names, they make six columns. In Column One, they put an R if the person if a relative, an F if he is a friend, and O for others. In Column Two, they put an M if the person's manners bother them. In Column Three, they place a star next to the names of the persons they were really glad to see. In Column Four, they put an X next to names of persons they would rather never came back. In Column Five, they put an S or a D if the person's religion is the same or different from theirs. In Column Six, they put an SR or DR if the person's race is the same or different from theirs. The typical response in each column is looked at and discussed, so that students can compare the profile of their friends with those of their classmates.

The "What Is Important" Song. The teacher plays the following song on the guitar or the piano (see p. 26 of *Values Clarification,* Simon *et al*); when the line "Tell me if you know" is reached, any child who wants to fills in his idea.

Baker's Dozen. The teacher says, "Make a list of 13 things you use around your house that run on electricity. If you can't think of 13, make a list of as many as you can. Draw lines through the things you don't really need. Now draw a circle around the three things you'd be lost without." A discussion, as usual, follows.

The Suitcase. Pretending that the class is going to take a long trip, the teacher asks the students to list what they would pack in one large suitcase. To vary the situation, the teacher can describe what the land to which the class is traveling is like; agricultural and very poor, an oasis, and so forth.

Twenty Things You Love To Do. In this series, participants are asked to write down 20 things in life they love to do. If students have trouble thinking of 20 things, suggest that they think of the seasons of the year for things that they love to do. When the lists are done, students are told to make a number of columns on the right hand side of their list. The number of columns depends on how many of the following ratings the teacher wishes to use. Each of the 20 choices is then rated on the basis of the following characteristics:

  a. If the item costs more than $5 each time it is done, place a dollar sign after it.
  b. If the item is usually done alone, the letter "A" is placed in the next column. If it is usually done with other people, a "P" is placed in this column instead.
  c. The letters "PL" are placed after items which require planning ahead.
  d. If the choice would not have been listed five years ago, an "N5" is placed in the next column.
  e. An "I" is placed next to any item which involves intimacy.
  f. An "R" is placed when the item has an element of risk.
  g. An "M" is placed next to items the student would not mind telling his mother about.
  h. Put a "U" next to those activities that other people would say are unconventional.
  i. A "CH" is put next to things which the student hopes his own children will do some day.
  j. The numbers 1 through 5 are placed next to the favorite five activities.

Whereas a large variety of values clarification techniques exist for school-aged children, practically no strategies have yet been designed for pre-schoolers. It seems clear, however, that the major goal for three and four-year-olds should be to improve their ability to make a simple choice. The following activities should be carried out in small discussion groups. The parent or teacher should encourage each child to explain his choice as much as possible.

Which Is Better? In this game, two choices are offered and the child must choose one as better than the other. If possible, a picture of each choice in the pair (perhaps cut from a magazine) is first held up for all to see. Of course, the actual objects are best.

    a. Tastes:
       Ice cream or spinach?
       Stones or jelly beans?
       Mashed potatoes or french fries?
       Pickles or carrots?
    b. Touch sensations:
       Bunny fur or bricks?
       Mommy's hand or Grandma's hand?
       Mud or snow?
       Warm sudsy water or icy cold water?
    c. Sounds:
       Crying or laughing?
       Singing or yelling?
       Truck horns or police sirens?
       A motorcycle or roller skates?
    d. Smells:
       Cookies or soap?
       Mommy or Daddy
       Rain or snow?
       Coffee or coke?
    e. General:
       Clean or dirty?
       Short or tall?
       Hot or cold?
       When using the toilet, standing up or sitting down?
       Biting or kissing?

Who Can Tell What I'm Thinking Of? This is played the same way as the above example.

    a. Things that are nice to take to bed with us.
    b. Things that make us scared (happy, sad, angry, proud, etc.)
    c. Clothing that is hard to put on (easy).
    d. The best part of a "busy box."
    e. The best animal in the world.
    f. Favorite toys.
    g. Things that are easy to lose and hard to find.
    h. Favorite relative.
    i. Things that hurt people's feelings (cheer them up, etc.).

Although only two examples are given here, others would have to be quite similar to these two. A large variety of value objects can be readily imagined. They should be chosen on the basis of relevancy to the interests and experience of the children being dealt with.

Several new books on strategies for values clarification are listed in the bibliography. Together they present a wealth of ideas for these on-going activities.

The major criticism that has been made of values clarification has been of its central tenet: whereas teachers must never evaluate the values expressed by the students, nevertheless some students occasionally espouse "unacceptable" values. Certainly, it does happen that a student says he favors a value that almost no one else in our society would share. Simon argues strongly, however, that teachers must allow such value statements to stand, relying on group pressure to change that student's mind. Another criticism is that most teachers will use subtle means to condition the values they want chosen. Experience seems to indicate, however, that teachers do this anyway, and that values clarification training makes them less likely to do it.

Educator John Stewart (1975) has added his own list of criticisms:

1. V.C. is too shallow. It gets at the context (the what), but not the structure (the why) of values.

2. It fosters group coercion.

3. It pushes all members of the group toward acceptance of the average position; this is usually in the middle of the continuum.

4. The question of certain values, such as those toward premarital sex, can be very embarrassing for some students.

5. Frequently the only students who really tell the truth about their values are the most popular ones. Often the others merely acquiesce.

6. The premature public affirmation of a value which the students, particularly teenagers, have not thought carefully about, can force them to stick to their position even in the face of overwhelmingly contrary evidence.

7. Raths' and Simon's criteria of a value are extremely stringent. It would appear according to their criteria, only martyrs have values.

8. Some of the activities betray the values biases of the designer's activities.

Summary

After a long hiatus, moral education is recovering its once important role in American schools. This is due in part to a growing concern among educators and parents over the ethical values (or lack of them) in today's society. It is also partly due to the innovative research of several psychologists.

This research has led to two major theories of moral development. Piaget suggests that there are four stages of the practice of moral behavior, and three stages of understanding. Each is closely governed by the unfolding of mental processes, and proceeds in stages covering several years. Kohlberg describes six levels of morality which are also developmental. He believes that this development is governed far more by experience than does Piaget, however. He finds that the majority of adults never progress beyond the middle two levels, and argues that only with appropriate education will they be likely to reach the highest levels.

Kohlberg's approach to moral education is quite directive. He poses moral dilemmas to students, and then attempts to raise each person's morality by exposing him to resolutions one level above his current level. Simon and his associates have taken a more non-directive approach. This technique, called "values clarification," relies on the discussion of moral dilemmas by a group to expose the irrationality of unethical opinions in the group. Over 100 strategies for clarifying values have been designed.

References

Beck, C.M.; B.S. Crittenden; and E.V. Sullivan. *Moral Education.* New York: Newman Press, 1971.

Bee, Helen. *The Developing Child.* New York: Harper & Row, 1975.

Dacey, J.S. "Moral Education in Early Childhood," in *The New Children.* Edited by J. Travers. Stamford, Conn: Greylock, 1976.

Hartshorne, H., and M.S. May. *Studies in the Nature of Character,* (3 vols). New York: Macmillan, 1928-30.

Hoffman, M.L. "Moral Development" *Carmichael's Manual of Child Psychology.* (3rd ed.), Vol 2. Edited by P.H. Mussen. New York: Wiley, 1970.

Howe, L., and M. Howe. *Personalizing Education.* New York: Hart, 1975.

Kohlberg, L. "Development of Moral Character and Moral Ideology," in *Review of Child Development Research,* Vol. 1. Edited by M.L. Hoffman and L.W. Hoffman. New York: Russell Sage Foundation, 1964.

Kohlberg, L. "Moral Development and Identification," in *Child Psychology, 62nd Yearbook of the National Society for the Study of Education.* Edited by H.W. Stevenson. Chicago: University of Chicago Press, 1963.

Kohlberg, L. "The Development of Children's Orientation Toward a Moral Order: I. Sequence in the Development of Moral Thought," in *Visa Humana.* 1963, 6, 11-33.

Kohlberg, L. "Moral Education in the Schools: A Developmental View," in *School Review,* 74. 1966, 1-30.

Kohlberg, L. "Moral Education, Religious Education, and the Public Schools: A Developmental View," in *Religion and Public Education.* Edited by T. Sizer. Boston: Houghton Mifflin, 1967.

Kohlberg, L., and E. Turiel. *Research in Moral Development: The Cognitive Developmental Approach.* New York: Holt, Rinehart & Winston, 1971.

Lefrancois, Guy R. *Of Children.* Belmont, California: Wadsworth, 1973.

Milgram, S. "Behavorial Study of Obedience", in *Journal of Abnormal and Social Psychology.* 1963, 67, 371-378.

Milgram, S. "Some Conditions of Obedience and Disobedience to Authority," in *Human Relations.* 1965, 18, 67-76.

Piaget, J. *The Moral Judgment of the Child.* New York: Collier, 1962.

Raths, L.; H. Merrill; and S. Simon. *Values and Teaching.* Columbus, Ohio: Merrill, 1966.

Sears, R.R.; L. Rau; and R. Alpert. *Identification and Child Rearing.* Stanford: Stanford University Press, 1965.

Simon, S.B.; L.W. Howe; and H. Kirschenbaum. *Values Clarification.* New York: Hart, 1972.

Stewart, John. "Clarifying Values Clarification: A Critique," in *Phi Delta Kappan.* June, 1975, 684-688.

Sverdlova, O., ed. *Ot Nolya Do Semi (From Zero to Seven).* Moscow: Znanic Publishers, 1967.

Turiel, Elliot. "An Experimental Test of the Sequentiality of Developmental Stages in the Child's Moral Judgements," in *Journal of Personality and Social Psychology.* 1966, 3, 611-618.

Chapter 7

Communicating
Well

Four women and three men sit facing each other in a circle. Two members of the group are chain smoking. One woman continuously rubs her palms on her jeans. The group's task is to decide which of the seven will go into a nearby fallout shelter, a shelter that will hold no more than five people. They have fifteen minutes to make their decision, at which time all the people in the world but the five in the shelter will die. The conversation is as follows:

Jim: "We have only fifteen minutes. We have to vote right now as to who gets to go into the shelter. Miriam, which five of us do you think should be chosen?"

Bill: "Wait a minute! Who appointed you boss? I say we should talk about our strengths and weaknesses, and then vote."

(Several people talk at once. It is hard to make out what they are saying.)

Jane: "Why don't we decide what we want for the new world to come. After all, everyone will be dead except those in the shelter so we want to know what kind of world we want to build."

Jim: "I think I should be allowed to stay—I am the strongest person in the group, and I've had some medical training."

Bill: "Jim, let someone else talk!"

Harriet: "We're going about this in a really jumbled way. I think we should first elect a leader for the group."

(Another confusion of voices is heard; it is impossible to understand what is being said.)

Nina: "The most important thing is to reproduce the species. I have two kids, so we know that I can have babies. I think we should find out if anyone else here has proven ability to have children."

Jim: "Now we're down to eleven minutes. I say we should vote right now and not take any chances."

These people were not really discussing survival outside a germ warfare shelter. They were participating in a communications skills exercise. But having engaged in a number of other exercises leading up to this one, they treated the situation as though it were deadly serious. At this point in their exercise the group leader called time out and played back a tape recording of the discussion. Returning to reality, the group proceeded to analyze the strengths and weaknesses of its communications abilities.

From kindergarten to graduate level study, the communications game is fast becoming a common activity in American classrooms. There are a number of reasons for this, the most important of which is a growing concern over the importance of future shock (described in Chapter One). Back when most Americans were born in rural villages, and generally stayed there, they had a lifetime in which to build adequate communications with people around them. Through extensive contact with their parents and relatives, they learned to understand and express themselves. But times have changed.

Johns Hopkins sociologist James Coleman specifies three alterations in American living patterns that have caused this critical change. First, children no longer learn their occupational skills from their parents. At the turn of this century, 91 percent of all boys went into the same jobs as their fathers (mostly farmer or small merchant). Almost 100 percent of all women went into the occupation of their mothers, that of housewife. Today few boys and fewer and fewer girls are going into the same jobs as their parents. Second, American youth used to be an economic asset to the family. Children worked on the family farm or in the store. Today children are an economic drain on the family's assets for the most part. Finally, people no longer stay in the towns in which they were born. The average family moves three times in the first ten years of its existence.

As Alvin Toffler explains it, we have many more friends during the course of our lives than our grandparents did, but we know them for a shorter period of time and much less well. If we are to achieve the kind of intimacy and sense of identity called for by Erik Erikson (Chapter Two), we will have to learn to communicate better and more quickly than ever before. This chapter describes some innovations which help children improve their ability to communicate.

The Language of Acceptance

In his book, *Parent Effectiveness Training*, psychologist Thomas Gordon has suggested a number of important principles to help parents communicate more effectively with their children. He refers to his overall principle as "the language of acceptance" by which one person shows another that he accepts him. Gordon believes that:

> It is one of those simple but beautiful paradoxes of life: When a person feels that he is truly accepted by another, as he is, then he is free to move from there to begin to think about how he wants to change, how he wants to grow, how he can become different, how he might become more aware of what he is capable of being (Gordon, 1972, p. 31).

This principle applies as strongly in the classroom as in the home. The language of acceptance has been taught to many teachers in recent years, and the results have been gratifying. But before looking at the rules governing the language of acceptance, let us look at the kind of language teachers usually use.

Gordon believes that almost all the responses that teachers make to student's statements fit into one of twelve categories: 1. ordering, directing, commanding; 2. warning, admonishing, threatening; 3. exhorting, moralizing, preaching; 4. advising, giving solutions or suggestions; 5. lecturing, teaching, giving logical arguments; 6. judging, criticizing, disagreeing, blaming; 7. praising, agreeing; 8. name-calling, ridiculing, shaming; 9. interpreting, analyzing, diagnosing; 10. reassuring, sympathizing, supporting, consoling; 11. probing, questioning, interrogating; or 12. withdrawing, distracting, humoring, diverting.

Each of these ways of responding, Gordon says, is nontherapeutic at best, and frequently destructive. Whereas any one of them might be appropriate under certain circumstances, none of them has the effect of making the child feel that he is non-judgmentally accepted by the teacher. Whatever it is that the teacher is trying to say, the child may well conclude one of the following: "You don't accept my feeling as I do, so you want me to change." "You don't trust me to work out this problem by myself." "You think it's my fault that...." "You think I'm not as smart as you." "You think I'm doing something bad or wrong."

Clearly non-acceptance is implied. The teacher who wants to make his students feel accepted tries to do one of the following:

1. Listen actively. The teacher shows the student that he is attending carefully to what he is saying, and does not interrupt. Even when the student seems to have stopped talking, if the teacher remains silent, the student often goes on and adds important information. The teacher can show acceptance in a number of ways, by saying "uh-huh", or "yes" or nodding, thus encouraging the student to continue speaking.

2. Restating what the student is saying to be sure that it is understood. Often the teacher can be helpful to the student's understanding of himself by positively restating what the student has expressed negatively and asking him if that's what he meant. For example, a sixth-grader says, "I hate my mother because she is an alcoholic." The teacher's response would be, "It makes you feel unhappy because you think your mother drinks too much, doesn't it?" Here the teacher took the label "alcoholic", which sounds permanent, and supplanted it with a more temporary description. This also removes the self-critical label, "son of an alcoholic" from the student, and shows the teacher's acceptance of him.

3. Use "I-messages." Often a teacher has a problem, but states it as though the problem belonged to the students. For example, when students are talking in the back of the room, they don't have a problem; the teacher does. Nevertheless, the teacher usually states it as though it were the students': "You kids have no respect for anyone!"

The problem could be more accurately stated this way: "I am getting angry because your talking is disturbing my train of thought." In this statement, the teacher admits that he is the one who has the problem, but because he does, soon the students will have one too. The goal here is for both parties to work out the problem so that neither of them suffers from it.

Gordon has developed a communications technique which he calls "the no-lose method of resolving conflicts." The method involves employing six steps, none of which should be skipped if the method is to work well:

Step 1: Identify and define the conflict. The language of acceptance is quite helpful here. Frequently children are unable to say what's bothering them because they fear the consequences of mentioning the difficulty. Even when he doesn't like what he hears, the teacher must open-mindedly attempt to get at the real problem.

Step 2: Generate possible alternative solutions. The problem-solving guidelines and the brain-storming techniques described in Chapter Five are useful here.

Step 3: Evaluate the alternative solutions.

Step 4: Decide on the best possible solution.

Step 5: Work out ways of implementing the solution.

Step 6: Follow up and evaluate how it worked.

Teachers can greatly enhance the no-lose method by employing active listening and "I messages" whenever appropriate. The combination of these techniques has been shown to improve the communications and cohesiveness of the classroom. Chapter Eleven treats this more fully.

Communications Models

Communications models may be used by both experienced teachers and teacher-trainees to analyze and understand the reasons for communication problems in the classroom. One well-known model is the "Laswell Formula," developed by Yale law professor Harold Laswell. The formula consists of five essential variables which embody the communication process:

Who
Says what
In which medium
To whom
With what effect

Looking at the communication process in terms of these questions allows us to analyze particular situations by focusing on a specific question. For example, the question "to whom" is an important one to teachers. Typical questions which arise from this are: "What are the characteristics of my audience?" "What expectations do they have?" "What is the best way to reach them and encourage two-way communications?" Answers to these questions generate modifications in teaching methods and lead to a better organized class. Similarly, many questions arise when a teacher asks, "What do I hope to achieve?" "How do I expect them to show interest?" "What will demonstrate to me that they have understood?" In answering these questions, greater clarity concerning the goals and expectations of teaching is attained.

Another useful model is the Shannon-Weaver model (Figure 7-1).

Fig. 7-1. The Shannon-Weaver Model

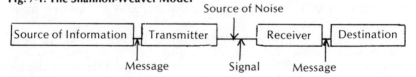

The information source, a teacher's brain, for instance, chooses a particular message. The message is then transmitted. In speech, the transmitter is the voice, and the signal is language. This message, traveling through a communication channel (air, in the case of oral speech) is then received. At this point the message is decoded and, it is hoped, understood. As you can see, this model incorporates all the mechanical prerequisites for communication into one diagram. The theory behind the Shannon-Weaver has specific value for teachers. The problems involved in "coding" and "noise" demonstrate the applicability of this model to education.

"Coding", the symbolization of messages, underlies all communication. In terms of the diagram, coding refers to the specific form a message takes when it is transmitted, received. and understood by someone else. A code may be verbal or non-verbal; for example, gestures, images, musical forms, or dances. It is important that the person receiving the message have an adequate understanding of the code being used. This is too often taken for granted.

There is a simple classroom exercise that can be used to demonstrate the importance of coding. The teacher invents a code of nonsense words which stand for specific instructions. For example, "karm"=leg. When the words are combined, they form simple messages. Then the teacher constructs a "fake" code of similar words whose meanings are different. In this exercise, the two codes are distributed to the class so that some students get the "real" code and others the "fake" code. The teacher then writes an instruction (e.g., "Put your leg on your desk") in code on the board, and the students are told to follow it. This will lead to much confusion since the message will be clear to some students and unintelligible to others. When the teacher pushes his class to work quickly, many of the students who had received fake code keys pretend to understand by imitating their classmates. In this case, social pressure and the teacher's insistence on speed forced some students to conform to the behavior of the others, even though they had no idea why they were doing so. Teachers should realize that this often occurs in the classroom, especially when all the orders come from the teacher. The best way to alleviate social pressures to conform is to solicit honest feedback from the students, in order to learn who doesn't understand the code.

Another problem in communicating is "noise." Technically, noise is anything that distorts a signal. In the Shannon-Weaver model, noise can be anything from radio static or "snow" on a television screen to a child screaming in your ear while you're trying to talk to a friend. In the classroom, psychological noise such as daydreaming and alienation accounts for many communications disruptions. Here are four ways of counteracting the distorting effects of classroom noise:

1. The deliberate use of redundancy can be helpful. The more ways you can repeat an important message, preferably through different but similar examples, the more likely you are to break through noise.

2. Use a variety of media to present your message.

3. Try to gear your presentation to the interest patterns of your audience.

4. When speaking your message, vary the way you use your voice. Move about the room so that you are heard from different directions. Avoid speaking in a monotone. In making an important point, pause for a moment, then raise your voice, and slow your words. Great actors use these and many other speaking tricks to capture your attention.

Sensitive observation of one's own behavior is the essence of effective communication. The Laswell and Shannon-Weaver models can promote observation by helping us identify and analyze the various steps in the information process.

Group Communications Processes

Studies of how individuals interact in groups grew largely out of the work of Kurt Lewin, a psychologist who developed the notion of "field theory" in the 1930's. Field theory is a method for analyzing the relationships and communications within groups.

For teachers, the most important concept of field theory is that all group processes involve change of the people involved. Lewin found that the perceptions, beliefs, motivations, or cognitive understanding of individuals change much more readily when they participate in a group process. He found that while lecturing can be quite effective in teaching new concepts, it is less useful in the application of such concepts. Students who have learned by discussion methods are better able to apply the concepts learned to new problems. Not all discussion groups produce superior application, however. What seems most important to the success of this method is the skill of the instructor.

Teachers are often faced with group dynamics problems. In large part, classroom learning is a group process. For this reason, it is important for teachers to study and understand the way groups function.

The teacher is both observer and participant in his class. By examining his own motives, a teacher can better appreciate the problems students have. One way to diagram the dynamics of awareness has been developed by Joseph Luft and Harry Ingham, two social psychologists. They call their diagram (Figure 7-2) the Johari Window. The window is divided into four quadrants.

	Known to Others	Not Known to Others
Known to Self	1 Open	2 Blind
Not Known to Self	3 Hidden	4 Unknown

Fig. 7-2. The Johari Window

The first quadrant refers to those aspects of ourselves which we and others know and share together. The second quadrant consists of those things which other people see in us, but of which we are unaware. The third quadrant relates to the parts of ourselves which we know, but don't divulge. The fourth quadrant contains the motives which neither we nor others are aware. We can assume its presence, because as we grow, we often become aware of motivations which were influencing us even when neither we nor anyone else knew of their existence.

The Johari Window can be used to analyze the way you and your class act as a group. For example, at the beginning of the year the size of quadrant one would be small, since you and your pupils know little about each other. But as you share more, quadrant one would grow larger, while quadrant three would grow smaller, since you and your pupils would hide less of yourselves. In your role as a teacher, an important concern would also be to reduce the size of quadrant two in your pupils. Helping students become aware of their motives and of how they relate to others is an essential goal of good teaching (and of any successful group). The development of a relationship between the teacher and his pupils involves several principles of change that help us structure the class.

The first, of course, is that a change in one quadrant will affect the others as well. As you share more, you hide less. This principle implies another; increased trust leads to greater awareness, while a sense of insecurity will lead to a withdrawal from sharing. In interpersonal terms, then, learning means an increase in all those behaviors and motives that enlarge quadrant one.

Keeping the Johari Window continuously in mind provides a necessary guard against authoritarianism and rigidity, whether in the classroom or any other group function. Another model for improving the effectiveness of group communication is described in the next section.

The Borton Model for Group Effectiveness

Terry Borton, author of the popular *Reach, Touch, and Teach,* suggests that "the most critical element in making the group function well is to keep decisions open, explicit and shared" (*Learning,* Jan. 1976, p. 59). He offers three techniques to achieve this goal. These techniques are especially helpful in group work at the secondary level.

1. Employ a group "navigator," instead of a leader or chairperson. This navigator helps the group by regularly asking one of three questions: "Where are we now?" "Where do we want to go?" "How can we best get there?"

The navigator does not try to impose his own will; he is merely an instrument to help the group find its own way. Thus the group, which at first will naturally look to the navigator for leadership when problems arise, will be forced to look to all its members for a solution.

2. Use basic problem-solving processes. The group should systematically attempt to answer each of the following five questions: "What is the problem?" "What are the possible courses of action?" "What

will be necessary to make the idea work?" "How is the solution working out?" "Has support been offered throughout the problem-solving process?" For further suggestions here, see Chapter Five.

3. Hold regular feedback sessions. At least one feedback session should be held during every meeting, Borton suggests. These sessions should deal with three concerns: 1. the rules by which the group is governing itself ("Should we continue to meet here?", "Should things said at meetings be kept confidential?"); 2. feelings ("Is anyone in the group feeling angry about the behavior of another member?"); and 3. the outside environment ("What resources should the group call on?", "Are other groups competing with this group?").

Borton believes that when groups apply these three communications principles, they can achieve the kind of effectiveness that makes members feel proud of sharing in the process.

Communications Games

This section offers thirteen games for use in classrooms to improve students' abilities to interact with each other. An extremely useful resource in this area is *Communication Games* by Karen Krupor, from which many of these activities have been adapted. Krupor's book has a companion student workbook which facilitates use of the games.

1. *I See X.* This exercise is aimed at helping students improve their observation skills and, more importantly, their ability to express honestly the things they observe. The class is divided into halves and positioned on opposite sides of the room in lines facing each other. One person at a time in each group selects a member of the other groups, and says, "I see X (something about that person) and I like it." For example, he might say, "I see Barb smiling, and I like it." When one group has finished, then members of the other group make observations about the first group.

Other ways of using this exercise include the following statements:

A. "I see X and I don't like it."

B. "I see X and I sense that you are feeling Y."

C. "I see X and it makes me feel Y."

D. "I see X and I think you should do Y about it. What do you think of that?"

E. "I have noticed X. How many other people in this group have also noticed X?"

One of the most important aspects of a well-functioning group is the sense of trust that the members feel in each other. Therefore, in establishing an appropriate classroom climate it is essential to help students be aware of the level of trust they feel for the other members of the class. There are many ways in which we feel trust or distrust for others, the most basic of which is whether or not we trust them with our physical safety. The following exercises help us examine our feelings about this kind of trust.

2. *Massage train.* Members of the class stand in a circle, then face the back of the person to their left. They gently massage the neck and shoulders of the person in front of them. After a time they change and

massage the person who has been massaging them. A discussion of emotional reactions follows.

3. *Trust walk.* Students choose a partner and are led around blindfolded by that partner. The partner leads them up and down stairs, asks them to touch things along the way, varies the speed of the walk, and so forth. After a time the partners switch roles.

4. *Face exploration.* Keeping the same partner, the students sit on the floor facing each other. One partner is blindfolded and then proceeds to explore the other partner's face with his hands. The partners should not talk to each other, but should make a mental note of how they feel while doing this.

5. *Trust fall.* Students form groups of seven to ten members, and form a circle. One member of each group stands in the center of the circle and is blindfolded. With his feet together and flat on the floor, the person allows himself to fall backwards into the arms of the student behind him. He is then gently passed around the circle, without moving his feet. This is done with a circle four feet in diameter, and then repeated with a six-foot circle. Everyone in the group should take a turn in the center.

6. *Trust run.* This exercise should be performed in a large room; a gymnasium is usually best. Members of the class stand on each side of the gym. One member of the class is then blindfolded and placed at the end of the gym. He is to start running down the center toward the other end. When he is approximately two-thirds of the way down the auditorium, the class should yell to him to stop. He must trust that they will not allow him to crash into the wall at the other end. Each person in the group also takes his turn at this.

Each of these exercises tends to generate strong feelings. Therefore, it is appropriate to allow a discussion of each exercise immediately after it has taken place.

7. *Identity card.* Each student writes the answer to one or more of the following questions on 3x5 cards. The students then put the cards on their collars and place them on their desks.

"In one word, what is:
    a. the thing you are proudest of?
    b. your favorite activity?
    c. your most serious fault?
    d. your favorite famous person?
    e. the thing that most frightens you?
    f. the thing that most saddens you?
    g. your favorite food?"
    h. other similar questions may be used.

Students read each other's cards and give their reactions. A variation calls for students to guess what others will say before seeing their cards.

8. *Crazy K-D Game.* Probably the most significant deterrent to effective communications is the lack of clarity in the message being sent. The purpose of the Crazy K-D game is to demonstrate to students the im-

portance of being precise in the wording of a communication. Students are requested to choose a partner and seat themselves back to back, with one partner facing the wall of the classroom, and the other partner facing the center of the room. The partner facing the wall is partner A; the partner facing the center of the room is partner B.

The A partner is given the loose pieces of the puzzle for the letter K (see Fig. 7-3 below), but is not told what it is.

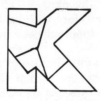

Fig. 7-3. Crazy K

The B partner, facing the center of the room, is given a picture of the completed K puzzle. Partner B is to describe to partner A how to put the puzzle together. The A partner is not allowed to ask any questions or say anything. Only the B partner, who has a picture of the puzzle, is allowed to talk in this part of the game.

After approximately five minutes, the teacher tells the partners that they may now talk to each other, but they must still remain back to back and not look at what the other is doing. This two-way communication usually helps the partners put the puzzle together. When one pair has completed the puzzle, the teacher asks them to go to the center of the room so that everyone can see that someone has finished. After about ten minutes, or when about half of the groups have been successful in completing the puzzle, the teacher stops the game. A discussion of what went on then follows.

The teacher asks those in the center of the room why they think they were successful, starting with the pair who finished first. After they have talked about their success for a while, those who were unsuccessful are asked why they think they failed. When this discussion has gone on for an appropriate period of time, the other half of the game starts.

Now the partners switch positions, so that the B partners are facing the wall, and the A partners are facing the center of the room. The teacher then gives the B partners who are facing the wall the loose pieces of the D puzzle (Fig. 7-4).

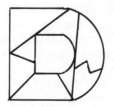

Fig. 7-4. Crazy D

The A partner, facing the center of the room, has a picture of the completed puzzle, and the game proceeds as before. As in the first session of the game, only the partner with the picture of the completed puzzle may talk. Again, the two partners may not look at what the other is doing.

After approximately five minutes, the teacher allows both partners to talk to each other as in the first session of this game. After about ten minutes, or when half the teams have been successful, the game is terminated.

This time the teams should finish more quickly. The teacher may want to wait until all teams are successful, so everyone feels good about the game. The teacher again asks successful and/or unsuccessful players why they think the game went as it did this time, particularly concerned with what improved in this phase of the game.

This game allows students to discern what it was that helped them sharpen their statements in directing their partners. The importance of precision in language should become abundantly clear.

9. *Tinker-toys.* This game also helps students realize the importance of being accurate and specific. The large set of tinker-toys will be needed for the game. Separate each type of tinker-toy part into piles, then divide them equally into three envelopes, so that you have three matched sets. The class should be divided into four teams: Team A, the makers; teams B and C, the copiers; and team D, the observers.

Tell team A to go into the hall with its set of tinker-toys, and make something. Also tell them they are going to have to described whatever they make to teams B and C, who will try to copy it with the other two sets of tinker-toys.

Teams B and C may do what they wish with their tinker-toys (most teams immediately sort their toys into types, but don't tell them to do this). Each of the teams should elect a messenger who is to go out to team A to get information for his team. The teams should go to the opposite corners of the room so they cannot see or hear what the other team is doing. As the messenger brings them information, they use it to try to copy team A's structure which they can't see. Team D should be given pads to make notes on the interactions between the other teams. The observers are allowed to roam about the room and station themselves out in the hallway so that they can watch and report on the communications and miscommunications that occur.

Having allowed team A sufficient time to complete their structure, tell them to pick someone to represent them to the messengers from teams B and C. Instruct them that they are to give "one piece of information" to each messenger when he comes up to the door, but don't specify what. If the messengers come at different times, they should be given the information individually. You will find that most teams give too much information at one time, which causes many problems for the two copying teams. Instruct all teams that the only people to speak when the messengers come to the door should be the team A person delivering the information. No body signals may be used by team A. The messengers may ask no questions in this first part of the game. The messengers take the information back to their respective teams, who then try to follow the instructions. It will soon be obvious to you that if one miscommunication occurs, all instructions after that will go awry.

After fifteen minutes stop the action and inform both teams that the messengers may now ask questions. The messengers should confer with their teams as to what questions they should ask, since they can ask only one question each time they go to the hallway.

After another fifteen minutes have passed, team A brings its structure into the room and places it on a table. Teams B and C place their structures next to team A's. You will encounter a great deal of laughter, as the copiers will undoubtedly have made something quite different from team A.

Now the observers should report what they noticed. Each observer should make a report, and should be encouraged to be frank and honest about what went on. All members of the class should suggest how they might have done better.

10. *Stand in the middle.* This game tests the ability of the class to express feelings and emotions in a non-verbal way. The teacher asks for one volunteer to stand in the middle. This person should stand with his eyes closed, saying and doing nothing, surrounded by the rest of the class. The others are to express some feeling of emotion to the person in the middle without saying anything. These feelings need not be sincere ones.

Sometimes this exercise puts a lot of pressure on the person in the center. Students have expressed anxiety about what people will do to them and have also felt intense loneliness. However, the greatest pressure is on the rest of the class. One person may get up and shake hands with the person in the center, signifying admiration for his standing all by himself. Someone else may come up and pat or squeeze his arm, or make some other fairly safe expression. It soon takes some imagination to do something different. Usually a period of long silence follows, and the pressure really builds up in the class. Students may attempt to whisper to each other, but should be reminded that no talking is allowed. After a time, individuals start to do all kinds of things, because they can no longer stand to just sit there. People may come up and kiss the person in the center, give him a chair, pat him on the back, or shove him. Teachers should be on the lookout for someone who seems to want to harm the person in the center. This is hard to tell in advance, but almost never happens.

After a fairly long period of time, about twenty minutes, and when you think that no one else is likely to do anything, tell the person in the center of the circle that he can open his eyes and sit down.

Ask the person who stood in the center to tell how he felt being there. Ask him to describe what various people did, and how he felt about those things. Ask him also if he knows who did what.

Then go around the circle and ask each student why he did what he did, or why he decided to do nothing. If the person responds that he did nothing because he thinks it's a dumb game, pursue this too.

Usually you will find that the people in the outside circle speak about their own feelings rather than the feelings of the person in the center. This is the point of the game. Most people have a difficult time expressing feelings in front of other people, and this game provides a good format for doing so.

11. *Patterns.* In this game students will learn the effects on communication of several different arrangements of groups. Although each group supposedly has an equal chance to win this game, groups arranged in one pattern will be more successful that groups in other types of patterns. The class is divided into groups of five with extra members used as referees. These groups are then arranged in seating patterns A, B, or C, as shown in Fig. 7-5 below.

Fig. 7-5. Three Communications Patterns

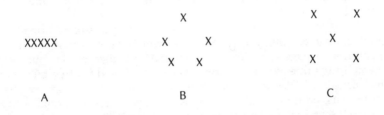

Students should be divided evenly into the three patterns; if you have six groups, two should be formed in pattern A, two in pattern B, and two in pattern C. Participants are told that they are to remain in these patterns and must not get up from their seats during the course of the game. The purpose of the game is for each of the members of the group to complete a square puzzle (see Fig. 7-6 below).

Fig. 7-6. The Square Puzzles

The puzzle pieces are cut out of plain cardboard; colors should not be used since these will give clues to the assembling of the puzzles. Pieces of the puzzles are shuffled up in five sets of three or four pieces (there are seventeen), and one set is given to each group member. Their task will be to pass pieces among each other, without talking, until each member has completed a square. When a team has finished the five squares, they should raise their hands.

Persons seated in pattern A, a straight line, can only pass pieces to persons on their left or right. Chairs in pattern A should be set far enough apart so that people in the line have difficulty seeing from one end to the other. In this and other patterns, when a piece is handed to another member, the member must take it.

Persons in pattern B, the pentagon pattern, may pass pieces to any other person in the group. However, they may not talk to each other, nor may they use hand signals.

Persons forming the figure of pattern C can pass pieces only to the person in the center. The person in the center, however, may pass pieces to any other member of the group.

Pattern B will almost always win. This should demonstrate to students the value of open communication between all members of a group. Pattern C usually comes in second, followed by pattern A. Sometimes, however, pattern A finishes before pattern C; if the person in the center of pattern C is not astute, he can slow that group down considerably.

The discussion following the playing of this game often brings up a number of interesting points. Students will usually discuss feelings of frustration at seeing which piece another member needs, but being unable to tell this person. Persons in patterns A and C often talk about the frustrations of seeing people in pattern B freely passing information, and remark on how unfair this seems to them. Students should then be led to a discussion of where these patterns occur in life.

12. *The Survival Game.* This is probably the most demanding, but most productive, of the communications games. The second part is definitely not recommended for young children. It is best employed with groups of fifteen to thirty.

Start by asking for seven volunteers. Only choose volunteers whom you know fairly well, so that you can avoid choosing participants who may have personality problems. The best mix is four females and three males, for reasons which will become apparent. Arrange the seven in a circle around a tape recorder, near enough to the microphone, but far enough from each other so that they will have to speak somewhat loudly. The other people are arranged in a surrounding circle. They are to take notes on the communications patterns of the inner group.

On the blackboard or on a handout, write the following role descriptions:

1. Politician (M)
2. Lawyer (F)
3. Husband (M)
4. Wife (F)
5. Four-year old daughter (F)
6. Teacher (F)
7. Priest (M)
8. Doctor (M)
9. Artist (F)
10. Football player (M)

Here are your instructions for the inner circle:

"Imagine that these ten people are located on a remote mountain near a newly developed germ warfare shelter. This shelter is the only one of its kind. Germ warfare has just broken out, with all sides unleashing their total capacities. The result will be the complete annihilation of the human race, with the exception of those in the shelter. Nothing else will be harmed. All animals, vegetation, and man-made things will be intact. You are to consider yourself a god-like committee, with the task of deciding which of these ten people will survive. The "M" after each role stands for male, the "F" for female. The husband, wife, and daughter are a family. That is all I can tell you about these people. Remember, you are not only to save seven of them, but, in doing it, you must try to communicate well. You have fifteen minutes to make your decision."

Start a tape recorder. Almost invariably, the participants will begin talking at once, without listening to each other. After about five minutes of this, stop the tape, and replay it. Usually the participants will find the tape embarassing, but do not let them discuss it yet. Ask the members of the outside circle to comment on the group's performance. They should have noticed a lack of concern for each other's ideas, that no coordinator has been appointed, that no criteria nor method for selection has been chosen, and so forth. Your role here is to help both groups *discover* what good communication means. Have the outside circle vote, on a scale from one to five, on the group's communicating ability. Next let the participants respond to the criticisms, and vote on themselves. When discussion is adequate, allow the final ten minutes of the session to begin.

If you think the group can handle the second part of the game, say: "You may now play this game a second time if you like, to see whether you've learned to communicate better." (See if they want to—usually they will.) "However, there is a slight change in the rules: the shelter now holds only five people, and seven are outside it. Those seven are you! Try to take the game seriously, but you need not reveal anything you don't want to." Use the game with discretion, and be ready to stop it if necessary. You will have no problem motivating discussion at the end of this section. Statements of feelings, reactions of non-participants, and ideas for improving communications should prove abundant!

13. *Non-verbal awareness.* This exercise is used as the last in a series of communications exercises, when the members of the class have had considerable interaction with each other. Its goal is to help students recognize that they communicate in many ways, and their non-verbal habits can sometimes interfere with effective communications.

The class is divided into groups of four. This exercise can be tried with groups formed of close friends, and another time with people who do not regularly associate with each other.

On one sheet of paper each student should write the word "Me" and list five different types of non-verbal communication that he feels he regularly uses. If possible, he should give an example. On separate pieces of paper, he should put the names of the other individuals in the group, and should list at least three non-verbal habits of each of them.

When all the members have completed each of the four sheets, one group member at a time should read his observations of each of the individuals in the group. After these are read, the person being discussed reads his own "Me" sheet aloud and reacts to the group's perception.

When the discussion period has ended, the teacher should call all students together for a discussion of the following topics:

1. "How many people thought the observations of them by the other members of the group were mainly accurate?

2. "How did you feel having your non-verbal habits discussed with other people?"

3. "In what ways were your perceptions the same or different from the other members of the group?"

Summary

Teachers can be a critical factor in resolving the problem of ineffective communications. It often appears that they are the only ones in a position to effect improvement. Teachers who would improve the communication climate of their classroom will do well to follow the example of Dr. Tom Gordon, who expresses his feelings in his:

"Credo for my Relationships with Youth"

You and I are in a relationship that I value and want to keep. Yet each of us is a separate person with his own unique needs and the right to try to meet those needs. I will try to be genuinely accepting of your behavior when you are trying to meet your needs or when you are having problems meeting your needs.

When you share your problems, I will try to listen acceptingly and understandingly in a way that will facilitate your finding your own solutions rather than depending on mine. When you have a problem because my behavior is interfering with your meeting your needs, I encourage you to tell me openly and honestly how you are feeling. At those times, I will listen and then try to modify my behavior, if I can.

However, when your behavior interferes with my meeting my own needs, thus causing me to feel unaccepting of you, I will share my problem with you and tell you as openly and honestly as I can exactly how I am feeling, trusting that you respect my needs enough to listen and then try to modify your behavior.

At those times when either of us cannot modify his behavior to meet the needs of the other and find that we have a conflict-of-needs in our relationship, let us commit ourselves to resolve each such conflict without ever resorting to the use of either my power or yours to win at the expense of the other losing. I respect your needs, but I also must respect my own. Consequently, let us strive always to search for solutions to our inevitable conflicts that will be acceptable to both of us. In this way, your needs will be met, but so will mine—no one will lose, both will win.

As a result, you can continue to develop as a person through meeting your needs, but so can I. Our relationship thus can always be a healthy one because it will be mutually satisfying. Each of us can become what he is capable of being, and we can continue to relate to each other with feelings of mutual respect and love, in friendship and in peace.

(Gordon, 1972, pp. 305-6).

References

Gordon, Thomas. *Parent Effectiveness Training.* New York: Nyden, 1972.

Henning, Dorothy G. *Mastering Classroom Communication.* Pacific Palisades, California: Goodyear, 1975.

Luft, Joseph. *Group Processes.* Palo Alto, California: National Press Books, 1970.

Otto, Herbert A. *Group Methods to Actualize Human Potential.* Beverly Hills, California: The Holistic Press, 1970.

Perlmutter, Joel; and Fred Stokley. *Let's Get it Together.* Newton, Massachusetts: Education Development Center, 1971.

Phillips, Gerald M.; David E. Butt; and Nancy J. Metzger. *Communication in Education.* New York: Holt, Rinehart and Winston, 1974.

Wittmer, Joe; and Robert D. Myrick. *Facilitative Teaching: Theory and Practice.* Pacific Palisades, California: Goodyear, 1974.

Chapter 8

Part III

Controlling The Classroom

A cold drizzle was falling as we drove up the hill toward Morningstar Free School on a typically gray day in mid-November. Rounding a bend, we were startled to see a group of barefoot teenagers racing across a meadow toward us, waving their arms wildly. We pulled over, and they ran up to the window.

"Come to have a look at us, have you?" asked one. "Tell us what you expect to find," said another.

"For one thing, I expected to find kids with shoes on in this weather," my friend Jule said. "Aren't you afraid you'll catch cold?"

They smiled at each other as a third said, "No one ever catches cold at Morningstar."

Children are basically bad.

Children are basically good.

Children are neither good nor bad; how they turn out depends on their education.

If you look closely, you will see that all teachers make one or the other of these basic assumptions about the nature of children. The view that children are bad was held by New England Puritan educators in seventeenth-century America. Teachers who make this assumption also believe that children need a great deal of control, and that this control should come directly from the teacher. The idea that children are basically good is exemplified in the writings of Jean Jacques Rousseau, the French philosopher, who believed that bad behavior is caused by unreasonable societal demands. He argued that if children were allowed to develop in their own way, they would turn out to be useful, happy citizens. Teachers who take this view of the nature of children believe that the less control exercised over them the better. The view that children are neither innately good nor bad is typified by the writings of most psychologists in America today. Teachers who make this assumption believe that children need to be controlled to some extent, but that this control should be indirect and should lead ultimately to self-governance.

This chapter looks at three types of educational control, and compares them as to their views of children. The no-control view is represented by the free school. The indirect view is represented by open education. The direct-control view is represented by many traditional classrooms in this country.

No-Control— The Free School

Although there are probably no more than 500 "free" schools in the United States today, there were virtually none in 1960. This phenomenal growth got its main impetus with the publication of Alexander S. Neill's best-selling book, *Summerhill*. For over fifty years, Neill experimented with the implications of the free school in the rustic setting of Leiston, England. The small school (never enrolling more than forty-five students) received international recognition with the publication of that book. Throughout his life (he died in 1975 at 80), Neill questioned the values, morality, and psychological restrictions that society imposes on children. He designed his school to have the absolute minimum of such restrictions.

In the introduction to his book, Neill quotes a poem by the Lebanese philosopher and poet, Kahlil Gibran. Four lines of the poem express the philosophy of the free school:

"Your children are not your children.
They are the sons and daughters of Life's longing for itself.
They come through you, but not from you.
And though they are with you, yet they belong not to you.

Neill considered the notion that unless the child is learning something he is wasting his time, to be nothing less than a curse, and one that blinds most teachers. He thought that parents should realize how unimportant the learning in school is. Children, like adults, learn what they want to learn. He added that prize-giving and marks and exams sidetrack proper personality development. Only teachers claim that learning from books is education. Books, he said, are the least important apparatus in the school. "All that any child needs is the three R's; the rest should be tools and clay and sports and theater and play and paint and freedom."

The principles underlying the free school can be summarized as follows:

All children are innately good.

The aim of education, as should be the aim of life, is to work joyfully and find happiness.

Intellectual development is not enough. Schools must also instruct children in emotional development. People today are too fact-oriented. The separation between the intellect and feelings is driving man to a schizoid state of mind, in which most people are incapable of experiencing anything that they cannot label.

Because their psychic needs are so seldom met, children often appear to be selfish. Only when these needs are met can the child develop a sense of mature love.

Discipline, dogmatically imposed, creates fear, and fear creates hostility. Extensive disciplining of children is harmful to sound psychic development.

Freedom does not mean license. Neill believed that the child should be perfectly free to do whatever he wants to do with two exceptions: he should not be allowed to be harmful to himself, nor interfere with the rights of others.

Teachers should be completely sincere and honest with children. There is no excuse for lying to a child.

It is necessary that children eventually cut the ties between themselves and their parents. Only in a state of freedom is the child able to develop the kind of responsibility and self-confidence that allows him to cut parental ties. Most adults today have not achieved this goal.

Children have little that they need to feel guilty about; most guilt feelings interfere with the child's growth toward independence. Guilt feelings start a cycle which oscillates between rebellion, repentance, submission, and then new rebellion. Teachers should avoid making children feel guilty, especially about their schoolwork.

All religious education is inappropriate. When children are assisted to clarify their own values, they grow up to be more highly ethical people.

Neill was fond of saying that most education only occurs from the neck up. He believed that when children are emotionally honest with themselves and open and trusting with others, their intellectual needs will naturally take care of themselves. He argued that when children feel free to express their emotional needs, their innate curiosity manifests itself willingly.

The organization of the school day at Summerhill reflects this philosophy. Lessons are held between 9:30 a.m. and 1 p.m. every day. Attendance, however, is never compulsory. There have been students at Summerhill who didn't attend formal classes for years at a time. Most of the students attend the classes because they want to. The classes are made up largely of workshops, including sewing, needlework, mechanics, and art. Academic classes are also offered. For the most part, the staff is willing to establish any course students want. Afternoons are completely unscheduled, except that in the late afternoon, there is another one-hour period for lessons.

In the evenings a variety of activities are scheduled. A typical week looks like this:

Sunday—theater evening.
Monday—go to local movies.
Tuesday—lectures on psychology and education for staff and seniors.
Wednesday—faculty-student dance.
Thursday—nothing special scheduled.
Friday—special events; changes weekly.
Saturday—general school meeting. Dancing usually follows this.

The general school meeting is an essential part of any free school. Free schools are self-governing and democratic. Anything connected with social life, including punishment for social offenses, is settled by vote at these weekly meetings. Each member of the teaching staff, and each child, regardless of his age, has one vote. Neill himself was allowed only one vote at these meetings.

The meetings are governed by a different chairman at each session, appointed by the previous week's chairman. The success of the meetings depends largely on whether the chairman is weak or strong, for maintaining order among forty-five vigorous students is no easy task. The chairman has power to fine noisy members, and if the chairman is weak, these fines tend to be frequent.

At these meetings, the social features of the community as well as the laws of self-government are discussed. Anyone who has a grievance or a suggestion may bring it up at these meetings; if necessary new laws and the sanction to back them are legislated.

One observer of these meetings described them as follows: "The loyalty of Summerhill kids to their own democracy is amazing; they seem to have no fear of it and no resentment even when they are fined. They have a fantastic sense of justice, and their administrative ability is much greater than you would believe." Neill suggested that one weekly school meeting is of more value than a whole week's curriculum in most schools.

Free schools are almost always live-in communities. Proponents argue that only when students have the chance to experience democratic interaction with their peer group are they able adequately to transfer these skills to their adult life. This concept includes complete coeducation, extending to living quarters. Most students have private rooms, but all floors of the dormitory are open to males and females. Free-school advocates argue that this is really no different than brothers and sisters living in a house together. While the students are not strictly forbidden to engage in sexual encounters, it is explained to them that sexual activities could get the school in serious trouble with the authorities. The teachers insist that loyalty to the school usually keeps sexual activity to a minimum.

Another important feature of the free school is the "private lesson." Children request such lessons with members of the staff at various times. These lessons are requested under the guise of academic interest, but often they wind up dealing with psychological problems. Children who come to a free school usually come to it from a more traditional education. Neill found that most children have a difficult time adjusting to freedom at first. Private lessons usually serve as a source of re-education. Their object is to remove complexes in the child's psychological life by allowing the child a place for safe, emotional release. Neill found that as children engage more and more in creative work, they need fewer private lessons.

Fostering creativity is the central concern of the free school. Such creative forms as dancing, art, and theater are believed to trigger the release of inhibitions against creativity. When the child is free to express his creative self, Neill urged, he begins to grow toward psychological health. Creative art forms play a major part in the curriculum of the free school.

Neill's criterion for the success of his students is growth in the ability to "work joyfully and live positively." Several studies have shown that Summerhill graduates do as well or better in life as do graduates of more conventional schools. Neill cites some examples of this:

Winifred, thirteen, was a new pupil when she told me (Neill) that she hated all subjects. She shouted with joy when I told her that she was free to do exactly as she liked. "You don't even have to come to school," I said.

She set herself to have a good time, and she had one, for a few weeks. Then I noticed that she was bored.

"Teach me something," she said to me one day; "I'm bored stiff."

"Righto!", I said cheerfully. "What do you want to learn?"

"I don't know," she said.

"And I don't either," I said, and I left her. Several months passed. Then she came to me again. "I am going to pass the college-entrance exams," she said to me, "and I want lessons from you."

Each morning she worked with me and other teachers, and she worked well. She found that the subjects did not interest her much, but the aim did interest her. Winifred found herself by being allowed to be herself; she eventually did pass her exams at the same age as other students.

Tom, eight, was continually opening my door and asking, "By the way, what'll I do now?" No one would tell him what to do.

Six months later, if you wanted to find Tom, you went to his room. There you always found him in a sea of paper sheets. He spent hours making maps. One day a professor from the University of Vienna visited Summerhill. He ran across Tom and asked him many questions. Then the professor came to me and said, "I tried to examine that boy on geography, and he talked of places I've never even heard of."

Barbel, fifteen, was with us for about a year. In all that time she found no work that interested her. She had come to Summerhill too late. For too many years of her life, teachers had been making up her mind for her. When she came to Summerhill, she had already lost all the initiative. She was bored. She eventually went back to a more traditional school.

As you can imagine, Summerhill and its free-school concepts are not without critics. Some of the criticisms which have been leveled at this approach are:

Free schools work well if the leaders are exemplary personalities. Unfortunately, there are not enough of these exemplary personalities to go around. In the hands of the wrong person, the free school would be extremely damaging to a child.

Not enough attention is paid to providing equipment for intellectual learning. Free schools rarely have well-equipped laboratories and resource centers which are available in the more traditional schools.

Neill is wrong when he says that teaching method does not matter. Millions of children have had their curiosity permanently stifled by poor teaching. Some children may be independent enough to learn in a free school environment; however, a great many children desperately need the control of a teacher.

A stay of a year or two at a school like Summerhill may well be good for children, but the atmosphere is too unlike the real world. An extended stay there gives them artificial ideas of what the world is like.

The Summerhill philosophy is an invitation to anarchy and chaos. Only when children are disciplined can they learn to discipline themselves.

Free schools place too much confidence in the innate morality of children. If they are allowed to be irresponsible in their school, they will continue to be irresponsible in their later lives.

Although some children learn to use their time wisely in a free school, many do not. This waste of time is especially disadvantageous in these critical years of their development.

Neill and his free school followers pay too much attention to the theories of Sigmund Freud.

All adults attempt to influence the lives of children in their presence. Teachers in a free school simply use this influence in a more subtle, insidious way. Children are manipulated at these schools, but they don't know it. It is better for children to be aware of the power of adults and to face it.

Probably the most telling criticism is that this approach cannot be used outside of its specific setting. Critics argue that, while the Summerhill approach may be appropriate for small, wealthy, private schools, it is not applicable in the average American classroom. I know of no successful attempt to apply the free-school idea in a classroom atmosphere, a fact which lends credence to this complaint.

Although many of these criticisms are clearly valid, I believe there is much worth imitating about Summerhill. The open education approach, which has gained considerable acceptance in American schools in the past few years, does incorporate some of the best ideas of the free school movement.

Indirect Control — Open Education

The open classroom method also had its start in England, in the 1940's. At that time Nazi Germany was attacking the large cities of Britain, and children were sent *en masse* to the rural heartland of the country. This created a number of serious educational problems.

The children were frightened at being separated from their parents. They had to live closely with their teachers. There was a shortage of teachers, so older amateurs filled the ranks. Classes were large; they usually had forty or more, so teachers had to develop a different approach to the classroom. These conditions led to the birth of the open classroom.

When open education was introduced in this country several

decades later, it was built upon the heritage of the progressive education movement of the 1920's and 1930's. Both of these predecessors, English informal education and American education, held many instructional principles in common. They subscribed to these basic tenets:

Education, to be effective, must be compatible with the natural growth of the child.

Free movement, physical activity, and the affective component are as much a part of education as cognitive and intellectual processes. Therefore, activity units requiring construction, use of drama, and physical activity are central to the curriculum.

Wholeness is emphasized. Life at the school is not divorced from life outside; moreover productively living in the present is seen as the best preparation for life in the future.

Learning by doing is a natural part of education; therefore, activity units based on children's experiences should be developed.

Activities are not to be pursued capriciously, but should reproduce selectively conditions of real life, within the boundaries of students' understanding.

Within the school there must be concern for children's making choices and evaluating consequences.

The open classroom and school differ from the free school and the traditional school in a number of ways. Although open classrooms differ greatly among themselves, their main characteristics are similar.

The open classroom frequently expands beyond the walls of the room into the corridors and to the community outside. Many schools have created spacious classrooms by knocking down the walls between one or more traditional classrooms. The open classroom is usually arranged in learning centers. Rather than sitting in rows of seats all day, students are free to move between the learning centers as long as they accomplish the tasks that have been agreed on.

Figure 8-1 is a diagram of an open classroom taught by Mrs. Phyllis Rantz in the West Memorial School, Peabody, Massachusetts. In this classroom, students have their own desks, but they use them only as a home base to keep the materials they are personally working with. Mrs. Rantz' classroom demonstrates that openness can also be created strictly within the walls of a traditional-sized classroom.

Students may be seen working at learning centers, either individually or in small groups. Many classrooms use the "take-a-key" system. On a large board a number of hooks are arranged. Over each hook is the name of a learning center. On the hook is a key or necklace or some other symbol, color-coded to go with that learning center. Students may choose any key they want, but when all the keys for a learning center are taken, no more students may use that learning center until a key has been returned.

The teacher in the open classroom serves as a guide, facilitator, and persuader to the students. He is a resource person, but not the source of all information. He is also a classroom team manager. Open classroom are usually staffed by several aides as well as the teacher. These aides can

Figure 8-1. Mrs. Rantz' Open Classroom

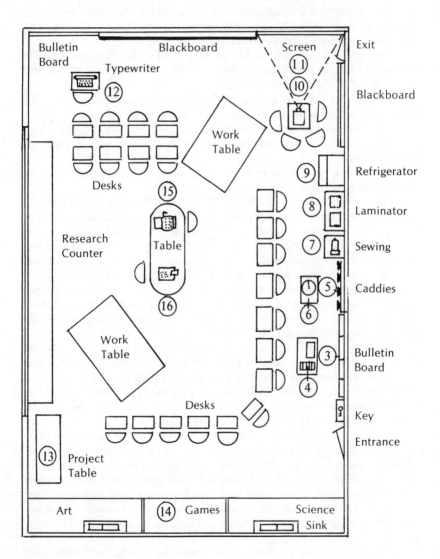

Key to Figure 8-1

1. Entrance
2. Pass key for lavatories - students sign out and sign in.
3. Newspaper bulletin board.
4. Film strip and tape cassette machine.
5. Paper Caddies - daily papers completed are placed in corresponding subject box for teacher to evaluate.
6. Record Player.
7. Sewing Machine.
8. Double-sided lamination machine.
9. Refrigerator.
10. Film strip projector (Current events on film weekly).
11. Bulletin board screen.
12. Typewriter - beginner book allows students to practice basic keyboard skills during free time.
13. Project table - Shoebox displays of Bicentennial readings.
14. Individualized teacher games and ideas - coordinated with subject matter being covered.
15. Cash register - used for teaching change-making and restaurant project.
16. Adding machine.

be student teachers, parents, or grandparents, even older students from the higher grades. Thus the teacher sees himself as a manager of a variety of resources, both human and material. These means of control, persuasion and selection of materials, give the students a strong sense of choice, but they also allow the teacher to give the class a strong structure, without always being "the boss."

Roland Barth, an elementary school principal who has pioneered open education, says that there is no such thing as unstructured learning; there must be a framework within which to learn. he says that the job of the teacher is to provide disorder that will challenge the child, and block him from his desired goals. The teacher then helps each child develop order (guidelines) that enable him to remove those blocks. The teaching art should be looked at as assisting the child to create order out of disorder. The major subject for the student in an open classroom, Barth suggests, should be *management*—management of tools and resources, time, and goals. When the teacher is the sole source of order in the classroom, children are unlikely to learn this kind of management. Barth argues that there should be as much or more structure in the open classroom as there is in the traditional classroom. The real difference is that this structure is imposed in a more informal way in open education.

In the open classroom there needs to be a greater variety of materials available to students. This approach is founded on the idea that students need direct experience with materials; reading about them is simply no substitute.

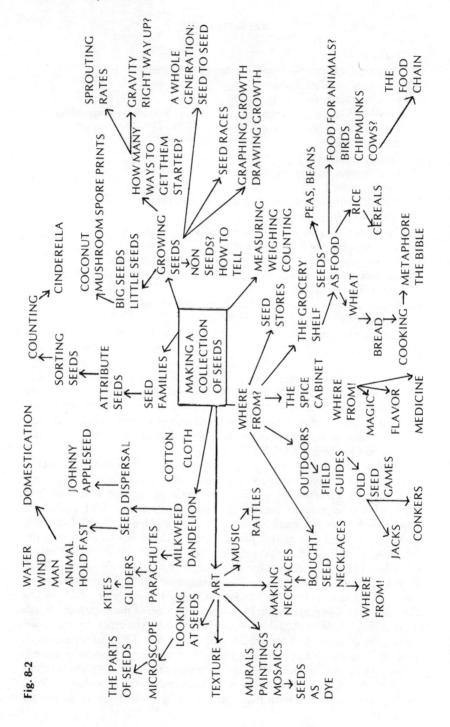

Fig. 8-2

The integrated day is another important factor. In open classrooms, the day is not broken down into periods or subject matters (social studies, science, etc.). Rather these various aspects of life are integrated into the various projects that the students pursue. An example of how completely the various academic subject matters can be integrated into a project may be seen in Figure 8-2, a matrix drawn by Phyllis Morrison (1971, p. 9).

An example of the goals of open education may be seen in Table 8-1 as suggested by psychologist David Miles (Spodek and Walberg, 1975, p. 90).

Table 8-1. Goal Priorities in Open Education

Affective Goals	High Cognitive Goals	Low Cognitive & Psychomotor Goals
Self-esteem	Critical thinking	Subtraction
Resourcefulness	Problem solving	Haiku poetry
Curiosity	Learning skills	Worm anatomy
Self-direction	Communication skills	Xylophone playing
Openness	Creativity	Paragraph writing
Self-awareness	Quantitative reasoning	Economic theory

Affective goals, which are the highest-priority goals, are teacher- determined and are the basis for such decisions as the physical and social arrangements of the classroom as well as motivational, learning, and evaluation strategies.

High-level cognitive goals, which are given second priority, are also determined by teachers and guide decisions regarding alternative learning activities, plus equipment and materials to be made available. These decisions are made in light of and must conform to those decisions made regarding the affective goals.

Low-level cognitive and psychomotor goals are selected by students alone, or by students and teacher together, and include various specific subjects. These goals are selected within the context of both sets of higher-level goals and are based in part on a student's current interest or concern and in part on the teacher's and student's perception of what would be useful to know and be able to do.

(From Spodek & Walberg, 1975, p. 90.)

The first three chapters of this book should have made it clear that children need to move through stages to develop in a healthy way. It should also be clear that children do not move through these stages at the same time. Therefore, the open classroom emphasizes individual pace. Teachers and students work out together what assignments each student should complete, and on what projects he should work. This is done on the basis of the needs of each student. It creates considerably more work for the teacher, not only in planning these activities, but in guiding and evaluating them. This is an essential component of the open classroom, however, and can make teaching much more successful and rewarding.

Direct Control—The Traditional Classroom

The model that describes traditional education states that there is a body of knowledge students need to know. This body of knowledge is translated into a curriculum, which in turn is interpreted by teachers. Finally, teachers try to get students to internalize their interpretations of the curriculum.

In traditional education, the teacher is the font of all knowledge and the central point of all communications between members of the class. All students study the same material at the same time. I doubt that much more needs to be said about this model of education, since I assume that most readers of this book were educated by this technique, and are familiar with it.

A Comparison of Open Education and Traditional Education

I have never liked the term "open" education, because I think it makes all other approaches to instruction appear to be "closed." This is obviously an unfair comparison, and I would rather talk about the degree of directness of control; that is, the continuum from no control through indrect control to direct control.

One way to consider the differences between these approaches is to look at the interest factor in learning. A comparison of the two approaches has been offered by educator George Morrison. His view of the interests of the child in the traditional classroom may be seen in Table 8-2 (Morrison, 1976, p. 108). His view of interest factors in the open classroom is shown in Table 8-3 (Morrison, 1976, p. 109).

A Comparison of All Three Types of Educational Organization

Table 8-4 compares the three types of educational organization presented in this chapter. I hope you will study it carefully, because it not only compares the three approaches, but should make the definitions of each clearer.

Environment

1. Difficult for students to become committed to learning task because of lack of interest.
2. Teacher spends much time and energy controlling behavior due to lack of interest.

Method

1. Learning occurs in same way for all students.
2. The same rate of learning is generally maintained for all students.
3. Generally all students learn same thing at same time.

Child
in
Restricted
Interest
Atmosphere

Curricula

1. Predetermined curricula.
2. Material may or may not be interesting—student has no control over this.
3. What is studied is determined mainly by textbooks and/or teacher.
4. What is studied is generally not matched to students' previous achievement or experiences.
5. Most problems for work and study are posed by the teacher.

Motivation

1. Limited opportunities to become interested in things.
2. Restriction of choices.
3. Students who are not already highly motivated have difficulty learning (especially disadvantaged).
4. Motivation basically extrinsic, i.e., grades.
5. Success mainly a function of how well school tasks are mastered.

Table 8-2. Interest as a Factor in Learning—Traditional Classroom

Environment

1. Teacher and students *viewed* as partners in learning.
2. Teacher provides a setting (prepares the environment) to encourage and promote interests.
3. Teacher has empathy for students.
4. Teacher spends less time controlling behavior.

Method

1. Learning tends to be individualized, based on interests.
2. Creativity is encouraged.
3. Student is repsonsible for his own learning.
4. Many opportunities for success in self-selected activities.

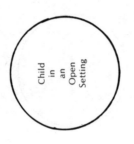

Child
in
an
Open
Setting

Motivation

1. Child is encouraged to become interested in a wide range of topics.
2. Opportunities to make decisions and choices.
3. Motivation is basically *intrinsic*, i.e., the interests of the child provide the motivation.

Curricula

1. Predetermined goals, i.e., reading may be required.
2. Student encouraged to select own goals based upon what he knows.
3. The "what" which is studied determined, in part, by interests of students.

Table 8-3. Interest as a Factor in Learning — Open Classroom

Table 8-4. A Comparison of Three Types of Educational Organization

Educational Aspects	Traditional Classroom	Open Classroom	Free School
1. Organization of classroom activities	Work at desks	Activity centers	Little exists
2. Emphasis on the use of books and other written materials	Great	Moderate	Slight
3. Reliance on foundations	Great	Great	Moderate
4. Position taken on how much subject matters should be integrated	Highly separate	Highly integrated	Highly integrated
5. Emphasis on teacher planning.	Great	Great	Slight
6. Main type of evaluation used	Written tests	Teacher observations	Seldom used
7. Emphasis on cognitive or affective learning	Cognitive	Balanced	Affective
8. Emphasis on sequential aspects of learning	Great	Moderate	Slight
9. Emphasis on respect for materials and housekeeping skills	Great	Moderate	Slight
10. Emphasis on "individualizing" the curriculum	Moderate	Great	Great
11. Emphasis on communication skills	Moderate	Great	Great
12. Emphasis on future vs. present needs of child	Future	Balanced	Present

Continued

13. Degree of "role playing" engaged in by teacher	High	Medium	Low
14. Tolerance of noise	Low	Medium	High

Another way to look at educational control is seen in Table 8-5. This table compares the degree of teacher control with the degree of student control. Some have suggested that there is bias in this comparison, in that quadrant IV, the one in which both teacher and student control is high, is really an idealistic situation. These critics argue that while you can have both low student control and low teacher control (for example, in educational television), it is not feasible to have both high teacher control and high student control.

Table 8-5. Four Approaches to Educational Control

Hi

I. The Traditional Classroom (Directly Controlled) Most Parental Teaching

IV. Open, or Leicestershire, or Integrated Day, or British Primary School (Indirectly Controlled) Classrooms

Control

Lo — Student — Control — Hi

Teacher

II. Educational Television Programmed Instruction Computer Assisted Instruction Most Educational Kits and Games

III. Summerhill-Type Schools, or Free Schools

Lo

This is a question of the directness of the control. The students in an open classroom have a high degree of direct control over what they choose to learn and how they choose to learn it. At the same time, teachers have a high degree of indirect control by deciding what the range of those choices shall be. This is no mere semantic quibble. There is ample evidence that children who have options in their education are more highly motivated learners. On the other hand, there should be no doubt that teachers generally know better than students what the options ought to be.

Summary

I believe that for most students, and for those teachers who sincerely wish to be effective, the open education approach is really the best one. We have a saying in education: "Beware of cure-alls." That is no doubt good advice, but if any instructional approach comes close to being appropriate for all students, it is my opinion that the open education model is the one.

Educator Herbert Kohl, who also favors the open education approach, has made a number of suggestions for fostering personality growth within the classroom:

1. Do not read the record cards of your students. Instead learn about the children through:

a. giving them numerous opportunities to interact, and observing same.

b. talk to them about yourself, what you care about.

c. talk to and watch them out of class.

d. ask their previous teacher to tell you only about *serious* problems.

Kohl argues that children often try to start the new semester off on a new footing, only to find the new teacher's expectations of him to be the same as those of last year's teacher. Then at the middle of the semester, it should be quite revealing to compare your evaluation of each of these students with the observations of his previous teachers.

2. Examine each of the rules and regulations governing your classroom. Eliminate any which are not entirely necessary. A strict rule system tends to encourage compulsivity, authoritarianism and dogmatism, and to discourage adventurousness and creativity. Try to let rules emerge as a result of the class's perception of the need for them. In this way, more appropriate rule structures will develop for each class (and subgroups within the class). As evidence of whether or not there is productive freedom in your classroom, see whether or not the room looks markedly different at the end of the year, compared to the first day. It should.

3. Work to increase your ability to follow up divergent thoughts, to loosen up areas of rigidity in your lesson planning.

4. Understand that conflict in the classroom, emotional as well as intellectual, can be a healthy, necessary release of tensions and other feelings. Conflict should be an integral part of the class, not a suppressed part.

5. Highly detailed lesson plans cause rigidity in the teacher, and dependent, overly cautious, teacher-pleasing students. Lesson plans written in a categorized style (topic, sources, aim, objectives, methods,

evaluation, follow up, etc.) promote such behavior. Lesson plans might better be written in a narrative style, for example:

> Teaching O. Henry's *The Retrieved Reformation.* Perhaps I can talk about other O. Henry endings? Maybe they'll like talking about what it's like to be a prisoner? Or even what it means to be a criminal? I used to like this story, but it seems phony now—will they think so? And so on...

Of course when lesson plans are done so vaguely, they can only be done one day at a time, but this, too, can increase the teacher's flexibility and responsiveness to students.

6. Let the older children in the school teach the younger children, and sometimes let the older ones decide *what* to teach.

7. Increase student involvement in the use of audio-visual aids. For example: obtain 100 feet of blank film leader and let students make a movie with ink and magic markers.

8. Hold class in as many places other than the classroom as possible: supermarkets, theaters, beaches, hospitals, bank, gas stations.

9. Provide places for students to be by themselves when they need to.

10. It is imperative to students' healthy understanding of the world that we stop teaching school subjects in isolation from each other. Kohl has numerous suggestions on this.

11. As to disciplinary problems:

a. To punish is to have been defeated. Punishment should be used only after other efforts have failed.

b. All infractions of your rules should be examined for evidence that the rule is impractical.

c. Never make absolute rules. There are inevitable exceptions, and in such cases, you cannot help but lose face, whether you enforce the rule or not.

d. Noise may be a problem in an open classroom because children will need to talk to each other. Let them help solve the noise problem while you try to negotiate truces with the teachers on either side of you.

e. At all ages, making messes can be a healthy way to express emotional conflicts. But you may need to place a drawing over the window of your room to prevent the disapprobation of your colleagues.

12. It is hard to make a classroom a relaxing, healthy place to be, and changing a classroom can be no less difficult that changing one's own personality. One way to start is to devote 10 minutes a day to unstructured activity. If the experiment proves successful, it can be expanded as new ideas are developed.

13. It helps to have an understanding colleague.

References

Carswell, Evelyn M., and Darrell L. Roubinek. *Open Sesame.* Santa Monica, California: Goodyear, 1974.

Goodell, Carol. *The Changing Classroom.* New York: Ballantine Books, 1973.

Hassett, Joseph D., and Arline Weisberg. *Open Education.* Englewood Cliffs, New Jersey: Prentice-Hall, 1972.

Hertzberg, Alvin, and Edward F. Stone. *Schools are for Children.* New York: Schocken Books, 1971.

Neill, A.S. *Summerhill.* New York: Hart, 1960.

Nyquist, Ewald B., and Gene R. Hawes. *Open Education.* New York: Bantam Books, 1972.

Silberman, Melvin J.; Jerome S. Allender; and Jay M. Yanoff. *The Psychology of Open Teaching and Learning.* Boston: Little Brown, 1972.

Spodek, B., and H., Walberg. *Studies in Open Education.* Agathon Press, 1975

Stephens, Lillian S. *The Teacher's Guide to Open Education.* New York: Holt, Rinehart and Winston, 1974.

Author John Dacey instructing student on Ropes Course.

Chapter 9

The Camp-School Idea

Two major problems in our classrooms today are the general boredom that many students experience, and the too frequent disruptions caused by emotional maladjustments, interracial friction, and other tension. These dilemmas seriously interfere with our children's intellectual and creative growth.

The camp-school is a new instructional approach that has been developed to overcome these problems. It has been tested a number of settings and there is convincing evidence that it works.

The Idea

The basic premise of the camp-school is that children with school-related difficulties often need to be taken away from school for short periods to overcome their problems. The place to which they go should be refreshingly different from school, and basically non-academic in activities. The out-of-doors naturally fulfills these requirements.

Several types of camp-school are currently in use. The one described in this chapter has operated for five years out of two cabins in a large wooded area which had previously been used as a summer camp. Elementary and junior high students are brought there from their nearby schools one day a week as an alternative to their classroom experience. Instruction is designed to handle such problems as low motivation, emotional disturbance, and racial antagonism. Operated throughout the educational year, it is staffed mainly by education majors, from undergraduate to doctoral levels, from a nearby university. They work closely with school faculties to plan the program.

Although this camp-school is located in a large woods, it could be set up in any place with an informal atmosphere and comfortable shelter. An unused barn, a country church, or a city park are examples. Camp-schools can be established inexpensively and with surprising ease. Most importantly, it can powerfully affect a youngster's self-confidence, control, and motivation. The following vignette demonstrates how.

Danny

Anxiously, Danny steps out onto the log.

The log is five feet above the ground, and stretches ten feet to the other end. Hesitantly, he starts side-stepping his way toward that other end. Danny's only support is a rope which hangs from a branch some 50 feet above his head, and 20 feet in front of him. He clings tightly to it.

Once Danny reaches the end of the log, he will be facing a rope net which hangs like the rigging of an old pirate ship, some 45 feet away. That net is his goal. To get there, he must grip the rope and swing in a great arc from the log into the safety of the net. Any fantasy of playing Tarzan has totally vanished for this ten-year-old.

In a soft voice, Peg, one of the counselors, says, "Now take a deep breath." She stands on the ground in front of Danny. She has been watching his movement, ready to protect him if he should slip.

Danny wonders how he ever let himself get into this situation. He inhales, and the tenseness in his muscles eases a little.

Peg has been through the ordeal herself, and she knows how he feels. She tells him about the many minutes that passed before she could pull together the courage to make the leap. Now Danny can say it out loud; he's kind of scared, too.

Peg tells him to continue deep-breathing. Gradually, the tension fades, and he feels ready to jump. He checks with his "spotters." These counselors and campers line the path he will swing through, ready to cushion him should he fall. In one voice, they shout "Ready!"

Danny leans forward slightly, but the fear returns and he halts.

"You don't have to go if you don't want to," Peg reassures him.

"I know," he says, "but I've got to try it." He asks again if his spotters are ready. They are. He grits his teeth, and jumps.

The difference between the look on Danny's face as he starts the swing, and his look as he safely clutches the net, is striking. In an instant, panic has given way to pride.

As he turns to acknowledge the applause of his spotters, Danny's face is radiant.

Danny used to be afraid of just about everything. He is of average intelligence, but doesn't do particularly well in school. His many fears prevent him from taking social or intellectual risks. His fifth grade teacher describes him as shy, withdrawn, and not very happy.

Danny has just felt the anxiety of uncertainty, uncertainty about what will happen, about how he will cope with the situation, and whether he will succeed or fail. With help, he has found that he can succeed.

Danny's elementary school sends him to the camp-school every Tuesday morning. As part of the program, the staff is introducing Danny and his fellow campers to controlled, mildly anxiety-producing situations, and is helping them succeed in handling these situations.

Danny's anxieties serve as internal barricades to learning. By creating non-academic situations that are fun and exciting and helping him succeed at them, the staff is helping Danny learn new patterns, new self-confidence, and self-reliance. He is getting a new outlook on himself, and thus can better accept academic risks.

It is beginning to make a difference.

The Tuesday Camp

Judy, 9, was selected for the camp-school because school officials, particularly the school's psychiatric social worker, recognized that she was "emotionally disturbed." In Massachusetts, funds are available for special instruction for children who are classified as emotionally disturbed. This must be official, agreed upon in writing by the school psychologist, a psychiatrist, and the child's parents.

Special instruction normally consists of tutoring and personal counselling sessions held at the school three times a week, and lasting one to two hours each session. The Tuesday morning camp was set up as an alternative approach.

Recently, money was found missing from several counselors' purses. There is no doubt that Judy is the thief. George, one of the counselors, is trying to get Judy to talk about it. He doesn't threaten; he wants Judy to talk it out and understand what happened.

"I guess you were feeling bad last week, weren't you," George says.

"It was my birthday," Judy replies. "And my mother didn't even remember it."

"Forgot your birthday? I can see why that would make you sad. So you decided to take the money—so you could treat yourself to a party?"

"Yeah. And I had a really good time, too."

George is sympathetic. "I'm glad you had a good time, Judy, but those counselors needs their money, too. I think we should try to figure out some way that you could pay them back."

With that, Judy smiles coquettishly, reaches out and grasps the zipper on George's trousers. George moves her hand away. She learned to trust George as a friend, so he doesn't want to shame her, and as calmly as possible, he asks, "Why are you doing that, Judy?"

"Sid lets me do it."

"Who's Sid?"

"My mother's boyfriend. He likes me to play with it."

Then, there unfolds a story of sexual abuse which would dismay a seasoned psychiatrist. Subsequent investigation by the school system and the local social agency revealed that, in addition to Sid, two other of her mother's boyfriends, and even her mother, had been involved in her sexual abuse. Eventually, with her mother's agreement, nine year old Judy was placed in a foster home.

Judy's story may seem extreme. However, Judy's home situation is not as unusual as we would like to believe; such problems are on the increase.

The real point is that Judy's problem had been going on for several years, and she had said nothing. There was no adult in her life in whom she could confide. And her harried teacher, with 26 other children in the class, wasn't able to give the hours of attention it took George to gain Judy's confidence. The Tuesday camp is designed to provide the atmosphere and the opportunity needed for such counseling.

Each Tuesday morning, 50 children, fourth, fifth and sixth graders, pour out of the buses that bring them to the camp from four nearby schools. About one-half of these children are classified as emotionally disturbed. The others are selected because their teachers felt they would benefit from the program. The 25 counselors are mostly education majors.

When the kids arrive at the main cabin, a meeting is held in the rough "living room." There is a free discussion period, and then choices of activities for the day are explained. Soon everyone scatters to take part in the seven to ten activities offered. Later, after a hot lunch (prepared by the students), a wrap-up meeting is held and the children return home. The counselors then meet to discuss psychological problems, curricular results, and plans for next week's session.

Although the activities are school-related and therefore valuable in themselves, the main purpose of the activities is to provide a safe setting for counseling. Since there is one counselor for every two kids, "rap" sessions abound.

Over the weeks of camp meetings, counselors are often able to become quite close to the children, able to gain an understanding of their problems, and in an impressively high percentage, help them to solutions.

The Thursday Camp

The primary objective of the Thursday camp is to develop a positive interaction between black and white fourth graders, in addition to developing the normal academic skills. Black children from the inner city and white children from the suburbs are bused to the camp each Thursday. This vignette will illustrate what is meant by "positive interaction."

"The lions are coming! The tigers are coming!"

Huddled in front of the eight-foot high wooden wall are ten fourth-graders, half of them black, half white. Neither group has seen the other before today.

They have been told the rules of the game: unless each member of the team is over the wall within ten minutes, they will be eaten by lions and tigers. They've been given two minutes to plan their strategy.

"I'm the tallest. I'll go first."

"I'm too scared. I don't want to do it."

"Somebody think of something! We've only got a minute left!"

Suddenly Teddy bursts out, "Listen! I've got a plan. We gotta push each other up. You—I dunno your name—you're the strongest, so you go first. Angela, you're the tallest, so you gotta go last 'cause there's nobody to push you up."

Excited now, they grab the first kid's legs and heave him toward the top. Soon he's on top and ready to help the next kid up. He extends his black hand to the next kid, a white. There is a moment's hesitation, but someone shouts, "Hurry up!" He grabs the outstretched hand and is pulled over.

One by one, they go up. The frightened girl is told that all she needs to do is try going up halfway. Reluctantly, she agrees. Before she has time to think about it, someone has grabbed her hands and she is pulled over the top. She looks pleased.

When the ten minutes have run out, everyone is over the wall except Angela, who is eaten by a tiger.

What is happening here? Essentially, black and white children are forced to depend on each other (see Fig. 9-1). Not forced in an authoritarian way, but forced as a matter of choice and necessity.

This is but one of a number of outdoor games used to break the racial ice. They are all exciting, enjoyable, and require cooperation. Other games include:

Fig. 9-1 Infinite Wall.

Fig. 9-2 Trust Fall.

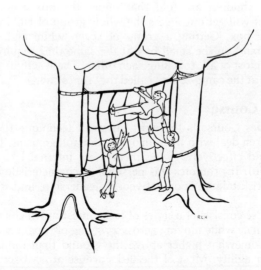

Fig. 9-3 Alligator Pit.

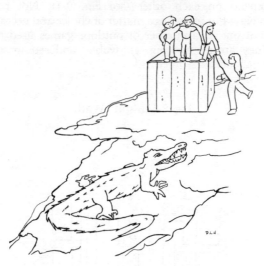

Trust Fall (Fig. 9-2). One at a time, each child climbs up the cargo net (a rope net) which hangs between two trees. The other children crowd in front of the net under the climber, with their arms held up over their heads. The climber leans back with arms, legs, and back straight. On the count of three, the climber lets go and falls into the supporting hands of the children below.

Because there are so many "supporters" below, this is actually a very safe activity. But it takes a lot of trust to let go, and the fact that children of another race are playing a crucial role in the climber's safety creates an important and lasting impression.

The Alligator Pit. (Fig. 9-3). This involves a wooden box, 2′ x 2′ x 2′ in size. The children are told that under the box are twenty-three alligators that will get out unless the whole group of children is able to stand on the box. Getting a group of seven white and seven black children to stand on the small box at the same time requires planning, agility, and, most of all, touching each other. These activities are part of a course held at the camp-school called the "ropes course."

The Ropes Course

The Ropes Course is the most powerful technique I know of for helping children deal with their anxieties and antagonisms. It is a means of rapidly and effectively giving them more internal locus of control (Chapter Two). It promotes this personality characteristic by affecting four others: risk-taking, cooperativeness, leadership, and sense of competence.

The course consists of a series of tasks, most of which involve keeping one's balance while moving across a rigging of rope. Each task in the sequence is somewhat higher above the ground than the last, and requires greater agility. Most of the tasks arouse at least some degree of anxiety in almost everyone. As each task is mastered, the child's anxiety is reduced, and he or she is ready to attempt the next.

The participants are not sure what is going to happen in most of the events, and they are not sure how they are going to react to them. As the child becomes more sure of himself, he becomes better able to tolerate the ambiguity of this situation. This, too, leads to a more internal locus of control.

The Ropes Course is a sensory rather than an intellectual approach to improving the self-concept. So many times, school involves talking about things rather than actually doing them. It has been our experience that to improve a child's self-concept, actual experiences are essential. The Ropes Course provides a chance to test oneself against a variety of graduated obstacles. In that sense, it is not unlike the initiation ceremony into adulthood that is common in other societies, which some theorists think we badly need here.

Although the course is chiefly physical, gains the child makes transfer to the emotional and cognitive aspects of his personality. As he becomes more daring in the physical sense, he becomes more willing to take risks in the classroom. He becomes more willing to respond to quesitons. He becomes more willing to take on a math problem which he didn't think he could do before. He becomes more willing to disagree with others. He becomes more successful.

We want children to *like themselves* better than before. We count on reinforcements from counselors and the peer group for this. Applause, backslapping, and compliments are frequent as participants go through the course. Especially important, though, is the intrinsic value of succeeding at something you didn't think you could do. Negative feedback such as scapegoating, teasing, and mocking are strongly discouraged. When children understand that earlier experiences such as falling often create their present fears, they become more understanding of their lack of success, and the failures of others.

Students' Introduction to the Course

When students first come to the course, they are given the following six rules:

Listen to and obey instructions. The course is very safe as long as this first rule is followed.

Try to encourage each other and never discourage each other. For instance, no calling people "chicken," "no guts," etc.

Everyone should *try* each task. However, you may always refrain from a particular task by saying "I pass." There will be no questions asked.

Even though some of the tasks in this course seem difficult, you will find that if you do the first ones, the later ones will be easier than you think.

Cooperate with each other. Everyone will be frightened at times and will need the help of others.

One way we make sure you're safe is "spotting." Spotters are the children and counselors who surround you when you're doing one of the tasks. They stand with their hands held up so that if you should fall, several hands would cushion the fall and prevent you from hurting yourself. Once in New Orleans, several people jumped from the eighth floor of a burning hotel into the outstretched hands of a large number of spotters below. The jumpers suffered only minor injuries.

The Tasks of the Ropes Course

Each of the tasks in the ropes course is designed to help the child feel more confidence in his body, give expression to his feelings, and strengthen his relations with those around him. Tasks can be altered or eliminated, depending on each situation. The following tasks are typical and are presented here in the usual sequence followed:

Balance Log. This activity calls for a straight log, twelve feet long, hung between two trees. It should be one foot off the ground and three feet away from the trees so that is can swing freely. The child stands on one end and tries to walk all the way to the other end. Spotters are spaced around the log in case somebody slips and falls to the side. Alternatively, children can stand facing the log at the center and try to jump onto the log.

Tension Traverse. This task calls for a rope stretched 15 to 20 feet between two trees with another 25-foot rope hanging from one of the trees. A child stands on the horizontal rope, balancing himself by clinging to the rope suspended from above. He then tries to walk across the rope sideways while holding the vertical rope behind his back for balance. This event is not particularly frightening, but it requires practice.

Bosun's Chairs. In this task, several bosun's chairs are suspended at different heights from a rope hung between three trees. The chairs are from four to eight feet above the ground. The child starts by climbing to the first one, which is hung fairly low. He then makes his way across the several chairs and down the knotted rope that is suspended from a tree branch at the end of the task. Spotters are particularly important in this event as students sometimes fall because their strength gives out.

The Rat Crawl. This is composed of a horizontal rope stretched 30 feet between two trees, five feet above the ground. The rope passes along the participant's chest, under his hips and through the instep of one foot. The other foot dangles down and is used for balance. Progress is made by pulling oneself along the rope head first.

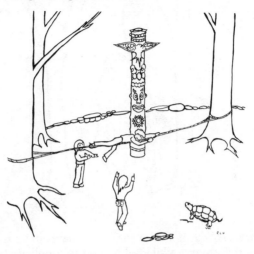

Postman's Walk. The child must climb the tree using the support steps provided. Then he climbs out along a horizontal rope strung 10 feet above the ground. He uses a rope strung four feet higher and parallel to the rope he's standing on for support. The child is protected from falling by a "belaying line" which runs from a harness at his waist, over the top rope, and then to an adult on the ground. After mastering walking the rope, this task calls for the child to stand in the center, lean back with arms and legs straight and, on the command of the belayer, let go and fall backwards from the walk. Obviously, this demands a great deal of trust, as well as freedom from too much anxiety.

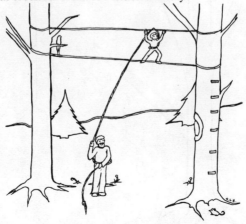

Tire Climb. The child must climb up six tires that are strung vertically to a branch of a tree. The task sounds easy but is actually quite difficult; spotters are stationed all around the tires.

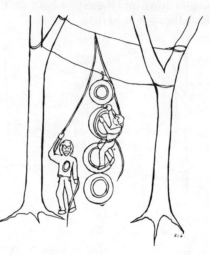

The Space Trolley. In this event, participants jump from a platform 12 feet above the ground while holding on to a pulley attached to wire cables. They travel 85 feet to a tree at the other end of the cable. The other end is attached four feet above the ground, however. The child grasps the trolley at the low end of the cable and the instructor pushes him along to give him a feeling of the ride. This is done several times, each time pushing the child successively higher, until he feels comfortable. Finally, he climbs the rope ladder to the platform and when seated, pushes himself off and slides down the whole way. Spotters are spaced along the first 20 feet of the ride.

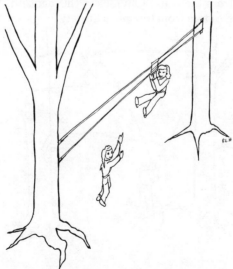

Swing Rope. This task is quite simple but is good preparation for the task which follows it. The child swings out and back three times. If he is nervous the first time, he may stick his foot through a loop at the end of the rope. Afterwards, he should attempt swinging on the rope supporting himself only by his hands. Spotters are necessary in this event, both at the maximum point of the swing and at the place of return.

The Cargo Net Swing. This is the event described earlier in this chapter with Danny and Peg. The child walks out on the log, balancing himself with the rope hung from overhead. When everyone is ready, he jumps and tries to pull himself up at least one foot on the rope. As he swings, he must keep his knees high. The "G's" naturally increase at the bottom of the arc of his swing; therefore, it is necessary to have adult spotters at this point. The child swings into the cargo net, where he has at least two seconds to grab on to the cargo net. He should grab the cargo net before releasing the swing rope.

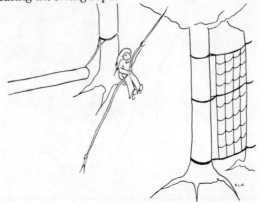

Cargo Net Climb. In this event the child climbs to the top of the 25-foot net, swings one leg over, then his body, and climbs down the other side. It is obviously an anxiety-producing task. It is perfectly safe, however, because a belaying line is always attached to the climber. Children are not told that they must climb over the top of the net, but rather that they should climb as high as they like. Climbing to any height is always considered a success and should be applauded.

Rock Climbing and Rappelling. For climbing up, rocks of various grades are needed, depending on the age and skill of the child. We use rocks from 10 to 30 feet high. A belaying line attached to the child passes to the top of the rock, through a carefully secured carabiner (a metal ring) and down to the belayer. In rappelling, ropes are used to climb down a flat-faced rock. The same belaying set-up is used. In addition, the child uses a rope secured at the top of the rock which winds through his legs. He lets himself down by slowly allowing the rope to slip over his body as he descends. An experienced rock climber should supervise this especially effective event.

The Burma or "Monkey" Bridge. This bridge extends 40 feet between two trees and is hung 35 feet in the air. It is made up of a bottom rope on which the child walks, and two side ropes hung three feet above the walking rope used for balance. Another three feet above these railings is a safety rope which is hung parallel to them. The climber climbs up a rope ladder, steps on to the bridge, walks across and comes down the other side.

A belaying line runs from a harness at his waist, up over the safety rope and down to an adult belayer. He descends on the other side of the bridge by floating to the ground on his belaying line, which is slowly released by the belayer. The ultimate in trust falls is possible in this event. The climber goes to the center of the bridge, leans back, and falls off, trusting his belaying line to keep him safe. This task is considered the most difficult of the Ropes Course.

Pin the Tail on the Tree. We often use this task at the end of the course to see if there has been improvement in cooperation and group cohesiveness. A group of six students is given a ribbon with a thumb tack through it. Their task is to pin it as high on a tree as possible. They can stand on shoulders, hold each other, etc. But the tree is too thick to climb. The record height achieved by a group is marked on the tree, and all are encouraged to beat the record. This is competetive, but calls for great cooperation among group members to achieve success.

Orientation of Instructors

I would like to mention here a number of the directions that we give to Ropes Course instructors. I think they further demonstrate the philosophy of the course:

Be as open and honest about expressing your feelings to your students as you can. It is important that you serve as a model in expressing fears and hopes, beacause our goal is to get the children to be able to express these to you, as well as to each other.

Try to have each member of the group develop a sense of commitment to the other members of the group.

Ask at least one child to repeat your instructions for each task, in order to check that they have fully understood you.

Try to create a non-threatening atmosphere. A sense of humor is the most valuable asset here.

Without hurrying the students, try to keep everyone active. Try to move to the next task as expeditiously as possible. More than six participants in a group make this difficult.

Reinforce any level of success, but avoid favoritism in your reinforcements.

Try to get individuals to talk about their own successes and failures, and about the effectiveness of the group.

Encourage cooperation, discourage competition.

Be as precise as possible in your instructions.

In order to encourage our instructors to be effective observers as well as to insure their complete attention at the Ropes Course, we ask them to fill out an observation sheet on each of the children involved in their group after each session. This serves as an effective means of encouraging instructors to be observant of their charges. In addition, it helps them get an idea of the changes in the students' performance. We have also had non-observers use this form to evaluate the course. The form that we use for this evaluation method may be seen in Table 9-1.

Table 9-1

Ropes Course Evaluation

Name	Grade	School

Date of Evaluation	Weather Conditions	Evaluator

A. Low risk —
   Avoids task
   Overly cautious

1	3	5	3	1
I	I	I	I	I

High risk —
Impulsive, foolhardy

B. Low competence—
   Ineffective

1	2	3	4	5
I	I	I	I	I

High competence—
Capable

Continued

C. Low leadership—
   Needs direction

1	2	3	4	5
I	I	I	I	I

High leadership—
Encourages others, uses
initiative

D. Low cooperative-
   ness—
   Refuses to spot, im-
   patient, disregards
   others

1	2	3	4	5
I	I	I	I	I

High cooperativeness—
Regularly spots, helps
others

E. Low self-
   confidence—
   Self-doubting
   fearful

1	2	3	4	5
I	I	I	I	I

High self-confidence—
Self-reliant, assured

F. Total Score

Ropes Course Summary

The Ropes Course is especially beneficial from the stand point of locus of control. There is good reason to believe that the beginnings of the child's locus of control stem from his early attitude toward his own body. If he feels incapable of manipulating his body to achieve the kinds of physical tasks that most other children are able to achieve, then he begins to feel incompetent in general. Therefore, it makes sense to go back to his underlying variable, body image, to make a start toward a more internal locus of control. The Ropes Course, with its graduated tasks, makes it possible for almost anyone to achieve a respectable level of performance, hence greater internality.

Camp-School Summary

The camp-school offers new opportunities. Because of these opportunities, children can discover new enjoyment in learning, enjoyment that makes learning easier, but is often difficult to generate in traditional classrooms.

Some of the advantages are:

The camp-school is an informal setting, and therefore offers more opportunity for communication, the genesis of many good things. In contrast to the more formal classroom, the camp setting is relaxed, and offers the security of being able to talk to the teacher-counselors as people. There is more opportunity for one-to-one and small group discussions.

For many students, the camp setting offers a temporary escape from the threat of academic failure. For some, school is a source of anxiety, of forced achievement or the disgrace of failure. Sometimes kids need to get away from school in order to re-examine their relationship to it. The camp school offers this fresh start.

There is more opportunity for children to learn how to learn. Times are changing so rapidly that new problems are multiplying faster than old solutions; *what* you know is less important than knowing *how* to find answers. The camp-school can go beyond the study of textbook solutions to textbook problems. It can present new tasks and challenging situations, and then provide guidance and practice in problem-solving.

Because of the camp experience, school in general is seen as a more interesting place. Kids feel that something special is happening to them, and they discover their own motivations. Teachers report a noticeable improvement in the classroom motivation of students attending.

Camp-school gives the teacher a better opportunity to identify and meet the needs of individual students. The teacher sees students participating in activities quite different from those in the classroom, and can gain new insights into each child's strengths, weaknesses and needs. The teacher is then better able to create imaginative ways to develop strengths and meet needs.

Prejudices and fears can be examined and dealt with. The camp-school is "neutral turf." The setting is new to all racial and ethnic groups. In this neutral setting, activities can be developed to create better understanding through the necessity of cooperation.

Children gain a better understanding of, and respect for, the out-of-doors. The trend toward a return to the wilderness is burgeoning. As more people turn to the countryside as a refuge from urbanization, a better knowledge and understanding of those surroundings becomes important, if not critical. No less important is the fact that children can see firsthand the inter-dependence of our natural resources.

The camp-school can save tax dollars. Setting up a camp-school does require some capital, but since the camp is informal, these requirements are minimal. However, the camp-school can save considerable money when a school system becomes too crowded or when antiquated buildings must be replaced. Rather than appropriate millions for new buildings, a camp-school could be established, which students could attend on a rotating basis, at great savings.

Since the camp-school was conceived as a response to the ideas presented in Chapters One, Two, and Three, we should expect it to be an acceptable innovation from those standpoints, and I think it is. In terms of Erikson, its operation coincides with Stage Four, the elementary school years, and Stage Five, Adolescence. Erikson argues that the main goal of the fourth stage is to develop a sense of industriousness through the use of technological elements. Teaching these "tool skills" is one of the things a camp-school does best. Physical skills like knot-tying, rock-climbing and rope-walking are not the only kinds meant here, although children of both sexes seem to be eager to master them. Motivation to read, write (in the camp newspaper, for example), and measure is also high. As for the identity crises occurring in Stage Five, the camp-school is also an excellent solution. Weekly one-to-one discussions with an interested, capable counselor in an informal setting is clearly of assistance in dealing with the many problems that regularly arise in an adolescent's life.

One basic technique for helping children to handle "future shock" is to place them in unfamiliar settings and then assist them to cope. The camp-school offers a variety of unusual settings and situations for this purpose. As to McLuhan's non-linear, non-print-oriented person, the camp-school is clearly more appropriate than almost any classroom. Activities there usually involve at least two senses. The aptness of McLuhan's proposition can be seen in how much more children seem to enjoy these tasks than they do the workbooks, textbooks, compositions, test papers and written resource materials of the classroom.

The camp-school was specifically designed to promote a more internal locus of control in it participants. An indication of its success may be seen in a recently completed study done at the Tuesday Camp. All the fourth, fifth and sixth graders in the several participating schools were administered the Nowicki-Strickland (1973) Test of Locus of Control (Chapter Two) in the fall. This test has nineteen items, and the higher the score, the more internal the person is considered to be. The mean score was 14.3, considered quite desirable for this age group. Scores of the children selected for camp-school were separated and averaged. These scores yielded a mean of only 9.2, indicating that these children were considerably more external. At the end of the school year, all children were retested, and the total group averaged 14.5, no real change. The camp-school children, however, scored a mean of 14.9!

This does not necessarily prove the effectiveness of the camp-school; for one thing, the teachers of these children were no doubt making special efforts for them, too. Nevertheless, it is exactly the kind of change in locus of control one hopes for.

Finally, in terms of Maslow, the camp-school may be seen as one new way to individualize instruction, aimed at helping youngsters and counselors achieve their own self-actualization.

The author wishes to acknowledge the contributions of Drs. Dan Joynt and Gordon Ulrey in designing and researching the ropes course.

References

Boy Scouts of America. *Fieldbook*. New Brunswick, New Jersey. 1967.

Dacey, J.S. "The Camp-School Idea," in *Learning*. In Press.

Hammerman, Donald R., and William R. Hammerman. *Outdoor Education*. Minneapolis, Minnesota: Burgess, 1968.

Lentz, Robert R. *Adventure Curriculum: Physical Education*. Hamilton, Massachusetts: Project Adventure, 1974.

Maud, Charles L. *Outdoor Education*. New York: Pratt, 1967.

Storer, John H. *The Web of Life*. New York: Signet, 1956.

Troost, Cornelius J., and Harold Altman. *Environmental Education: A Sourcebook*. New York: Wiley, 1972.

Van Matre, Steve. *Acclimatizing*. Martinsville, Indiana: American Camping Association, 1975.

Van Matre, Steve. *Acclimatization*. Martinsville, Indiana: American Camping Association, 1972.

Chapter 10

Promoting Process Learning

A large truck screeches to a halt at the entrance to a railroad bridge. The sign on the bridge reads: "Bridge height—10'8"." The truck driver climbs down from his rig and scratches his head. He glances at the sign on his door: "Height—11'." He tries to imagine a way to get under the bridge, but nothing comes to mind. Soon a small crowd gathers; horn honking and shouting add to the confusion. It is a difficult problem; the driver knows from the map that this is the only road leading to his destination. Furthermore, the road is impossibly narrow and he would have a very hard time turning around. After almost half an hour, a young girl watching at her father's side says, "Why doesn't he take some air out of his tires, Daddy?"

Although we are often charmed by stories of children solving problems that adults cannot, it really doesn't happen very often. Most difficult problems require a knowledge of facts children seldom possess.

However, there is clear evidence that imagination is an increasingly important human ability (see Chapter One). Consider, for example, the stockroom at the back of every large manufacturing plant. Not long ago, the manager of that stockroom was invariably a fellow with an excellent memory. he could describe every product the company manufactured, and knew how many parts were on hand at all times. His memory was a great asset to the company. Today, however, computers are taking over his job, and are better at it that any person's memory could be. Due to the complexity of modern inventory control, what is needed today is a stockroom manager with imagination to create new and better uses for the computer.

For most of this century, our schools have concentrated on teaching facts and skills, and this is certainly still true today. Curriculum in our schools has been "content-centered" education (CCE). It concentrates on choosing and organizing the body of factual knowledge and skills (or content) that children need to be adequately prepared for life.

CCE is based on dividing the school week among seven subject areas: "the big four"; math, science, language arts, and social science: and the "little three"; art, music, and physical education. Each subject is allowed a certain number of hours per week, depending on the subject's supposed importance in real life. Teachers are expected to stick to this curriculum model faithfully in order to maintain the balance among the seven. Educators may tinker with the scope and sequence of each of these subjects, but little else has changed in this type of curriculum. Almost all of the schools in this country, elementary and secondary, operate on some form of CCE.

Recently, however, there has been a growing interest in the counterpart of CCE; "process-centered" education (PCE). Rather than memorizing facts, PCE concentrates on showing children how to acquire knowledge for themselves. PCE focuses on showing children *how* to learn, rather than *what* to learn. It is based on the contention that the relative importance, and sometimes even the truth, of factual information today is changing rapidly.

The differences between CCE and PCE are not always easy to discern. These differences apply more to the philosophy of instruction rather than to specific teaching strategies. It is a question of emphasis. Obviously, we cannot teach the processes of learning without content. We must think about what content is most appropriate, so all curriculum must be "content-centered" to some extent. The difference is that PCE is more concerned with the child's attitudes toward learning and his ability to learn for himself. Therefore, if one content will achieve this better than another, the PCE approach would favor using it.

The educational assumptions made by these two approaches are summarized in Table 10-1, an adaptation from Ripple (1970, p. 5). It should be pointed out that these two sets of assumptions are meant to represent the opposite ends of a continuum.

Table 10-1
Opposed Value Positions Underlying CCE and PCE

Educational Variable	CCE	PCE
Knowledge is:	Absolute and true.	Tentative and arbitrary.
Learning is:	Unnatural and difficult.	Natural and enjoyable.
The Learner is:	A humble and passive recipient of knowledge and experience.	An eager and active seeker of knowledge and experience.
The School is:	The authoritative transmitter of established values and knowledge.	The setting for emergence of values and knowledge through inquiry

PCE is not new. Socrates' method of teaching may be classified as PCE, in that Socrates was trying to teach his pupils how to solve problems more effectively. He was teaching them how to think.

Philosophers from Descartes to Dewey favored the process-centered approach to education; their writings are the foundation for the current movement. The major impetus for PCE today, however, can be traced to Jerome Bruner's innovative book, *The Process of Education* (1961). Many of the ideas in this chapter are based on Bruner's theory of intellectual growth, described in Chapter Three.

While the philosophy of PCE may not be new, the implications for classroom strategies are seen by some as radically new. It is true that PCE fits better in the open classroom and in the camp-school than in the traditional classroom. However, the more traditional teacher can use the PCE approach for selected parts of his curriculum, and many do. For example, some teachers allow "project afternoon," during which students may study anything they wish to know more about.

The two major aspects of PCE are inquiry strategies and supporting competencies. These will now be described.

Inquiry Strategies

Learning how to learn means learning how to inquire. A number of researchers have investigated the inquiry process, and it is variously defined. My view of the problem-solving process includes six phases, and I believe that an understanding and appreciation of each phase will prove invaluable to the student in later life. The six phases, or inquiry strategies, are:

1. *Formulating an inquirable question.* To produce an inquirable question, students must ask themselves a number of other questions: "What do I care about?" "What do I like/need to know more about?" "What kinds of things am I interested in?" Chapter Six, which deals with helping children clarify their values, gives suggestions for this phase.

2. *Formulating researchable questions* related to the inquirable question. In order to clarify aspects of the inquirable question, the student develops a series of sub-questions which are researchable. These sub-questions can be more easily answered and documented than the complex inquirable question.

3. *Developing a plan* for locating and gathering information.

4. *Organizing and analyzing* the collected data.

5. *Evaluating the data* and drawing conclusions about the researchable questions.

6. *Formulating an answer* to the inquirable question based on these conclusions.

The inquiry process seems to be the most fruitful way to learn how to learn. It is the best suited to looking at problems as wholes, but it can also be used well when study is restricted to one of the seven subject areas in CCE. This is particularly true when teachers help students integrate each of the inquiry strategies with what I call supportive competencies. These competencies are made up of instrumental skills, skills in self-direction, creative thinking, self-evaluation, self-analysis, and communication.

Supportive Competencies

1. *Instrumental skills.* These are the basic tools one needs to effectively obtain and use data. Listed among these essential skills are:

operating equipment
reading
listening
speaking
computing
measuring
charting, mapping
observing
identifying
note-taking
classifying

These skills are also important under CCE, but PCE treats them less as ends in themselves, and more as vehicles to higher levels of understanding.

2. *Self-direction.* Experience has indicated that the greater the amount of involvement the child has in planning and organizing his study, the more he is motivated to do it. On the other hand, there is the now-famous statement made by a student in a progressive school: "Please, teacher, do we have to learn whatever we want today?" Children have to be gradually taught to be self-directive. This means purposefully going from total teacher direction to total student self-direction. It also usually means that the teacher should move from goals for the whole class to goals for small groups to goals for each individual student. Many children are far from eager to be self-directive; it often takes a great deal of encouragement. The teacher might start by supplying the students with answers to researchable questions (Phase 5) and requiring them to form conclusions about an inquirable question (Phase 6). Gradually the students can take over all six phases. Bruner suggests that the following important benefits will derive from assisting children to be more self-directive.

The child develops confidence that he is able, by himself, to responsibly solve problems through using an orderly, well-planned approach.

The student's dependence on extrinsic rewards, such as the teacher's approval, is replaced by an increasing reliance on intrinsic rewards, such as the feeling of pride in personal success.

There is evidence that self-directed learning is more readily applicable to more kinds of problem situations. That is, the transfer of such learning to new situations is greater.

Students learn to interpret and store information according to their own cognitive style rather than that of the teacher. In creating their own mental structures, students become better able to retrieve information from memory when it is needed. Their learning, therefore, is more durable over the years.

Self-discovered solutions to problems are best, because people are much more likely to use their own remedies than those given them by someone else.

3. *Creative thinking.* This concept was explored in detail in Chapter Five. Here is a brief reiteration of it:

A creative act results in a product which is original, at least for that creator, and which is particularly appropriate (useful, beautiful, insightful, etc.). The creative person tends to be open to new experiences, tolerant of ambiguity, independent in his judgment, and enjoys "fooling around" with ideas and things. Creativity may be considered as a process in itself, and as an attitude which pervades all mental processes. The process-centered educator assumes that all persons are creative to some degree, and that creative ability can always be improved.

4. *Self-evaluation.* Closely allied to self-direction is the process of self-evaluation, whereby a student becomes skillful in objectively evaluating his own performance in a learning situation. In most classrooms today the ability to perform well on a variety of types of examinations is the major criterion of evaluation. CCE is based primarily on mastering skills related to *following instructions* and solving problems *set by others.* These abilities are clearly of great importance in many occupations and should certainly be developed in the schools. However, research indicates that too much emphasis on these skills has a strong suppressing effect on curiosity, imagination, and ingenuity. The process-centered educator is more concerned with encouraging students to refine their own learning, than with seeing whether or not they "got it right."

Also, when teachers are the sole source of information, the student may rationalize his failures ("She flunked me!") and thus defer responsibility for understanding and evaluating his own learning. Conversely, some children, especially adolescents, feel that they are failures no matter what marks they get ("She only gave me an A because I've got her snowed!"). Learning how to evaluate themselves helps students go from dependence on extrinsic rewards to intrinsic motivation and self-reliance.

The basic skill involved in self-evaluation is the student's ability to compare a measure of his own capacity in an area (knowledge or skill) with some criterion of that area. Criteria may include national norms, the average score of the rest of the class, the student's prior scores, or the student's forecast of what he thought his score would be. Of particular importance is the development of an appropriate attitude toward this comparison. It is essential that the student accept the comparison as valid and relevant to him, but that he not be discouraged or forced to resort to defense mechanisms (see p. 77) when the comparison proves unfavorable to him. This attitude will most likely develop when the student is personally responsible for his own evaluation.

5. *Self-analysis.* This process, almost totally disregarded in most classrooms, is considered by psychologists to be essential to the development of humans, and the most important task of adolescence (see Chapter Two). While self-evaluation is concerned with a student's

analyzing his performance, that is, *what he did* in a given situation, self-analysis is concerned with a student's analyzing *why* he performed or reacted as he did.

The student needs not only to learn content and processes, but also to be aware of himself as he is learning. Thus, he is able to analyze not only his performance, but the mental processes and attitudes that are responsible for that . performance. With practice, he becomes self-correcting in his approach to problems. It is natural and in some cases essential that the youngster use defense mechanisms to protect his overly sensitive self-concept from the onslaught of reality. Sometimes being realistic is temporarily more that the ego can bear. Teachers should become adept at helping the student discover for himself when he is fooling himself about reality. This does not mean that the teacher should directly tell a student that he is using a defense mechanism. Indirect methods such as class discussion about defense mechanisms and empathetic questioning of the individual are more useful.

6. *Communication.* Each phase of inquiry requires that the problem-solver use one or more of the communication processes described in Chapter Seven. Communication includes all the skills related to encoding and decoding information in various ways. Bruner has described encoding systems as "systems for representing information." He suggests that man encodes and disseminates information through action, through imagery or pictures, and through the symbolism of languages (see Chapter Three). In order to efficiently record or encode the data related to each phase of inquiry, a problem-solver would need considerable skill in using each of these systems of representation. Conversely, a problem-solver would need skill in decoding examples of each kind of representation during his quest for data.

Teachers in subject areas (that is, CCE) are predominantly concerned with encoding and decoding in terms of just one of these representational systems. For example, the mathematics teacher is concerned with the symbols of mathematical language. Physical education and dramatic arts teachers help students learn to use physical gestures in systematic ways to communicate thought and feeling. The specialization is unnecessarily artificial.

A major aim of PCE is to provide students with instruction combining these representation systems, as means of clarifying ideas in each phase of an inquiry. In a given subject area, one system of representation may be more efficiently used than another. Nonetheless, students need training in *integrating* all systems as means of conceptualizing ideas and relationships. PCE gives them that.

Matrix of PCE Goals

Table 10-2 shows diagrammatically all the various interactions between inquiry strategies and their supportive competencies. Teachers who wish to follow this model, whether during the whole school week or for some part of it, can use it to insure that each of these important goals is met. The idea is that activities should be designed to sharpen skills

Table 10-2
A Matrix of PCE Goals

Supportive Competencies

Inquiry Strategies	1. Instrumental skills	2. Self-direction	3. Creative thinking	4. Self-evaluation	5. Self-analysis	6. Communication
A. Formulating an inquirable question.	1A	2A	3A	4A	5A	6A
B. Formulating researchable questions.	1B	2B	3B	4B	5B	6B
C. Developing a plan for locating and gathering information.	1C	2C	3C	4C	5C	6C
D. Organizing and analyzing the collected data.	1D	2D	3D	4D	5D	6D
E. Evaluating the data and drawing conclusions about researchable questions.	1E	2E	3E	4E	5E	6E
F. Formulating an answer to the inquirable question.	1F	2F	3F	4F	5F	6F

represented in each of the thirty-six cells of the matrix. The matrix serves as a checklist for teachers as they plan their instructional strategies.

An Example of PCE in Use

The following is an example of the kinds of activities involved in the process-centered approach to learning. Students participating in this project attended a camp-school one day a week at a nearby wooded area. Each activity matches one of the cells in the PCE matrix.

A. *Formulate an inquirable question about living outdoors.*

1A. Instrumental skill. Prior to going to the woods, students make a list of possible questions by looking at tables and indices of resource books on camping and forests.

3A. Creative thinking. Brainstorming is used to add to the list from 1A. This calls for generation of many ideas as quickly as possible. No editing, of own ideas or those of others, is allowed. Even if silly, an idea should be contributed. (Note that cells need not be done in their numerical order.)

2A. Self-direction. The values clarification technique (Chapter Six) called "forced choice ladder" is used. Each student orders the ideas on the above list, starting with best and worst, and works toward the middle. Then students discuss their choices—this is tape-recorded. Finally, a vote is taken to select one inquirable question. The one chosen was "What is the best way to survive in the woods when you have no equipment?"

6A. Communications. The group listens to a tape from 2A. They analyze the effectiveness of the discussion, stopping the tape when anyone wants to make a point. Their ability to do this tends to be poor at first, but improves with time.

4A. Self-evaluation. The tape is replayed. Each student makes a list of his contributions and expressions of feeling and fact, estimates what percentage of time he talked, and whether he facilitated the discussion or not.

5A. Self-analysis. The child then writes an explanation of why he thinks he acted as he did.

B. *Formulate researchable questions as to "how to survive in the woods when you have no equipment."*

1B. Instrumental skill. Group looks through Yellow Pages of the phone book, and calls local American Camping Association chapter to get names of experts on survival training.

3B. Creative problem-solving. Selecting a park ranger, they discuss imaginative ways to get ideas from him. They decide to hold a contest among other classes at the school for the most creative approach.

6B. Communications. The best idea is selected: one student discovers the ranger owns a dog, so a note is tied to the dog's collar, inviting the ranger to call the school if he is willing to participate. He is.

2B. Self-direction. A committee interviews the ranger, and from their discussion with him, recommends several researchable questions. One of these is "What wild plants are good to eat?"

C. *Locate and gather information about "What wild plants are good to eat?"*

1C. Instrumental skill. Map reading techniques are studied so as to be able to negotiate wooded area in search of plants.

2C. Self-direction. Election of leaders for the five sub-groups that will search the area for plant samples is held.

6C. Communication. Semaphore (a hand signalling technique) is learned so that sub-groups can communicate between sites where plants are found. This will help avoid duplication of efforts.

3C. Creative problem-solving. A set of symbols are developed to show where various plants are to be found on map. Now the class goes to the woods and carries out its plans.

4C. Self-evaluation. A group discussion is held, after the collection effort, of:

a. Did leaders really lead?
b. Which kids made the best contribution?
c. Who really enjoyed the activity? Found it boring?

5C. Self-analysis. Pairs of students discuss the relevance of the finding of 4C for them personally.

D. *Organize and analyze the data on "What wild plants are good to eat?"*

3D. Creative problem-solving. Students write imaginative but accurate descriptions of each of their finds.

1D. Instrumental skills. Students then look up each plant in a plant book, and compare their descriptions of each plant with those in the book.

6D. Communication. Displays of the various plant types are made, which include information on the food value of the plant, distinguishing characteristics, etc.

4D. Self-evaluation. Each student completes a series of sentence completion tasks about this project, such as:

a. I felt proud that
b. I was scared when
c. The most fun was when
d. The most important thing this data on plants shows is

E. *Answer the researchable question "What wild plants are good to eat?"*

2E. Self-direction. The class decides to produce a guide booklet to common wild plants found in the woods, which will include recipes for their preparation. A leader is elected to assign the tasks.

1E. Instrumental skills. Recipe books are consulted for ideas on cooking the plants.

3E. Creative problem-solving. Each student must contribute at least one new recipe, using only wild plants.

6E. Communication. The recipe is prepared and explained to others (parents, friends). Students try to persuade them to eat the food.

4E. Self-evaluation. Each student writes a critique of someone else's recipe, and then reads someone else's critique of his.

Phase F, formulating an answer to the inquirable question, was not included in this activity, but it might well have been. As you can see, there is no problem in leaving out cells or whole lines or columns in the matrix, or in changing the order. The matrix is meant to serve only as a guide so that all PCE goals are considered in planning projects.

Most of the activities in a PCE strategy involve the same content areas as CCE, although in a different way. Examples are map-reading, writing, imaginative descriptions, and using fractions in recipes. Objectives are stated behaviorally to aid in measuring success.

Impressions of PCE

There are always a number of questions about PCE, and answering some of them here will assist your understanding.

How does a child learn to read? It seems as if there are no lessons in PCE.

First of all, reading is considered an instrumental skill. These skills are prerequisites for all of the other supporting competencies, and so of course they cannot be neglected. Nothing in PCE would be opposed to present techniques of reading instruction. Certainly there will be reading lessons, some of which the whole class will participate in, and some of which will be given to smaller groups. PCE does urge that the child's reading experience be integrated with his other experiences, for motivational purposes. To the extent that he learns to read because he is interested in inquiring about something, he is more likely to retain what he learns and apply it in new situations.

Aren't students going to miss important information? What about the child who only wants to study one subject?

PCE does emphasize that if the child is learning inquiry skills and supporting competencies by studying something that he's really interested in, then it will be all right to let him stay with that for some time. Such imbalances usually do not last very long.

Furthermore, we need to reexamine how much knowledge and how many skills are really all that essential. It is conceivable, for instance, that we may not even need handwriting or computation skills in the future. Imagine a twelve inch by twelve inch sheet of plastic, which can fold up and fit in your shirt pocket. Imbedded in the plastic are a number of microcircuits, including a radio receiver and transmitter. On the surface of the plastic sheet there is a typewriter and numerical keyboard. There might even be a small television screen. We would use this to transact business between the store and the bank, to write letters to each other, to take notes in class; all kinds of communications. Computers would make and keep track of all calculations. Thus handwriting and computational skills would really be unnecessary for most of the population. A great deal of the information our children are learning in school today will undoubtedly have to be unlearned, and new information learned, at some future date anyway.

Finally, it should be remembered that PCE goes from teacher- controlled to student-controlled learning. Teachers must judge for themselves to what extent they are willing to let students make decisions about what they will study.

Isn't this nothing but affective education?

Through its concern for self-evaluation and analysis, creativity, and communication skills, PCE does show a greater interest in the affective side of the child than CCE. It is, after all, a result of the humanistic movement in education. This position holds that our curriculum has been misdirected by the behaviorists, who have over-emphasized cognition, and the psychoanalysts, who have been too concerned with the "sick" personality. Too little regard has been paid to the need of all children to develop a healthy emotional nature.

However, by no means does PCE favor a complete swing away from cognitive education, as A.S. Neill did ("Educate the emotions and the intellect will take care of itself.") What it seeks to do, in a way that CCE has never been able to accomplish, is to interrelate cognitive and affective learning in a way that is productive to both.

How does the class go from being teacher-controlled to student controlled?

This is one of the more difficult questions, because the members of the class cannot move toward self-control at the same pace. PCE is in a better position than CCE to facilitate this change, however, because it favors the complete individualization of instruction. PCE follows the Skinnerian shaping techniques which were described in Chapter Three. The goal of the teacher is to relinquish more and more of the responsibility of the child's learning to the child. The teacher may find that he needs to retrench from time to time. However, with experience, this should become less necessary.

How do you report the student's progress to parents?

Clearly, letter grades are inadequate. As the teacher or the school moves toward the PCE approach, parents will have to be carefully advised as to what is going on, and why it is believed this will benefit the students. At least in this interim period, letter grades would be rather meaningless. Regular, substantial conferences between teachers and parents are the best solution.

What happens when the teacher in one grade is PCE-oriented and the teacher in the next grade is CCE-oriented?

This is unquestionably the most serious problem for the PCE approach. The simplest answer is to use the approach where at least one class at every grade level is PCE-oriented. The second best solution is for the PCE and CCE teacher to work out the best compromises they can between the two programs. The PCE teacher makes sure that each child has all the basic skills he will need for that CCE class, and the CCE teacher tries to individualize his instructions as much as possible. Actually, accomodations such as these can have a beneficial effect on the morale and effectiveness of a faculty. However, when such cooperation cannot be arranged, PCE will probably be disadvantageous for the children, and should not be used.

How can this approach work with younger children, who really need teacher control?

While it is true that young children need considerable guidance, it is not the case that they need a greater degree of control. Most teachers who have used PCE in the first four grades find it harmonious with children's perception of the world. At this young age, they do not divide knowledge into subject areas, and often find this difficult to do. Focus on process is more natural for them, hence they cooperate more readily.

How can this work with adolescents, who are so disorderly and confused?

As Erikson and others have documented, children in grades five through eight experience dramatic changes in physical and psychological make-up. The adolescent's attitude toward himself, his peers, and toward authority are in flux. A growing desire to make decisions and solve problems, independent of adult control, is also evident. All of these psychological changes derive from a major change in the adolescent's method of thinking and perceiving.

Piaget and his colleague, Barbel Inhelder, have described this as a period of development in the student's thinking processes when he is becoming more adept at solving abstract hypothetical problems. Moreover, the pre- and early adolescent is primarily self-centered and consequently less interested in the study of times, places, and customs other than his own. Less emphasis on memorization and preordered units is essential at this time. Adolescents are much more interested in their own attitudes and thinking processes, and are probably most open to efforts to alter and improve these processes. Hence PCE is particularly well-suited to the needs of this age group.

How can this work with high school students, who need to know a lot of information in order to get into college?

Students who have never experienced PCE until they reach high school often find it a pleasant change from the CCE approach. However, those who have had long experience in PCE frequently do reject it at the high school level. By high school, PCE-trained students often feel that they know very well what they want to learn more about and are highly motivated. They are more receptive to teacher lectures and other sources of direct information. They often seem in a hurry to learn more and don't wish to be forced to discover it for themselves. Thus if some choice of topic is allowed, the CCE approach can work well here. Far from being a detracting result of PCE, this is one of its important benefits.

How can this work with slow students?

Slow students usually display frustration and anxiety in a regular classroom, because they are unable to keep up with the other students, and are constantly "getting into trouble." It is true that in the beginning of a PCE program, these students tend to have a low motivational level. Therefore, they sometimes tend to abuse this approach. However, when the teacher maintains a great deal of control at the beginning and slowly shapes their behavior toward responsibility, these children learn well from the approach too. It should be noted, by the way, that the so-called "slow" student often is not slow because of lack of intelligence, but because of a general lack of motivation. The difference between learning and performance pointed out by Bandura in Chapter Three is relevant here.

Is PCE of benefit to gifted student?

In their highly respected book on PCE, Parker and Rubin argue that PCE is better that CCE in promoting the intellectual growth of the gifted because it makes it easier for a gifted child to pursue learning at his own faster rate. This student might work with a small group of other gifted students on some high-powered project, or he might serve as a tutor to slower learners. Also, gifted children are better able to get an overview of a complex problem, and are more interested in obtaining such an overview. PCE provides many opportunities for overviewing, through the integration of knowledge, skills, understanding, attitudes, and appreciations.

Summary

No teacher should choose the CCE approach merely because he is most familiar with it; at the same time he should recognize the risks involved in opting for PCE. There is no way to be comfortable with PCE *before* starting; it cannot be prepackaged as CCE can. PCE is a highly interpersonal approach and this can pose problems for those students and teachers who prefer some "distance." It will be far more difficult to tell administrators exactly what specific progress the class as a whole is making. These are a few of the problems faced by the PCE teacher.

Why then elect such a challenging course of action? Because PCE does better what American education must do:

1. It attempts to prepare children for an unpredictable future by helping them learn how to learn.

2. It recognizes the occurrence of a series of crises in our lives, and accepts repsonsibility for helping children resolve these crises, affectively as well as cognitively.

3. It is aware that stages of intellectual development are invariant, but that these stages do vary in age of onset. Therefore, it allows each child to learn in ways commensurate with his intellectual stage.

4. It encourages spontaneous, intuitive thinking patterns, as well as logical, reflective ones.

5. It helps each child increase his confidence in his ability to control his own life, largely through helping him become more competent.

6. It is cognizant of a hierarchy of basic human needs. It realizes that unless the lower deficiency needs are satisfied by the teacher, the higher being needs cannot be met.

7. It attempts to gear instruction to the distinctive learning styles of students (more on this in the next chapter).

8. It treats imagination with as much respect as intelligence.

I hope these eight characteristics of PCE will be recognized as corresponding well to the eight factors suggested in Chapter One as criteria for judging any educational innovation.

The author appreciates the assistance of Jane MacDonald, Linda Schulman, and Karen Zikoras with this chapter.

References

Bruner, J.S. *Toward a Theory of Instruction.* New York: Norton, 1966.

Parker, J.C., and L.J. Rubin. *Process as Content.* Chicago: Rand McNally, 1966.

Stephens, J.M. *The Process of Schooling.* New York: Holt, Rinehart, and Winston, 1967.

Chapter 11

Developing a Cohesive Teaching Style

What is a good teacher?

"You and I know who good teachers are. In a very short time, in a new school or faculty, we are able to state with a high degree of confidence who are the very best teachers in the group. We can do this even when we have never entered a teacher's classroom. Somehow we pick up the information we need to make such statements by a kind of osmosis. Why then, can't we *measure* good teaching? The answer is simple: because they are unique human beings. Like the children they teach, teachers, too, are individuals. No good teacher is like any other (Combs, 1969, p. 195)"

While I used to agree with Combs, I think his statement is less true today. The job of teacher is becoming increasingly complicated. Some teachers are especially good at some parts of the job, and others are better at other parts. Thus it is harder today to speak of the overall "good teacher."

There is much more for the teacher to know and understand today than in, say, 1965. There are three particular areas of change which are causes for concern.

New Curricula.

Consider the area of curriculum. Many things have been added to the schools' tasks. Today's teacher must be familiar with each of them. I think you will be surprised at the length of the list:

Technology.
Values clarification.
Drug education.
Communications skills.
Career education.
Early childhood.
Sex education.
The new math.
Metrics.
Black history.
Women's liberation.
Affective education.

Increased political awareness and knowledge, brought on by lowering of the voting age.

Process-centered education.

New health concerns (school breakfasts, dental health care, alcoholism, veneral disease).

Adult education.

The proliferation of electives.

Consumer education.

Greater specialization in all curriculum areas.

Increase in Problems.

The second area for concern is the increase in problems which affect every classroom teacher. Among these are:

Mainstreaming (the inclusion in regular classrooms of students with special problems, who previously had been sent to special classrooms).

The increased mobility of families. The greater number of students entering the class during the school year creates special problems for the teacher, but the long-range effects of the number of students *leaving* the school may be even more serious. Most teachers gain satisfaction in observing the results of their efforts as their students move on through the grades. As more and more children leave the school, this important satisfaction is correspondingly decreased.

The shrinking job market.

The shortage of money, and the commensurate consolidation of schools.

The striking increase in the divorce rate in this country, that often affects the cognitive ability and emotional equilibrium of the children involved.

The change in the record laws, in which anything the teacher writes about his students may be seen by the student and his parents.

The voucher system, which allows parents a choice between public and private schools in their area. Although not yet widespread, this system puts teachers and schools in competition with each other, thus creating a new type of pressure.

Bussing.

New pressures for "accountability", that forces teachers to spend more time demonstrating the effectiveness of their efforts to the general public.

Increased involvement of non-professionals in educational decisions.

Unionization and teacher strikes.

"Style."

A third area of changes, the one which probably provides the most difficulty to teachers, is that of teaching "style." Examples of these changes are:

Decrease in the kinds of sanctions teachers may use. In most states, physical punishments of all types are discouraged and in many cases completely disallowed.

The increase in in-service education. Teachers are required to update their knowledge of instructional strategy by attending courses, in-service workshops, etc.

Variety of roles. Teachers are expected to play a larger variety of roles in the classroom than ever before.

Individualization. Teachers are expected to be more responsive to the different learning styles of their students, and to provide instruction appropriate to these styles.

Teaching has probably never gone through so many changes so quickly as it has since 1950. As I have suggested elsewhere, rapid change tends to cause breakdowns in cohesion within social institutions. By cohesion, I mean a spirit of basic trust and cooperation among group members. Although difficult to measure, there is evidence that today's teachers find it harder to be consistent, and that the social cohesion in the average classroom has decreased. If so, this must inevitably suppress learning, creativity, curiosity, communications, clarity of values, and ultimately, healthy personal growth.

Numerous studies have investigated the factors that influence cohesiveness in the classroom. Of all the things that affect it (size of class, organizational rules, age of students, and so forth), the single most important factor is the cohesiveness of the teacher's behavior, that is, a consistent teaching *style*. The next section deals with this.

Teaching Style

A number of factors make up teaching style. This section reviews the five most important ones: goals of the teacher, leadership role, expectations, self-image, and directness of influence.

Goals

The goals of the teaching process may be seen from three distinctly different views. These three goal models reflect different attitudes toward knowledge and learning:

In one model, the teacher acts to *transmit the knowledge* that society considers relevant. The pupil is given the information considered important for his future role as an adult. As the transmitter of knowledge, it becomes the teacher's responsibility to initiate and direct all learning.

A second teaching model emphasizes the importance of revealing the underlying structure of a discipline. The aim here is to teach *the process of inquiry* rather than the facts. It is assumed that the excitement of intellectual discovery motivates the pupil to search, question, and actively learn. Primarily, the teacher asks questions which will stimulate the pupil to search for answers.

The third teaching model stresses *interpersonal* learning. According to this point of view, teaching is first and foremost a process of creating a positive atmosphere for learning. This model thus stresses the quality of the interaction between teacher and pupils: if the relationships between them are warm, genuinely affectionate and empathetic, then learning can occur.

The major proponent of this view, psychologist Carl Rogers, emphasizes the quality of experience and feeling, rather than thinking. This quality comes about because the teacher is "real, prizing, and understanding." "Realness" means being yourself, with all the likes, dislikes, faults, and strengths laid bare. It is saying what you feel as you feel it, and not putting up a false front that separates the real you from those you teach. "Prizing" is the knack of making a person feel important, accepted, and secure. If a classroom has an atmosphere of trust, confidence grows, communication expands, creativity flourishes, and learning is facilitated. "Understanding" is the ability to set aside one's own views and convictions long enough to see the problem at hand through someone else's eyes.

The three role models correspond quite closely to the three types of education described in Chapter Eight. The first relates to the traditional classroom, the second to the open classroom, and the third to the free school. However, it is clear that all three of these models must play a part in a well-designed classroom. Ideally, the strengths of each approach are integrated into a cohesive teaching style.

Leadership role

Another way to look at the effectiveness of teaching styles is to examine how various leadership roles affect classroom dynamics. For example, Bradford and Lippitt, two sociologists, studied the difference between democratic, laissez-faire, and "hardboiled" and "benevolent" autocratic types of leadership. Their findings are summarized in Table 11-1, and strongly indicate the superiority of the democratic leadership role.

Table 11-1

Types of Leadership, Characteristic of Leaders, and Students' Reactions

Type of leadership	Characteristics of this type of leadership	Typical reactions of students to this leadership
Hard-boiled Autocrat	1. Constant check on students.	1. Submission, but there is incipient revolt and dislike of the leader.
	2. Expects immediate acceptance of all orders - rigid discipline.	2. "Buck passing" is a common occurrence.
	3. Little praise is given as he believes this would spoil children	3. Pupils are irritable and unwilling to cooperate and may indulge in "backbiting".

Continued

	4. Believes students cannot be trusted when on their own.	4. The work slips markedly when the teacher leaves the room.
The Benevolent Autocrat	1. Is not aware that he is an autocrat.	1. Most students like him, but those who see through his methods may dislike him intensely.
	2. Praises pupils and is interested in them.	2. There is great dependence upon the teacher for all directions-little initiative on part of pupils.
	3. The crux of his autocracy lies in the technique by which he secures dependence upon himself. He says, "that's the way I like it," or "how could you do this to me?"	3. There is submissiveness, and lack of individual development.
	4. Makes himself the source of all standards of class work.	4. Amount of classwork may be high and of good quality.
The Laissez-faire teacher	1. Has little confidence in dealing with pupils or a belief that they should be left alone	1. There is low morale and poor and sloppy work.
	2. Has difficulty in making decisions.	2. There is much "buck-passing", "scapegoating", and irritability among students.
	3. Has no clear-cut goals.	3. There is no teamwork.
	4. Does not encourage or discourage students, nor does he join in their work or offer help advice	4. No one knows what to do.
The Democratic teacher	1. Shares planning and decision making with the group.	1. Pupils like work, each other, and teacher better.
	2. Gives help, guidance, and assistance to individuals gladly but not at expense of the class.	2. Quality and quantity of work are high.
	3. Encourages as much group participation as possible	3. Students praise each other and assume responsibilities on their own.

Continued

4. Praise and criticism given objectively.	4. There are few problems of motivation whether teacher is in the room or not.

(From Bradford and Lippitt, 1954.)

Expectations

Several studies have shown that teachers' *expectations* for their pupils can affect their teaching style. In one study where teachers were told that certain children chosen at random would have a "growth spurt" during the year, these pupils received more compliments from their teachers and did better on IQ tests. All of them showed better than average improvement on achievement tests. Pupils whom the teacher expects will improve often do, while pupils not expected to improve generally don't. Pupils who do well despite lower expectations of the teacher tend to be perceived negatively by the teacher. This phenomenon, the "self-fulfilling prophesy", is another aspect of teaching style which ought not to be neglected.

Self-image

The image a teacher projects to his students is an integral part of his style. Educational researcher Robert Thelan has enumerated seven self-images commonly held by teachers:

Some teachers perceive themselves as wise and Socratic. Their role, as they see it, is to stimulate thought through careful questioning and debate. Their image is that of a seeker promoting the growth of others by emphasizing insightful examination.

Other teachers see themselves mainly as democratic moderators. These teachers stress the development of cooperation and participation by all members of the class. In their teaching style they emphasize the interdependency and equality of their pupils.

Some teachers seek to teach a way of life or attitude toward living. These teachers often hold an attitude toward their pupils similar to that of a master toward his apprentices.

In contrast, there are teachers who treat teaching almost as business management. For these teachers, the main goal is productivity. This teacher organizes the class so that it will be efficient. He typically uses task charts and devises work contracts with his pupils to ensure that the work is done.

For the teacher who sees himself as a coach, the class may be treated as a team. Success, drive, and group spirit become the major goals.

A more disinterested self-image is that of the guide. Such a teacher usually stresses his expertise and his ability to give comprehensive answers to his pupils' questions.

Finally, a well-known self-image for teachers is that of the authoritarian who lays down the rules because he knows what's best.

This teacher values obedience and respect above all.

Of course, most teachers do not fit exactly into any one of these categories. Still, it is worthwhile to enumerate them since they represent different values or "hidden agendas" which are expressed in teaching style.

Directness of influence

Psychologist Ned Flanders has done extensive research on the question of teaching styles, and he concludes they can best be understood in terms of the directness of the teacher's influence over his students. This is quite similar to the concept of directness of control described in Chapter Eight. Flanders has devised a scale of ten observable categories of behavior that occur in classrooms; he suggests that every imaginable teacher-student interaction fits into one of these ten categories. As Table 11-2 shows, four of the categories involve indirect influence by the teacher, three indicate direct influence, and two have to do with student behavior. The tenth category indicates silence or confusion. Most studies by Flanders and others indicate that classroom interactions of the indirect influence type effect a greater amount of learning.

Table 11-2

Categories in the Flanders System of Interaction Analysis

Teacher Talk

Indirect Influence

1. Accepts Feeling: accepts and clarifies the feeling tone of the students in a non-threatening manner. Feelings may be positive or negative. Predicting or recalling feelings are included.
2. Praises or Encourages: praises or encourages student action or behavior. Jokes that release tension, not at the expense of another individual, nodding head or saying "um hm?" or "go on" are included.
3. Accepts or Uses Ideas of Student: clarifying, building, or developing ideas or suggestions by a student. As teacher brings more of his own ideas into play, shift to category five.
4. Asks Questions: asking a question about content or procedure with the intent that a student answer.

Direct Influence

5. Lecturing: giving facts or opinions about content or procedure: expressing his own ideas, asking rhetorical questions.
6. Giving Directions: directions, commands, or orders which a student is expected to comply with.

Continued

7. Criticizing or Justifying Authority: statements intended to change student behavior from nonacceptable to acceptable pattern; bawling someone out; stating why the teacher is doing what he is doing; extreme self-reference.

Student Talk

8. Student Talk-Response: talk by student in response to teacher. Teacher initiates the contact or solicits student statement.
9. Student Talk-Initiating: talk by students which they initiate. If "calling on" student is only to indicate who may talk next, observer must decide whether student wanted to talk. If he did, use this category.
10. Silence or Confusion: pauses, short periods of silence and periods of confusion in which communication cannot be understood by the observer.

It seems clear from the above research that the teacher who is most effective is one whose teaching style is cohesive, and includes:

1. A blend of the three goal models described.
2. Democratic leadership.
3. An awareness of the effects of his expectations on students.
4. A flexible self-image.
5. Indirect influence techniques.
6. Consistency.

How can the teacher really know what style he uses? How can he know whether he has a cohesive style, or whether he vacillates between several? By himself, he can't. Especially if he is a good teacher, he is usually too involved with the needs of his students to simultaneously observe himself. Besides, observing yourself teach is like watching your feet while you dance: you don't dance the same way as when you're not watching. Teachers need feedback from others. The next section describes effective ways of getting it.

Feedback Systems

Interaction Analysis

To study the teacher's style of influencing students, Flanders developed "interaction analysis." A classroom observer sits in the room and records the kinds of interactions taking place as the class proceeds, based on Flanders' ten categories of influence.

Using a tally sheet, the observer notes the number of the category of behavior that is occurring in the classroom at a particular point in time. He does this every five seconds for all or part of the period. This produces a list of numbers which give the history of the interactions during that observation. The teacher can see what percentage of the time was spent engaging in each of the ten behaviors on Flanders' scale. An I/D ratio (the ratio between indirect and direct influence) can also be computed. It is determined by dividing the sum of the tallies in categories one through four by the sum of categories five through seven.

While this is very helpful information, the use of an interaction matrix to analyze these data can be even more so. On a ten-by-ten matrix, adjacent pairs of numbers are entered in the appropriate cell (small square). Suppose that one minute of the class had yielded the following series of twelve tallies: 10, 6, 8, 5, 5, 5, 5, 6, 9, 5, 5, and 10. These numbers are separated into adjacent pairs (10-6, 6-8, 8-5, etc.) and recorded in the matrix. The first number indicates the row and the second the column in which the tally should be recorded. The interaction matrix for this series is seen in Figure 11-1. Obviously if the tallies for an entire period are to be recorded, more room in the cells would be needed. When this matrix is completed, the teacher is able to analyze graphically the types of interactions and the style of influence that prevail in his teaching. By noting in which shaded area most of the tallies fall, the teacher can discern more clearly the style of teaching he tends to employ. As Figure 11-2 shows, the more tallies in Areas A and D, the more effective the teacher is likely to be.

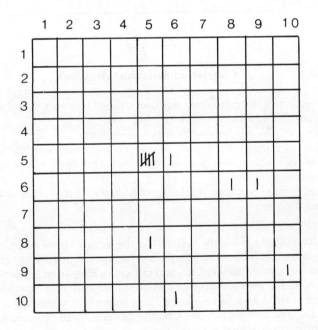

Fig. 11-1

Interaction Matrix

Pairs: 10,6 6,8 8,5 5,5 5,5 5,5 5,6 6,9 9,10

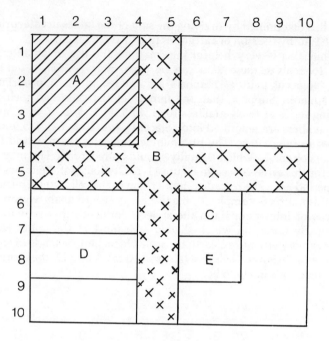

Fig. 11-2

Completed Interaction Matrix Area

A. Constructive Integration: teacher uses indirect influence to motivate students and uses their ideas constructively.
B. Content Cross: teacher emphasizes subject matter.
C. Vicious Cycle: teacher disciplines students and gives them direction.
D. Interested Acceptance: teacher is genuinely concerned with hearing and using student ideas.
E. Indifferent Acceptance: teacher ignores student participation and doesn't use their ideas.

Although the Flanders' system has the advantage of being relatively simple in format, devoid of complicated statistical procedure, and stated in terms familiar to teachers, several criticisms have been leveled at it:

Not all the interactions in a classroom are verbal, as specified in the Flanders scale. Often some of the most important communications are emotional and non-verbal (see Chapter Seven); these often do not show up in Interactional Analysis.

It is necessary to persuade a colleague and/or friend to give the time to do the observation(s). This is not always easily arranged.

Whoever is to do the observation must be trained in the Flanders system prior to the actual observation. This is somewhat time- consuming.

In some school systems, permission for classroom observation must be obtained from administrators, parents, and in some cases, students. This can be one more frustrating obstacle.

Nevertheless, I would suggest that the inherent advantages of this type of feedback outweigh the obstacles that must be overcome in using it. A number of other systems have been developed, but none of these, in my opinion, offers quite as much as the Flanders system. A chief advantage of this system is the well-designed research on which it is based. To sum up these studies, we may conclude that a higher percentage of indirect influence, a higher ratio of indirect over direct influence, and a more "constructive interaction" and "interested acceptance", will, on the average, result in more learning.

Micro-teaching

I have spent many hours watching teachers teach and thereafter telling them what I thought was good and bad about their performance. Usually they seem to understand, and most often agree with what I suggest to them. However, it is rather rare to see a teacher change very much as a result of this verbal feedback. They understand intellectually, but they don't internalize it. I find it far more effective to make a videotape (televised replay) of their performance and then discuss this tape with them. Micro-teaching is a technique in which teacher behavior is videotaped for a short (usually five-minute) period of time, immediately after which the teacher and observer(s) discuss what happened. Among the best observer-discussants of the videotape, I find, are the students who were being taught during the taping.

I have employed the micro-teaching technique over 500 times; I can only remember two individuals who were pleased with what they saw. The great majority were plainly mortified. For the most part, I think this is a good result. All of us in the educational profession have habits and traits that we should correct, if our teaching style is to be improved. The main problem is to admit to ourselves that we really do have those habits and traits. I am not merely speaking of such simple difficulties of speaking too softly, twirling our glasses, or saying "um" too much. There are many, much more subtle behaviors that defy verbal definition, but which, when we see them on film, clearly need correction. Videotape has the unique advantage of forcing us to see firsthand the way we look to others.

The Sociogram

The sociogram is an excellent way to get feedback on the amount of cohesiveness in the classroom. Cohesiveness here refers to the level of communication and the spirit of cooperation among the students. When a classroom is cohesive, students are willing to help each other with their assignments and to communicate with each other and to the teacher problems they may be having with their learning. A cohesive class is one in which students feel that they have friends on whom they can count when they run into difficulty. The emphasis in a cohesive class is on trust and cooperation, as opposed to suspicion and competition. A non-cohesive class is one in which students are divided into jealous cliques, small groups which have as their purpose the exclusion of other students from their interactions. The presence of cliques in the classroom depends to some extent on the age of the students (adolescents are more likely to develop cliques than students younger or older); however, the teaching style of the teacher has a large impact. One of the main purposes of a clique is to defend its members against the threat of an attack from the outside; a major source of the threat is the teacher who makes them feel unsafe. The sociogram is the best way to determine the social patterns of interactions in a classroom.

Another aspect of cohesiveness has to do with the isolation of certain students. "Isolates" are students whom no one else in the class has identified as a friend. The number of isolates in a classroom can show how uncohesive the class is.

Figure 11-3 is a diagram of the social interactions in one classroom. The teacher distributed 3 x 5 cards to the students and asked them to put their name at the top. Students were then told to list those students in the class whom they considered "good friends." They were allowed to name up to five students, but could name none if they felt they had no good friends in the class. The circles indicate girls, the triangles boys. The arrows indicate the choices that the students made; arrows in both direction mean a mutual choice as a good friend.

Fig. 11-3   **The Sociogram**

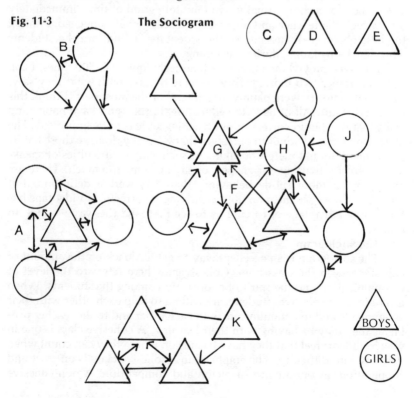

The questions below indicate some of the uses to which a sociogram can be put. You may wish to try to answer them; the answers I would give to these questions will appear later in this chapter.

a. At what grade level do you think this class is?

b. How would you categorize the cohesiveness of this class?

c. What predictions can you make for the relationships of students in groups A and B?

d. What conclusions can you draw about students C, D and E?

e. How many isolates are there in this class?

f. Which of the cliques in this class is the most popular one?

g. If you were to form discussion groups for this class, which students would you want to put in the same group?

h. For this sociogram, the question was asked, "Which students do you consider good friends?" What are some other questions that would be useful to ask students?

i. In what way does the cohesiveness of a class relate to the teacher's teaching style?

Neutrally Led, Tape Recorded Discussion

Often students have strong feelings about what is happening in their classrooms and would like the teacher to know, but they don't know how to speak of these feelings to the teacher's face. Under these circumstances. the neutrally led, tape-recorded discussion can be helpful.

The teacher makes arrangements with a friend, a fellow teacher, an aide, anyone he trusts, to take over his class and lead this session. If appropriate, he takes over the class of his fellow teacher. He then says to his class, "Miss Jones is going to come into our class for about an hour, and talk to you about the way our class is going. I will take over her class while she is here. She will ask you a number of questions and tape-record the answers. I hope that you will be as honest as possible when you answer these questions. I am very interested in how you feel about the way our class is going, and I thought you might be able to talk about it more easily if I were not in the room. Of course, you should know I will listen to the tape that you make and will discuss it with you later."

The neutral person then comes into the room, the teacher leaves, and a discussion is held on a wide variety of aspects concerning the classroom. The whole class might participate in the discussion, with various members taking the microphone to state their position. On the other hand, it may be well if only a part of the class takes part. These students could be selected by the teacher, or better yet, might be a sub-group elected by the class to represent their views in this discussion. Sometimes it is best to have seven to ten students participating in the discussion, with the rest of the class listening in.

I have found that these discussions can be greatly enhanced by periodically replaying the tape of what the group has just said. As they listen to what they have said, they very often have new thoughts about the subject. In one seventh grade math class, students started out by saying how unfair the teacher was in his homework assignments. They listed all the ways he had been unfair in the semester thus far. However, after they had heard the tape-recorder, they began to have second thoughts about how fair their own comments were. Soon they began to take part of the blame for the unhappy siutation that had developed in the class. Fruther discussion brought them to see their own role in what was going on, and they became far more reasonable about the situation. After the teacher had heard the recordings of the first and second session, he then discussed these issues with the class. A number of compromises were worked out, and the class became a more effective unit.

It may seem strange that students are willing to say things to a tape-recorder that they know the teacher will hear later, but are unwilling to say these things to the teacher's face. However, this seems to be the case, and often the older the child, the more likely it is to happen. And students seem to find it just as difficult to tell the teacher about things they like in the class as things they don't like. This simple strategy can work miracles for the atmosphere in the classroom. It helps clear the air of unspoken problems in a way that straightforwardly asking the class would not do. It is especially useful for student teachers who want to know in what ways they are or are not communicating with the class. Once children have been invited to participate in the analysis and reorganization of the classroom procedure, they become the teacher's allies in the endeavor.

Answers to Questions on Figure 11-3. The Sociogram.

a. At what grade level do you think this class is?

This class is a sixth-grade class, which is evident from the number of boy-girl interaction; the cliques.

b. How would you categorize the cohesiveness of this class?

This class is not very cohesive. The friendships within it are restricted mainly to a number of cliques; members of the cliques maintain few friendships outside.

c. What predictions can you make for the relationships of students in groups A and B?

You can expect some friction and possible hurt feelings among the girls in groups A and B. It is unlikely, especially in a sixth-grade class, that children of one sex who compete for the friendship of a child of the other sex are likely to be able to maintain their friendships for very long.

d. What conclusions can you draw about students C, D and E?

These children are clearly isolates. No one picked them and they did not pick anyone else. Student C is a black girl, student D a black boy, and student E is a Chinese boy. Each of these students recently joined the class and is bussed to the school from another neighborhood. It is easy to understand that no other students have picked them yet. However, it is also typical that they should not have picked each other. Usually when a student has a characteristic that makes him an isolate from the rest of the class, he does not want to pick a student who has the same "negative" characteristic.

e. How many isolates are there in this class?

Six. Students C, D, and E of course are isolates. Students I, J, and K, who were not picked by anyone else, should also be considered isolates.

f. Which of the cliques in this class is the most popular one?

Clique F, the members of which were most often picked by members outside the clique, is the most popular one.

g. If you were to form discussion groups for this class, which students would you pick for the same group?

I would try to form a group which included at least one of the isolates, at least one of the most popular students; for example, students G and H. Students G and H, who were chosen many times by other students, are ones who can most afford to befriend an isolate and help him into the group.

h. For this sociogram, the question was asked, "Which students do you consider good friends?" What are some other questions which it would be useful to ask students?

Some other suggestions would be: "Which students do you most like to work with?" "Which students do you admire the most?" "Which students does the teacher like the best in the classroom?" "Which students would you least like to work with?"

i. In what way does the cohesiveness of a class relate to the teacher's teaching style?

Research has shown that the teacher's style sets the climate of the classroom. A classroom in which the children feel psychologically safe and trusting of each other is one in which the most productive learning will go on. When a teacher is continually accepting and open to the contributions of the students, he constitutes a model which tends to be followed in all the members of the class. Hence drawing together in the protection of a clique becomes less necessary.

Adjusting to Learning Style Needs

There is reason to believe that if the teacher's teaching style is cohesive, it will be appropriate for at least eighty percent of the students in any particular class. Most students are flexible enough to adjust to almost any teaching style. However, some ten to twenty percent of students have learning styles that are so rigid, so different from the teacher's teaching style that the teacher will need to adjust his teaching style to these students.

Table 11-3 is a rating chart for evaluating the learning styles of the students in your class. There are five variables in this chart, each considered to be an important part of a child's learning style. Each of these variables is represented as two extremes on a continuum.

Table 11-3

Learning Styles— Rating Form

1. Cognitive	1	2	3	4	5	Affective

Continued

2. Fast Paced	1	2	3	4	5	Slow Paced
3. Single Information Input	1	2	3	4	5	Multiple Information Input
4. Independent	1	2	3	4	5	Dependent
5. Internal Locus of Control	1	2	3	4	5	External Locus of Control
6. Logical, Linear	1	2	3	4	5	Intuitive, Non-linear

These factors are defined as follows:

1. Cognitive—student prefers a highly intellectual curriculum, does not like having to react emotionally to anything he is studying.

1. Affective—student prefers a curriculum which gets at feelings and attitudes. He tends to prefer art, music, and drama to science.

2. Fast Paced—student enjoys an exciting atmosphere and willingly takes risks. This is not necessarily a smarter student; he is simply one who enjoys having things move along quickly.

2. Slow Paced—this student tends to be cautious and compulsive. This child wants to be certain he understands the lesson before going on to the next one.

3. Single Information Input—this child prefers to get information through only one of his sensory channels; for example, he is the type who really loves to read and is not interested in anything else.

3. Multiple Information Input— This is a child who enjoys all kinds of media.

4. Independent—this child seldom needs much guidance and prefers his own judgment to that of others, including the teacher's.

4. Dependent—this child prefers working with others and frequently needs to be reassured of the instructions he is to follow.

5. Internal Locus of Control—this child sees the control over his life as coming largely from himself; thus takes responsibility, credit, and blame for his actions.

5. External Locus of Control—this child sees life largely as a matter of chance or luck and tends to be rather irresponsible.

6. Logical, Linear—this child is highly methodical. He may be either side of the continuum on the other characteristics; for ex-

6. Intuitive, Non-linear—this tends to be the highly creative child who makes spontaneous mental leaps but is not too good

Continued

ample, he may be fast or slow paced, but he does tend to be the cognitive type.

at checking out his work for errors. He too can be on either side of the continuum, but tends to be the affective type.

The teacher should evaluate the learning styles of each child in the class, probably about one month after the semester has started. This evaluation should include not only observations of the child in social and learning situations, but also interviews and a written attitude survey of the child's preferred learning style. The teacher should also fill out one of the rating charts (Table 11-3) on himself as to his teaching style. Then he can easily see how well his style fits with his students' learning styles.

A number of interesting discoveries come about as a result of this exercise. For example, I have found that when a teaching style does not fit well with a child's learning style, but the teacher likes the child, that child is almost always quite independent and has an internal locus of control. When the same misfit occurs, but the teacher does not particularly like the child, it is almost always a child who is dependent and external.

Comparing teaching and learning styles this way is not as time-consuming as it may sound, and most teachers report that it is quite useful.

Summary

Educational researchers Jere Brophy and Carolyn Evertson (1976) argue that one of the most recent, and least useful, fads in education is that of blaming teachers for everything. The educational reformers of recent years may have done a good job at pointing out weaknesses in schools, but they have had very few specific solutions to offer. Brophy and Evertson propose that we stop trying to find out what effective teachers *are* (studying their personalities, for example), and instead spend our time seeking to learn what they *do*. For example, in their extensive study of the behaviors of successful teachers, they found that although these teachers were affectionate and student-oriented, they placed instructional aspects of teaching above interpersonal ones. Teachers who seemed primarily concerned with children's emotional needs tended to...."use relationships with students to satisfy their own emotional needs (the impression that our observers gathered after observing teachers who had an overblown, romanticized view of the child)" (Brophy and Evertson, 1976, p. 142).

Brophy and Evertson conclude:

> In summary, then, we think it is time for educators to abandon concepts of teaching based on the idea that successful teachers are those who have mastered a few techniques or who have acquired a few specific characteristics....Instead, attention should be turned to....linking specific situations....with specific teacher behaviors and specific student outcomes. (Brophy and Evertson, 1976, p. 147).

These authors are describing what my professors in graduate school used to call a "cookbook." If such a book existed, we could go to its index and look up Problem Situation Type 21, Child Type 42, and Teacher Type 15. The index would refer us to page 3116 (this would be a *very* thick cookbook), on which we would find a "recipe" for handling the situation. Those professors of mine were fond of saying, "There are no cookbooks in education." It would be wonderful if there were, but there still aren't. The best I can offer you, as a summary of the advice I have been trying to give in this book, is Albert Wight's excellent description of what he calls the "participative" teacher. In Table 11-4, he compares this type of instruction to traditional teaching.

Table 11-4

The Participative Instructor vs. the Traditional Instructor

The Participative Instructor	The Traditional Instructor
Focuses on the process of learning; learning how to learn.	Focuses on the presentation of content, facts, and information.
Involves the student actively in assuming the responsibility for his own learning.	Assumes the responsibility for deciding what the student needs and motivating him to learn.
Helps the student learn to be an active information seeker, identifying and making effective use of available resources.	Decides what the student needs and provides it through lectures, reading assignments, films, etc.
Expects the student to learn by exploration and discovery, asking questions, formulating and testing hypotheses, solving problems.	Expects the student to learn primarily by memorization and formulation of responses to questions.
Focuses on the creative process of identifying and solving open ended, real-life problems, with many possible solutions. There is no expert or one right answer.	Focuses on the completion of textbook-type exercises or problems with "one right answer." The instructor is the expert.
Formulates clearly defined objectives based on the needs of the student.	Formulates objectives, but usually based on covering a specified amount of material.
Involves the student in the identification of his own learning needs and objectives.	Expects the student to accept the objectives specified for the course.

Continued

Involves the student in assessment and evaluation of the learning experience, information obtained, and progress toward objectives.

Focuses on individual achievement in relation to the student's own needs and objectives.

Focuses on helping the student learn to work effectively with others in cooperative, problem-solving activities.

Focuses on group discussions and activities conducted and evaluated by the students themselves.

Works toward open communication between student and faculty and among the students.

Avoids giving "advice", but helps the student explore alternatives. Supports the student in making his own decisions.

Invites ideas, suggestions, and criticism from the students; involves the students in decision-making.

Encourages informality and spontaneity in the classroom; establishes informal relationships with the students.

Promotes a questioning attitude, constructive discontent, reliance on the student's own judgment.

Attempts to develop a climate of openness, trust and concern for others, with maximum feedback to each person of information he needs to evaluate his performance and progress.

Assesses and evaluates the material he presents, effectiveness of presentation, and performance and progress of each student.

Focuses on performance in relation to the group, with grading on the normal curve.

Focuses on competition with peers, for achievement, recognition, grades, and other rewards.

Focuses on lectures, group discussions, and other activities led and evaluated by the instructor.

Focuses on one-way communication from the instructor to the students, with little communication from or among the students.

Gives the student "advice" regarding actions he should take or perhaps even the career or profession he should select.

Makes the decisions or carries out decisions made by the faculty or administration; discourages suggestions or criticism from the students.

Establishes formal procedures and control in the classroom and formal relationships with his students.

Requires respect for the instructor as the authority, distrust of the student's own judgment.

Promotes competition among students, creating a climate of distrust and lack of concern for others; provides feedback to students regarding performance on examinations.

Continued

Structures the course so that unplanned and unexpected problems will be treated as learning opportunities.	Follows the course outline closely; avoids problems or dispenses with them quickly so they will not interfere with the schedule.

Being a traditional teacher is a tall order; being a participative instructor is even harder. Many teachers have no chance of being participative instructors because they come to this work for the wrong reasons. Some chose it because it seems to have good hours (it doesn't). Others opt for it because it is socially respected work. A surprising number become teachers because of their authoritarian needs. An authoritarian is someone who desires work where those subordinate to him obey blindly and those superior to him give him easily-followed commands. In a study of 400 occupations some years ago, teachers as a group placed third in authoritarian needs; only military officers and state policemen were higher!

So you must carefully consider your reasons for being, or wanting to be, a teacher. And even having all the right reasons is not enough. You must learn to combine these reasons and your behavior based on them into a consistent cohesive teaching style.

I hope this book will help you examine your role as a teacher. I sincerely hope it will make you a more successful teacher than you might otherwise have been.

References

Biehler, Robert F. *Psychology Applied to Teaching*. Boston: Houghton-Mifflin, 1974.

Brophy, J.E., and C.M. Evertson. *Learning from Teaching*. Allyn and Bacon, 1976.

Good, Thomas L.; Bruce J. Biddle; and Jere E. Brophy. *Teachers Make a Difference*. New York: Holt, Rinehart, and Winston, 1975.

Jackson, Phillip. *Life in Classrooms*. New York: Holt, Rinehart, and Winston, 1968.

Klausmeier, Herbert J., and Richard E. Ripple. *Learning and Human Abilities*, (third ed.). New York: Harper & Row, 1971.

Sprinthall, Richard C., and Norman A. Sprinthall. *Educational Psychology: A Developmental Approach*. Reading, Massachusetts: Addison-Wesley, 1974.

Index